FINANCING
PSYCHOTHERAPY

FINANCING PSYCHOTHERAPY
Costs, Effects, and Public Policy

THOMAS G. McGUIRE
Boston University

BALLINGER PUBLISHING COMPANY
Cambridge, Massachusetts
A Subsidiary of Harper & Row, Publishers, Inc.

Publication of this book was made possible by grants from the Maurice Falk Medical Fund and the National Institute of Mental Health. These organizations, however, should not be understood as endorsing any statement made or expressed herein.

International Standard Book Number: 0-88410-711-6

Library of Congress Catalog Card Number: 81-1706

Printed in the United States of America

Library of Congress Cataloging in Publication Data

Mc Guire, Thomas, 1950-
  Financing Psychotherapy.
  Includes bibliographical references and index.
  1. Insurance, Mental health—United States.
2. Psychotherapy—United States. I. Title. [DNLM:
1. Insurance, Psychiatric—United States. 2. National health
insurance, United States. 3. Psychotherapy.
W 275 AA1 M39p]
HD7102.6.U5M34   368.4'2   81-1706
ISBN 0-88410-711-6   AACR2

DEDICATION

To Lark

CONTENTS

PART III   PUBLIC POLICY

LIST OF FIGURES

LIST OF TABLES

PREFACE

Coverage for psychotherapy in health insurance has been controversial since first offered as part of major medical contracts of commercial insurers in the early 1950s. Intensive long-term psychotherapy for a few policyholders put upward pressure on premiums. Insurers, in response, dropped coverage for psythotherapy or imposed severe special limits on coverage that remain, by and large, in place today. Psychoanalysis is no longer the predominant form of treatment in psychotherapy, but it is still often argued that psychotherapy is uninsurable. Emotional distress is ubiquitions—anyone may qualify as needy—and treatment, once begun, may continue indefinitely. Premiums, however, cover costs for even generous benefits for psychotherapy. Until very recently, the five million members of the Blue Cross/Blue Shield High Option Plan for federal employees were covered for 80 percent of the costs of psychotherapy. This offers ample testimony that, in a technical sense, psychotherapy is clearly insurable.

Another more interesting question is whether coverage for psychotherapy should be included in health insurance. At first glance there might seem to be an easy answer to this question. Coverage for psychotherapy should be a matter of choice. If an individual or group decides it is willing to pay for coverage, then it should be free to do so; if it is unwilling to pay for coverage, then it should be free not to do so. Powerful arguments favor this position. Most of these rest on the attitude, widely held among economists (myself included), that individuals are the best judge of their own welfare. But this assumption does not immediately imply the conclusion that, in insurance markets as they are, individuals should have free choice of coverage for psychotherapy.

Public policies already interfere, in many ways, with choice of coverage for psychotherapy. Eleven states do not permit residents to decline coverage for psychotherapy in health insurance. All states limit choice of covered provider by licensing statutes. Thirty-one states forbid individuals to choose insurance for psychotherapy that only covers services of physicians (these statutes are often referred to as "freedom-of-choice" legislation). At the federal level, most proposed forms of national health insurance would severely restrict choice of form and extent of coverage. Moreover, even among advocates of national health insurance there is no consensus about whether coverage for psychotherapy ought to be included.

This book considers what choices individuals should have about insurance coverage for psychotherapy. Should some coverage be compulsory? Discussion of this will involve the mechanics of insurance markets (notably adverse selection), effects of psychotherapy, and costs of coverage. Should individuals choose what professionals and organizations are eligible to receive payment for psychotherapy under insurance? Discussion of this will involve the relative merits of medical and nonmedical psychotherapists, of various organized care settings, and the costs of different alternatives.

This book contains three parts. The first two chapters in Part I introduce the problem and survey the institutions providing psychotherapy. This survey is from the perspective of economics—the supply and demand for psychotherapy are the organizing concepts of the chapter. In many respects, psychotherapy is provided in a market, and the perspective of economics is crucial to understanding how insurance or regulations affect that market. Chapter 3 is the conceptual heart of the book, analyzing the arguments for and against interference with individual choice of insurance for psychotherapy. Although Part I uses some simple tools of economics, no prior knowledge of economics is needed to understand the discussion.

It will be evident at the close of Part I that in spite of some past research, there are no good estimates of the responsiveness of demand for psychotherapy to insurance coverage. This issue is, of course, crucial for policy. Part II (Chapters 4, 5 and 6) presents an extensive study of insurance and demand for psychotherapy. This is the first true study of demand for a mental health service, in which the effect of insurance is isolated from other factors. Technical discussion could not be avoided, and the reader without a strong background in statistics would be advised to skim these pages.

Part III draws the conclusions for public policy. Chapter 7 develops a set of general principles for policy. Chapter 8 is an attempt to describe how these principles could be implemented at the federal and state level.

Application of rigorous economic analysis to problems in mental health services is very new. As I hope will be evident, economic methods can provide evidence on some crucial points. This book should be of interest to economists concerned with health policy, but it was also written to appeal to those who provide mental health services and those of any background who are concerned with mental health policy.

I am indebted to a number of individuals and organizations for their advice, encouragement and support. First, my thanks go to Fritz Redlich, whose interest in the social aspects of mental health influenced me. In addition, his keen interest in economics helped me to see the value of tackling the very complicated economics of mental health policy.

My work on this project began with the substantial task of conducting an empirical study of demand for psychotherapy. That project required financial support, and I, a new Ph.D., knocked on many foundation doors without success. I am very grateful to the Falk Medical Fund and its President, Phil Hallen, for their willingness to support such a risky venture.

I am also very grateful to the National Institute of Mental Health for support in the job of putting my empirical work in the broader context of mental health policy. I want to thank a number of officials and researchers at the Institute, notably Larry Kessler, Darrel Regier, Steven Sharfstein, and Carl Taube, for their interest and help.

The Joint Information Service of the American Psychiatric Association and the National Association for Mental Health generously provided the data for the study in Part II. I would particularly like to acknowledge the cooperation and assistance of Patricia Scheidemandel, now of the American Psychiatric Association, who was primarily responsible for design of the survey, and for whose expertise there was no substitute.

I have benefited from the comments of numerous colleagues, in addition to those already mentioned, including Bill Capron, Thanos Catsambis, Dan Hogan, Lee Jones, Al Klevorick, John Krizay, Oldrick Kyn, Bob Lucas, Michael Manove, Ted Marmor, Randy Olsen, Jon K. Peck, John Quigley, Gary VandenBos, and Stan Wallack.

One of the things I enjoyed most about this project was working with Richard Frank, my extraordinarily able research assistant. In the course of this project, it was extremely gratifying to see Richard's growing interest and expertise in both economics and mental health.

None of the above-mentioned individuals or organizations necessarily endorse the methods and conclusions of this book. For these I bear sole responsibility.

Thomas G. McGuire
Boston University

THE PROBLEM AND THE SETTING

1 PSYCHOTHERAPY AND PUBLIC POLICY

This book is concerned with the role of insurance for psychotherapy in national health policy. In the past few years debate about health policy has focused on national health insurance (NHI). Coverage for psychotherapy is the most controversial component of proposed coverage for mental health services and an unsettled part of NHI proposals. At present the major legislative bills proposed for national health insurance provide much less coverage for psychotherapy than for other forms of outpatient health care. Meanwhile, organizations representing the consumers and providers of psychotherapy, the National Institute of Mental Health (NIMH), and the major professional associations, press strongly for coverage for mental illness equal to coverage for physical illness. In early 1981, consideration of national health insurance per se seems to be slipping from near the top of the national agenda. Issues surrounding public policy toward financing psychotherapy are no less pressing. The analysis presented here does not presuppose national health insurance of any particular form for the rest of health care, or even any explicit NHI program at all. Some NHI-type public policies, such as subsidies for purchase of private insurance or mandatory coverage for mental health benefits in private insurance plans, are already in force. States are proceeding with policies that mimic some characteristics of national health insurance. Presently, eleven states require insurers to cover psychotherapy—a form of compulsory insurance. In the words of Sharfstein and Clark (1978), we have national health insurance "in disguise" already.

3

In contrast to the literature on financing policy and general medical services, the literature on financing and psychotherapy is very limited. It consists mainly of publications of the National Institute of Mental Health, the American Psychiatric Association, the American Psychological Association, and other professional organizations of providers of psychotherapy. More often than not the literature contains position statements rather than analyses of the possibilities. Economists, sociologists, and others trained in policy analysis have simply not given thorough consideration to the question of how to organize payment for psychotherapy. It is remarkable, for instance, that the task panel on cost and financing for the recent President's Commission on Mental Health (PCMH) demurred entirely even from taking a position on national health insurance for psychotherapy. Like all the commission's task panels charged with assembling a report in a matter of months, the panel on cost and financing could do no original research and had to pull together previous work. Unfortunately, there was little to pull together. With NHI clearly the most important financing issue for mental health services, the group assigned to study cost and financing for this major effort of the executive branch confined its recommendations to reforming Medicare and Medicaid.

In 1980, $4 to 5 billion was devoted to providing psychotherapy (ADAMHA 1980). This figure might decline or rise depending on arrangements for financing mental health care under national health insurance and other policies. Five billion dollars is but a fraction of the country's $200 billion annual health care budget, yet the importance of mental illness—and the potential importance of psychotherapy in dealing with mental illness—are not proportionally small. Their importance would be vastly understated by anyone who might gauge it by comparison of monies spent. Little is spent in treating mental illness, but the costs imposed on society by the mental illness that remains untreated are enormous. The President's Commission on Mental Health calls mental illness the nation's "primary public health issue." The economic loss in productivity from mental illness vastly exceeds the cost of the resources devoted to treatment.[1] But the major "cost" of mental illness remains pain and suffering, which is hard to quantify, but which would clearly dominate the accounting if it could be included. As understanding of human behavior improves, the links between mental health and physical health, productivity, crime, and other social problems become more clear.

There is increasing evidence of a strong relation between mental and physical health. In a recent survey of progress in research in psychiatry, Freedman wrote, "Recent public health reports have reemphasized that *all* modalities of death—suicidal, homicidal and natural— are considerably higher in psychiatric patients than in the general population" (1978: 511).

Although no one would disagree about the importance of mental illness, there is considerable debate about the effectiveness of present methods of reducing both suffering and costs and doubts are raised about whether to include mental health benefits in national health insurance. The debate ranges far beyond the usual issues in health policy. While cost, quality, appropriateness of treatment, access, and distribution of services remain issues in both the general medical and the mental health sectors, within the general medical sector the outline of how services should be provided is reasonably well agreed upon. The public expects medical institutions—physicians working singly and in groups, as well as general hospitals and related institutions—to continue to provide general medical care as they do now. Compare this with the situation in mental health. Basic, disturbing questions receive attention: Is there a role for mental hospitals? Should we attempt another "reform," or should mental hospitals be phased down as rapidly as possible to free patients and resources for treatment in community-based settings? Is psychotherapy worth paying for? Is psychotherapy a medical treatment or is it something else? Who should be qualified to provide psychotherapy? What should be the relation of mental health services to the general medical sector? What is the proper role of government? Should the government ensure access for everyone? Should it provide services directly? Or should it just regulate providers? There is much less consensus on what the structure of the mental health system should be—what services should be offered, how they should be paid for, and who should be providing them.

A BRIEF HISTORY OF FINANCING OF MENTAL HEALTH SERVICES

Insurance coverage for medical treatment within hospitals first became widely available in the United States during the 1930s, years before coverage for outpatient care. During the Depression, hospitals' desire for a secure source of payment and patients' desire for insurance against large medical expense set the stage for the birth and growth of Blue Cross. Blue Cross was a creature of the private general hospitals, few of which had psychiatric beds. Hospitalization for mental illness took place primarily in state mental hospitals or private mental hospitals, neither of which were part of the early Blue Cross plans. Treatment in hospitals for mental illness largely fell outside early insurance coverage.

Control of nominal industrial wages during the Second World War diverted pressure for wage hikes into fringe benefits, including hospital insurance. By the end of World War II, 32 million Americans were covered for hospital expenses. Blue Cross and commercial insurance companies continued to expand their coverage, so that today over 90 percent of the total population has some insurance for hospital expense.

Coverage for hospitalization for mental illness was part of this growth, with commercial insurance companies offering coverage in all settings and for all illnesses, and Blue Cross plans gradually expanding to include treatment of mental illness. Although by the mid-seventies most Americans who were covered for hospital expenses had equal coverage for both mental and physical conditions, some insurance plans continued to feature lower benefits for treatment of mental illness. A Bureau of Labor Statistics survey of 148 employee health benefit plans found that 68 percent of the plans offered equal care for mental and physical conditions and 32 percent offered less care for mental conditions (Reed 1975). The BLS survey did not identify Blue Cross and commercial insurance plans, but Reed's (1975) survey of Blue Cross showed that Blue Cross hospital insurance plans discriminated against treatment for mental illness more frequently than did commercial insurance plans. Of seventy-four Blue Cross plans in 1974, fifty-two plans (70 percent) provided less coverage for mental illness in a general hospital than for physical illness under their most widely held contract. Twenty-two plans (30 percent) provided no coverage for treatment in private mental hospitals, and forty plans (54 percent) provided no coverage for treatment in public mental hospitals.

There was no significant insurance coverage for medical treatment of any kind outside of the hospital before the early 1950s, when commercial insurers began to offer "major medical" policies, primarily through group insurance plans. Blue Cross and Blue Shield followed, and the growth of this insurance was rapid.

Initially, during the early 1950s, under the major medical policies of commercial insurance companies, outpatient treatment for mental illness was covered on the same basis as other illness. Generally after the policyholder paid a deductible amount, the insurer paid 75–80 percent of the charges for treatment. Commercial insurers' early experience with this coverage, however, led them to draw back quickly from equal coverage for outpatient treatment for mental and physical illness and to institute discriminatory coverage for outpatient mental health benefits. Psychoanalysis was the predominant form of psychotherapy and presented special difficulties to insurers, as it still does today. "The companies became concerned over the appropriateness and equity of paying out significant portions of total benefit payments to a very few individuals who were not disabled and were continuing to earn or to carry on their usual functions" (Reed, Myers, and Scheidemandel 1972: 61).

Most private and public insurance for outpatient psychiatric care reflects this early experience. In a survey of group health insurance policies issued by commercial insurance companies in 1973, the Health Insurance Institute (1977) reports that although 96 percent of persons insured by the companies surveyed (representing 55 percent of the total insurance premium volume) were covered for mental and nervous disorders, maximum benefits were usually limited to $500 per year and $10,000 per lifetime, and the coinsurance rate was usually 50 percent. In Reed's (1975) survey of Blue Cross and Blue Shield outpatient coverage in 1973, of the eleven plans or pairs of plans reporting coverage, seven paid 50 percent or less for outpatient psychiatric treatment (as opposed to 80 percent for other conditions, and most of these had other restrictions on visits); three paid 80 percent of charges, the same as for other conditions; and one plan offered a variety of packages with coinsurance ranging from 50 to 80 percent with and without limits.

The pattern of broad, equal coverage, bad experience, and retraction of benefits has been repeated since the 1950s. The recent experience of federal employees is notable. Aetna insurance, one option for health benefits for federal employees, was cited by many as a model for national health insurance coverage for mental illness. Benefits were generous and equal for mental and physical illness. After a few years' experience with this coverage, however, Aetna found it necessary to restrict psychiatric outpatient coverage to twenty visits per year in 1975. Some of the complaints about improper utilization echo the story of major medical coverage in the early 1950s (Aetna

1974). More recently, Blue Cross/Blue Shield, the other nationwide option for health insurance for federal employees, has also reduced coverage for outpatient psychotherapy by increasing the coinsurance rate.

Blue Cross and Blue Shield plans in Massachusetts and California are following Aetna's lead and tightening coverage for mental health care (Herrington 1979). In the latest round, the reaction of insurers to unexpectedly heavy use of mental health services is less severe than in the early 1950s. In spite of publicized cutbacks in coverage, more and more people are gaining coverage for outpatient mental health care. Today, roughly 50–70 percent of the population has some coverage for outpatient mental health services, but few have benefits that match coverage for physical illness.

Federal programs have helped selected groups pay for mental health care. Since 1965, Medicare and Medicaid have insured the elderly and the poor for some treatment for mental illness. Medicare, providing for patients over sixty-five years of age, limits coverage for mental illness to both treatment in and out of hospitals in similar fashion to the limits specified in most private insurance plans. Under part A of the Medicare plan, coverage in a general hospital is the same for psychiatric as for other illness, but coverage for treatment in a psychiatric hospital is limited to 190 days in a lifetime. Under optional part B, coverage by a psychiatrist for treatment on an outpatient basis is limited to either 50 percent of charges or $250 per year, whichever is less. State Medicaid programs, serving the poor, may not make payment contingent on diagnosis; however, states may place limits on the amount of care covered, as by limiting fees or the number of visits to physicians, and thereby limit psychiatric coverage. The federal government also provides care for veterans at Veterans Administration (VA) hospitals and insurance coverage for dependents and retired personnel of the armed forces when they must obtain services in the civilian community through the Civilian Health and Medical Program of the Uniformed Services (CHAMPUS).

AN APPROACH TO POLICY

The essence of national health insurance is that it is *compulsory*. Coverage and payment for coverage cannot be avoided by personal choice. Compulsory insurance may be financed in many different ways. The government need not act as the collector of tax premiums and provider of benefits to have national health insurance. It is national health insurance if the government decrees that all citizens must buy coverage of at least a certain amount (for example, through group plans at place of employment) and pay for coverage by premiums to private suppliers of insurance. This is the effect of state mandates for coverage for mental health care. In many aspects, the alternatives to national health insurance differ, but each falls under the category of compulsory insurance.

In arguing for compulsory insurance for psychotherapy, one must address the following position: If psychotherapy is worth the cost, people will buy it for themselves; the government should not interfere. If insurance for psychotherapy is worth the premiums, people will buy coverage on their own; the government should not interfere. Insurance for psychotherapy is available to some people on a voluntary basis. Why should the government take this choice away by *forcing* people to pay through taxes for a service they could have purchased, if they wished, on the private market?

The answer to the foregoing argument—the justification for public action—must be based on the shortcomings or failures of mechanisms that rely on voluntary behavior in markets. The shortcomings of markets for psychotherapy are many. Pointing out that markets are imperfect is a necessary part of the case for public intervention in insurance for psychotherapy. But to make a *sufficient* argument it must be shown that markets are worse than the alternative.

It is tempting to recommend that the blatant failures in private markets be corrected by public action. But however bad a market may appear in relation to theoretical ideals of efficiency and fairness, the market may still be the best of any practical alternative. Having pointed out that a market fails in a certain way, it is naive to conclude that the appropriate response is to reassign authority to some public official to take the appropriate action.

The health sector of the national economy provides ample illustration of how "corrective" action by government, even when market failure is obvious and costly, may not be beneficial on balance. To simplify, we could say that with regard to pharmaceuticals, society's goals are to foster constructive research into new drugs and to bring to market only those drugs that prove safe and effective. Experience suggests that an unfettered private market would continually fail to regulate itself, so that harmful or ineffective drugs would too often be marketed. Market failure here would accordingly be judged to be severe. In response to this, Congress empowered the Food and Drug Administration (FDA) to take over a function of the market for drugs and to regulate which drugs are to be marketed. No one quarrels with the regulatory *goal* that only safe and effective drugs be marketed, but the regulatory *practice* of the FDA, its attempts to administer the goal, has come in for serious and pointed criticism. The FDA is charged with being overly cautious in approving or disapproving possible new drugs, and for the drugs it does approve, with taking years too long. There is broad consensus, even within the FDA, that as currently constituted, the regulation mandate of the FDA leads to an overly conservative stance.

Drug regulation is not an isolated case. Put in the position of allocating resources, the government is predisposed to certain problems. One particularly relevant to the present discussion is that governments are inherently limited in their ability to accommodate diversity in consumer choices.

Politicians and bureaucrats are inept at deciding how much goods and services the individual household ought to buy. Simple rules adopted in Washington, such as "Everyone must have insurance coverage of the following amount," would give too much to some and not enough to others. No matter what choice is made for coverage for psychotherapy under national health insurance, some will believe the government has not gone far enough ("At the tax rate I pay I would like to have seen the government require more coverage"), while others will argue the opposite ("At the tax rate I pay I would like to have seen the government require less coverage"). Even an NHI bill politically "right" in the sense of representing what the average citizen would want would be "wrong" for all but the average citizen. When the federal government provides services for national defense or state governments provide educational services, everyone is automatically enrolled. Citizens may not withhold their taxes to support these services if they would rather have the money than the defense or education.[2] National health insurance would take insurance for private psychiatric care out of the market and put it into the same category as national defense and education, imposing on all a uniform standard of coverage. But it is inherently inefficient because it imposes equal consumption (or at least an equal minimum level of consumption), neglecting differences in individual circumstance and preference.

Governments are not only imperfect in this regard, they are generally inferior to markets in their ability to offer consumer choice. Purchases in a market are basically voluntary. If a service is worth the cost to a consumer he buys it; otherwise he does not. At present there is a market in insurance for private psychiatric care. The market is highly imperfect, but it does offer some choice. For most people, the choices are very limited. Individual policies insuring against psychiatric expenses are unavailable or very expensive. Although a large portion of employee group insurance policies include some coverage for outpatient psychiatric care, employees often have little choice about how much or what type of coverage they receive. In this case, the price of buying more or less coverage would include resigning from one's present job and seeking another with a different firm, possibly in a different industry.

There are some people, though, for whom the market provides a wide range of options. Federal employees are the best example. The typical federal employee may join the Blue Cross "high-option" plan with very extensive benefits for all medical services, including outpatient psychotherapy; the Blue Cross "low-option" plan with fewer benefits for all services; the Aetna Insurance Company's plan with benefits essentially the same as the Blue Cross high-option but with special restrictions on outpatient psychotherapy benefits; or the local health maintenance organization (HMO) with its characteristic package of services, generally including limited outpatient psychotherapy. Differences among the insurance benefit plans concern more than just level and type of mental health benefits; employees make choices based on numerous considerations. Nevertheless, the federal employee has considerable scope for exercise of consumer sovereignty in choice of insurance for mental health care. The market's flexibility in accommodating differences in circumstance and preference can be lost in a move to compulsory insurance.

As is probably not surprising, the markets for psychotherapy and for insurance for psychotherapy are weak, beset by failures of various sorts (see Chapter 3). As this discussion has tried to make clear, it is necessary to go beyond making up a list of market failures to establish an effective case for compulsory insurance for psychotherapy; it is necessary also to demonstrate that government action (with its own set of failures) is likely to improve the situation.

Psychotherapy is practiced by a number of professions, including physicians, psychologists, psychiatric social workers and psychiatric nurses. Mental health services are provided by professionals in private practice and numerous institutions, some specializing in mental health care, some affiliated with health institutions, and some (like employee assistance plans) affiliated with businesses run for profit. Government, at all levels, already participates in many ways in supply of mental health services, ranging from regulating the work of professionals and terms of third-party payment plans to direct provision of care through hospitals and clinics. All this makes consideration of further government intervention in the provision of psychotherapy extremely complex. Questions arise about who and what to pay for, and about the effects of a new initiative on the existing system of financing and care. The next chapter is an overview of the present system of providing psychotherapy. The perspective is that of an economist—as will be argued, the present system can quite legitimately be called a market.

NOTES TO CHAPTER 1

1. The latest and best in a series of studies attempting to measure the costs of mental illness is by the Research Triangle Institute (1980).
2. "Public goods" such as national defense are characterized by "equal consumption" by all citizens. These goods are widely agreed to be an appropriate domain of government activity. Equal consumption is not an inherent characteristic of education or insurance. Government activity in these spheres comes only at the price of some diversity in choice and is controversial.

2 THE MARKET FOR PSYCHOTHERAPY

Expenditures for mental health care (outside of nursing homes) have been estimated at $14 billion in 1980. More than half of this amount, $8.3 billion, is spent for active care in inpatient facilities, predominantly in state and county mental hospitals and nonfederal general hospitals. More than $3 billion is spent on therapy at organized mental health facilities, and slightly less than $.5 billion at organized outpatient health settings. Expenditures for services of psychiatrists, other physicians, and psychologists in private practice total nearly $2 billion. Details on these estimates are contained in Table 2–1.[1]

SERVICES AND COSTS

Over 200,000 residents of nursing homes in 1980 received a primary or secondary diagnosis of mental disorder. These people are by far the most expensive to care for, although very little of the expense is attributable to active treatment. Levine and Willner (1976) estimated that the average cost per year of caring for a mentally ill person in a nursing home was $6,673, more than twice the $2,599 yearly average for the next highest setting, public mental hospitals. According to Levine and Willner this means that almost half again as much is added to total expenditures on mental health care by including nurs-

Table 2-1. Estimated Expenditure on Mental Health Care in the United States in 1980 (000's).

Inpatient Facilities[a]

State and county mental hospitals	$ 1,829,097
Private mental hospitals	403,873
Other public mental hospitals (VA neuropsychiatric, prison psychiatric)	364,588
Nonfederal general hospitals	
Without separate psychiatric unit	1,050,854
With separate psychiatric unit	2,472,270
Federal General hospitals	
Department of Defense	120,697
VA general hospitals	563,030
Public Health Service (PHS)	2,880
Indian Health Service (IHS)	7,808
Community mental health centers (CMHCs)	437,708
Children's treatment programs	205,911
Halfway houses and community residences	43,323
Physician visits to psychiatric inpatients	750,204
Total	$ 8,252,243

Organized Outpatient Mental Health Settings

VA general hospital (psychiatric unit)	$ 51,335
Nonfederal general hospital (psychiatric unit)	325,279
Free-standing outpatient clinics	710,368
State and county mental hospitals	773,917
Federally funded community mental health centers	874,642
Other mental health facilities	540,314
Total	$ 3,275,855

Table 2-1. continued

Organized Outpatient Health Settings	
Health maintenance organizations (HMOs)	63,999
General hospital outpatient departments	243,229
Neighborhood health centers	52,062
Migrant health programs	2,097
National Health Service Corps	1,340
Home health	265
Department of Defense	16,197
PHS	533
IHS	7,517
Total	$ 387,239
Private Office-Based Providers	
Psychiatrists	$ 1,236,000
Other physicians	93,677
Psychologists	533,000
Total	$ 1,862,677
Grand total	$13,778,014

a. Active care only.
Source: ADAMHA (1979).

ing homes as a setting for care. If nursing homes are included, expenditures for care of the mentally ill exceed $20 billion in 1980. This is about 14 percent of all health costs and roughly 1 percent of national income.

On behalf of the President's Commission on Mental Health, Regier, Goldberg, and Taube (1979) have compiled estimates of the number of persons treated for mental illness in various settings in the United States. The results of their investigation are summarized in Table 2-2. Regier, Goldberg, and Taube make a distinction among the specialized mental health sector, the general hospital inpatient/nursing home sector, and the primary care/outpatient medical sector. Although categories in the tables are not fully comparable, it is nevertheless interesting to compare the distribution of persons across facilities in Table 2-2 with the distribution of expenditures in Table 2-1. What Regier, Goldberg, and Taube call the specialized mental health sector accounts for about 25 percent of all the people treated for mental disorders outside of nursing homes but for about 65 percent of all the expenditures outside of nursing homes. Three-quarters of all persons treated for mental disorders are treated in general health settings. About one-third of expenditures for mental health (outside of nursing homes) go to care for this large group.

Significant changes in the treatment of persons with mental disorders have taken place in the past twenty-five years, some of which are evident in Table 2-3. The first striking fact is the quadrupling of episodes of care in facilities between 1955 and 1975, from 1.7 to 6.4 million. Only episodes in mental health facilities are counted. The growth in treatment outside facilities by practitioners in private practice has been even more dramatic.

The second major change in the past two decades has been the thorough reorientation of mental health facilities away from providing treatment on an inpatient basis toward providing it on an outpatient basis. In 1955, over three-quarters of all care episodes occurred on an inpatient basis. By 1975, three-quarters of all care episodes were on an outpatient basis. The relative importance of the inpatient services of state and county mental hospitals showed a dramatic decline, the only setting to show an absolute decline in the number of patients served between 1955 and 1975. Inpatient services of state and county mental hospitals accounted for one-half of all mental health care episodes at U.S. facilities in 1955, but less than 10 percent of all episodes by 1975. Including the 1-2 million visits of people seen outside facilities every year, well over 80 percent of

Table 2—2. Distribution of Persons with Mental Disorder by Type of Treatment Setting, U.S., 1975.

Setting	Persons	Percentage[a]
Specialized Mental Health Sector		
State and county mental hospitals	789,000	
VA—psychiatric units of general and neuropsychiatric hospitals	351,000	
Private mental hospitals and residential treatment centers	233,000	
Nonfederal general hospitals with psychiatric units	927,000	
Community mental health centers	1,627,000	
Free standing outpatient multiservice clinics	1,763,000	
Halfway houses for the mentally ill	7,000	
College campus mental health clinics	131,000	
Office-based private practice psychiatrists	854,000	
Private practice psychologists	425,000	
Subtotal	7,107,000	
Unduplicated sector total	6,698,000	26.7
General Hospital Inpatient/Nursing Home Sector		
Nonpsychiatric hospitals	893,000	
Nursing homes	207,000	
Unduplicated sector total	1,100,000	4.4
Primary Care/Outpatient Medical Sector		
Office-based nonpsychiatric physicians	13,047,000	
Neighborhood health centers	314,000	
Industrial health facilities	314,000	
Health department clinics, outpatient	941,000	
General hospital and emergency rooms	6,391,000	
Subtotal	21,007,000	
Unduplicated sector total	19,218,000	76.6
Unduplicated total	25,094,000	100.0

a. Sector percentages total more than 100 because some patients are seen in more than one sector.

Source: Regier, Goldberg, and Taube (1978), Table I.

Table 2-3. Number of Inpatient and Outpatient Care Episodes
in Selected Mental Health Facilities, U.S., 1955, 1965, 1975.[a]

		Inpatient			
Year	Total, All Facilities	All Inpatient	State and County Mental Hospitals	Private Mental Hospitals	General Hospital Psychiatric Services
1975	6,409,447	1,791,171	598,993	165,327	565,696
1965	2,636,525	1,565,525	804,926	125,428	519,328
1955	1,675,352	1,296,352	818,832	123,231	265,954

a. In order to present trends on the same set of facilities over this interval, it is necessary
to exclude from this table the following: private psychiatric office practice; psychiatric service modes of all types in hospitals or outpatient clinics of federal agencies other than the
VA (e.g., Public Health Service, Indian Health Service, Department of Defense, Bureau of
Prisons, etc.); inpatient service modes of multiservice facilities not shown in this table; all
partial care episodes, and outpatient episodes of VA hospitals.

Source: Provisional Data on Patient Care Episodes in Mental Health Facilities, Mental
Health Statistical Note No. 139 1975, Division of Biometry and Epidemiology, National
Institute of Mental Health (August 1977).

all episodes of mental health care in the mental health sector are
handled on an outpatient basis.

Policy needs to be formulated with recognition that mental health
care is increasingly and now largely provided in *market settings*, the
hallmark of a market being choice by provider and user of the good
or service. Mental health providers have always had plenty of choice
about where and how much to work. From their point of view the
market for mental health personnel has been little different from
many other professional labor markets.

The new force in this sector is that users of mental health care
are finding themselves with important choices, too, about whether,
from whom, and how much care to seek. Historically, most mental
patients were admitted involuntarily to mental institutions where
decisions about treatment were made for them in an authoritarian
manner by professionals. Increasing judicial recognition of patients'
rights and mental health professionals' desire to deemphasize institu-
tional care has returned to patients some of the decisions formerly

Table 2−3. continued

Year	Inpatient (continued)		Outpatient		
	VA Psychiatric Inpatient Services	Federally Assisted CMHCs	All Outpatient	Federally Assisted CMHCs	Other
			(non−VA)		
1975	214,264	246,891	4,618,276	1,584,968	3,033,308
1965	115,843	. . .	1,071,000	. . .	1,071,000
1955	88,355	. . .	379,000	. . .	379,000

made for them. Patients who have been treated with long stays in mental hospitals or who would in earlier times have been institution-alized are likely to be severely ill and require close management of their living and treatment arrangements to lead a satisfactory life out-side of the institution. But the large majority of people treated for mental disorder are not so severely ill and can make many of their own decisions about treatment. These people have significant choice about where to seek care—from general physicians, psychiatrists, psychologists, other mental health professionals, residential health centers, community mental health centers—and are likely to base their decisions on price, convenience, and quality.

For policy to have an effect in the market it must work through the decisions of the millions of users and providers of mental health care. The results of policy, never automatic, will emerge as the re-sponse of users and providers to changed market conditions. Insur-ance for some types of psychotherapy would change the relative prices for different types of care for a user of mental health services, perhaps causing a shift from seeking help at a subsidized public clinic to seeing a private practitioner. Another user in the presence of insur-ance might not shift but expand considerably the quantity of services demanded. New patients will be brought into treatment as the cost for receiving care falls.

A convenient set of tools for analyzing these sorts of responses is provided by market analysis in economics. Market analysis relies on the separate consideration of the forces affecting supply and demand for a service. Hence the rest of this chapter focuses on the supply and demand for psychotherapy, stressing the role of insurance in demand.

SUPPLY OF PSYCHOTHERAPY

There is tremendous diversity in the supply of psychotherapy. Policy toward financing and psychotherapy must include decisions about what organizations and what providers of psychotherapy will be eligible for payment. Psychotherapy is dominated by the four core mental health professions: psychiatry, psychology, social work, and nursing.

Growth of the Mental Health Professions

Since the Second World War, psychiatry has been one of the major "growth specialties" of medicine. The number of psychiatrists has increased by a factor of 10 between 1940 and 1980, to 30,000. At the same time, the ratio of psychiatrists to population has increased by a factor of 5. Psychiatrists as a percentage of all physicians has also been growing steadily. Between 1963 and 1973, the number of psychiatrists increased by 51.2 percent while the total number of MDs increased by 32.5 percent (AMA 1975). These increases have been fueled by the popularity of psychiatry among medical students. Throughout the 1960s, the percentage of first-year residents in psychiatry and child psychiatry hovered close to 10 percent, pushing the present percentage of all physicians in psychiatry to an all-time high of near 8 percent.

This wave of popularity of psychiatry among medical students now seems to have subsided. Table 2–4 shows the percentage of first-year residents in psychiatry and child psychiatry for selected years. For the first time, it appears that the percentage of residents choosing psychiatry is smaller than the percentage of all physicians who are psychiatrists. This means that barring major specialty crossovers by physicians not trained in psychiatry, psychiatrists as a percentage of all physicians will decline in the future. Table 2–5 reports a prediction of the number of psychiatrists to 1990. Note that although psychiatrists as a percentage of all physicians is predicted to fall, the

Table 2-4. Percentage of First-Year Residents in Psychiatry
and Child Psychiatry.

Year	Percentage
1960	9.8
1968	10.2
1974	9.8
1976	7.9

Source: Graduate Medical Education National Advisory Committee (1979, p. 49).

Table 2-5. Number of Active Psychiatrists and Child Psychiatrists
Projected to 1990.

	1974	1980	1985	1990
Number	27,470	33,020	35,870	38,420
Percentage of MDs	7.9	7.6	7.2	6.7
Ratio to 100,000 population	13.0	14.8	15.4	15.5

Source: Graduate Medical Education National Advisory Committee (1979, p. 153, 156).

rapid growth in the number of physicians relative to the population
over this period means that the psychiatrists-to-population ratio will
still be increasing.

There are conflicting indicators of whether this decline in the relative number of psychiatrists will constitute a shortage of psychiatric
manpower. This concern is derived from several factors:

• Erosion of federal support for psychiatric training. Between
1969 and 1976 NIMH support for psychiatric training fell from $46
million to $26 million. In real terms the decline was even more dra-
matic. (There has been a similar decline in funds for the other core
mental health professions.)

• Cutoff of foreign medical graduates (FMGs). "Less desirable"
residencies and staff positions in many mental health facilities are
often filled by FMGs. FMGs make up over one-half of all MDs in
state mental hospitals. The Health Professionals Education Act of
1976 (PL 94-484), designed to restrict the flow of FMGs into the
United States, threatens a major source of psychiatric manpower.

• Persistence of underserved areas. The number of psychiatrists per 100,000 population varies tremendously among states. Psychiatry may be the most severely maldistributed of any major medical specialty. Nationally in 1976 there were nine psychiatrists per 100,000 population. In the five states with highest overall physician density there were sixteen psychiatrists per 100,000, and in the five states with the lowest density there were only three per 100,000 (see Table 2-6). As the last column of the table shows, the ratio of specialists per capita between the best and worst served states is higher for psychiatry than for any other specialty except general surgery. These factors led the President's Commission on Mental Health (PCMH) to recommend that psychiatry be added to the primary care specialties now designated as shortage specialties under PL 94-484.

On the other hand, there are reasons to think that the declining supply of new psychiatrists may be appropriate. Psychiatrists have recently become the most poorly paid of medical specialists (Matterra 1979). Their income relative to other MDs' fell by 20 percent between 1970 and 1974 (Sharfstein and Clark 1979). Falling relative income is not characteristic of a shortage specialty. Further, if there

Table 2-6. Patient Care MDs (Nonfederal) per 100,000 Population by Selected States and Specialties, 1976.

Specialty	MDs per 100,000 Population	MDs per 100,000 in Top 5 States[b]	MDs per 100,000 in Low 5 States[c]	Ratio Top 5 to Low 5
All specialties	137	181	85	2.13
Primary care[a]	58	76	39	1.95
Obstetric gynecology	9	13	5	2.60
General surgery	14	17	3	5.67
Psychiatry	9	16	3	5.33
Opthalmology	5	6	3	2.00
Orthopedic surgery	5	6	4	1.50
Anesthesiology	5	8	2	4.00

a. General and family practitioners, internists, pediatricians.

b. High 5 are New York, Massachusetts, Maryland, Connecticut, and California.

c. Low 5 are South Dakota, North Dakota, Alabama, Alaska, and Mississippi.

Source: American Medical Association, *Physician Distribution and Medical Licensure in the U.S., 1976.*

is indeed a shortage, it should be regarded as a shortage of mental health *services* rather than of an input in production of these services.

In considering a shortage of any particular input, the notion of substitutability becomes key, and the supply of possible substitute services becomes relevant. The output of doctoral psychology programs is growing, and within this general growth, programs are producing an increasing number of students in specialties likely to lead to licensure and careers as health service providers. As Table 2-7 shows, about 3,000 psychology doctorates are awarded annually, roughly half of these being awarded to students likely to receive a license or certification. New health service providers in psychology exceed the roughly 1,200 psychiatrists per year graduating from residency programs (PCMH II: 489). The growth in masters degree programs in psychology has been even more dramatic. Over 8,000 masters degrees are awarded annually—a doubling of degrees in ten years (Scientific Manpower Commission 1978: 226).

Many more psychologists eligible to become health service providers are doing so. New psychologists are much more likely to be health service providers than are older psychologists (Scientific Manpower Commission 1978: 230). If this pattern holds, even without further increases in the number of graduates of psychology programs, it will mean a large increase in the total number of psychologists who provide health services, because there will be little depletion from the provider ranks due to retirement. Psychologists not trained in the clinical specialty are becoming health service providers. Dörken and Webb (1978) discovered that of licensed or certified psychologists in

Table 2-7. Doctorates in Psychology 1920-77.

	1920-72	1973, 1974	1975	1976	1977
All psychology	26,383	5,031	2,749	2,878	2,960
Clinical, counseling and guidance, school, and industrial and personnel specialties	9,202	2,263	1,208	1,363	1,405
Specialties likely to be licensed, as a percentage of total	34.9	45.0	43.9	47.4	47.5

Source: Scientific Manpower Commission (1978, p. 225).

full-time fee-for-service clinical practice, 18 percent were not originally trained in clinical psychology.

Currently, about 8 percent of physicians, 40 percent of psychologists, 10 percent of social workers, and 5 percent of nurses are primarily engaged in providing mental health services. Data on the number of physicians who are psychiatrists and where these psychiatrists
work is published annually by the American Medical Association (see
AMA 1979). Information on psychologists is somewhat harder to
locate. Since 1920 roughly 40 percent of psychologists have specialized in a field leading to licensure or certification. Presently 75 percent of licensed or certified psychologists are active health service
providers, and about 75 percent of all health service providers are
licensed or certified (see Table 2-8.). This makes the 40 percent
a good guess. Data on social workers and nurses are more reliable
because their work is almost exclusively within settings surveyed
by NIMH. Liptzin (1978) reports 24,000 of 300,000 social workers
provide mental health services. Rosenstein and Taube (1978) report
that 39,392 full-time-equivalent (FTE) nurses work in mental health
facilities. The PCMH (1978 II: 488) estimates there were 1,018,000
nurses in 1978.

Estimates of the number of workers from each profession are summarized for a recent year in Table 2-8. In the aggregate there are

Table 2-8. Members of Core Mental Health Professions Providing
Mental Health Services.

Year	Psychiatry[a]	Psychology[b]	Social Work[c]	Nursing[d]
1974			24,000	
1976	24,600			39,392
1977		25,865		

a. Sources: American Medical Association, Physician Distribution and Medical Licensure
in the U.S. annual.

b. Mills et al. (1979) report 18,882 licensed or certified psychologists were active health
service providers in early 1977. Among American Psychological Association members who
provide health services, 73 percent were licensed or certified (see Gottfredson and Dyer
1978). If 18,882 represents 73 percent of all health service providers, there were 25,865 in
total.

c. Reported in Liptzin (1978, p. 57).

d. This is full-time-equivalent nurses (all levels of qualification) working in mental
health facilities surveyed by NIMH (Rosenstein and Taube 1978). Of registered nurses,
there are approximately 11,000 with training at masters level or above in psychiatric nursing.

roughly equal numbers of workers from each profession providing mental health services.

The mix of professionals providing services in mental health settings varies greatly (Rosenstein and Taube 1978). In all hospital settings, medical personnel—psychiatrists and nurses—are more heavily used. Psychiatrists are most heavily used relative to other groups in psychiatric units of general (nonfederal) hospitals. In outpatient settings, such as free-standing clinics and community mental health centers (CMHCs), psychologists and social workers predominate. Members of the four core mental health professions make up less than one-half of the total full-time-equivalent staff at mental health facilities devoted to patient care. Other mental health workers outnumber the core professionals by over three to one in psychiatric hospitals (non–VA) and by roughly two to one in most other settings.

Psychotherapy in office-based practice, outside of mental health facilities surveyed by NIMH, is dominated by psychiatrists and psychologists. Dividing time between a private office and work in a mental health facility is a way of life for psychiatrists. Most psychiatrists who report the private practice office as their primary setting spend part of their time working in a mental health facility. And the large majority of psychiatrists working primarily in a mental health facility see some private patients. A survey of all psychiatrists, conducted by the Division of Manpower Research and Development of the Americana Psychiatric Association (APA), indicates that practice in private offices accounts for 41 percent of the total hours worked by psychiatrists (Reed, Myers, and Scheidemandel 1972). Applying this average to the total of 24,600 psychiatrists at work in 1976, about 10,000 FTE psychiatrists work in private practice.

Recent surveys of psychologists give reliable profiles of psychologists working as health service providers in all settings, including private practice (Mills, Wellner, and VandenBos 1979). In 1976 there were over 22,000 licensed or certified health service providers in psychology. Of these, about 19,000 were active as health service providers. About 5,000 were in full-time private practice; 10,000 in part-time private practice; and 3,500 were health service providers not in private practice. In terms of FTEs there are roughly 6,000–8,000 FTE psychologists in private practice. The vast majority of psychologists are in solo private practice. Only about 1 percent are employed by another mental health professional, presumably a physician. About 20 percent of psychologists in private practice work in a group setting. Some of these groups are interdisciplinary, including psychiatrists or other physicians.

The private practice of social work was first sanctioned by the National Association of Social Workers (NASW) in 1962. At that time there were only 400 social workers in full- or part-time private practice. This number has grown rapidly in recent years. In 1975, about 2,200 worked more than twenty hours per week in private practice, and another 6,600 devoted some time to private practice (Kole 1978). Little is known about the practice of social workers, but NASW seems to be following the lead of the American Psychological Association in compiling a *Register of Clinical Social Workers*. Mental health nurses are rare in private practice, with fewer than 300 nurses in full- or part-time private practice (Kole 1978).

Roles of the Mental Health Professions

One of the major issues in mental health policy is how much substitution among mental health workers should be permitted (or encouraged). Psychiatrists, as physicians, have broad mandates to provide health services, including mental health. Traditionally, psychiatrists have dominated the delivery of mental health services, in the same way other physicians dominate the delivery of general health services. Stereotypes from the 1950s determined that "psychiatrists treated patients, psychologists administered tests to them, social workers helped them make logistical arrangements for them after they were discharged, nurses handed out medications, and the attendants kept the patients company by playing cards. . . ." (Blum, Redlich, and Mollica 1979: 3). Although it is doubtful whether such strict roles were a fully accurate description of the division of labor among mental health professionals even then, they do reflect the original orientation of and perception about the major mental health professions.

Today these stereotypes are certainly inaccurate. Changed perceptions of mental disorders and their proper treatment have blurred the roles of the mental health professions. Psychiatrists, once indisputedly at the top of the occupational ladder in mental health, seem to have failed to maintain the intellectual leadership in definition and treatment of mental problems that their medical colleagues have achieved in other areas of health. Blum, Redlich, and Mollica (1979) refer to a professional "identity crisis," by which they mean a lack of consensus among psychiatrists about the model of disease and treatment and its relation to medicine. In the absence of a dominant medical model, the field opens to alternative models championed by other professionals. Society and the professions do not recognize psychiatrists' exclusive expertise in treating mental problems. Kole and Metnick have argued that payment for mental health services "should be on the basis of equivalence of service provided, rather than on the specific disciplinary background" (1978: 115). The broadening scope of recognized mental health problems and the introduction of innovative programs emphasizing community mental health have naturally drawn more heavily on the talents of mental health workers other than psychiatrists.

Studies of the work of professionals in the various mental health care settings apparently confirm the existence of considerable overlap in their functions. In an early limited comparison of the division of labor in two CMHCs in New York City, Sloan (1971) found major differences in the personnel assigned to various tasks. Recent studies have looked at the performance of tasks in mental health settings in more detail. Steinberg et al.'s 1976 study of 812 workers in CMHCs found a set of "core functions" done by all mental health professionals. These included receiving new clients, providing crisis intervention, observing and recording client's behavior, planning treatment programs for individual clients, referring clients to outside resources, and others.

Blum, Redlich, and Mollica (1979) questioned mental health professionals in a variety of settings in South Central Connecticut about the nature of their work. Some of their results are reported in Table 2-9. Most performed individual psychotherapy. The sharing of essential treatment functions appears so egalitarian in the mental health settings studied that one-half of all *nonprofessional* mental health workers, when filling out questionnaires on their activity, reported that they do invidual psychotherapy. About one-half of all workers led group therapy.

No doubt there has been considerable replacement of psychiatrists by other mental health workers in the past thirty years. In the rapidly growing service sector the share of treatment services being provided by psychologists, social workers, and nurses has increased, largely at the expense of psychiatrists. These facts are beyond dis-

Table 2-9. Performance of Treatment Tasks by Mental Health Workers in South Central Connecticut.

Function	Psychiatrists (N = 179)	Psychologists (N = 105)	Social Workers (N = 105)	Nurses (N = 106)	Mental Health Workers (N = 91)
Individual therapy	89.4	70.1	83.8	64.2	49.5
Group therapy	39.7	53.3	48.6	64.2	63.7
Evaluation upon admission	Not asked	35.2	44.6	26.4	33.0

Source: Blum, Redlich, and Mollica (1979, p. 20).

pute; but it should be kept in mind that the *nature* of this replacement is not clear. Taking a benign view one could say that over the last generation Americans have desired considerably more mental health services. Experience has shown that members of all mental health professions are capable of providing those services in a satisfactory way. It has been sensible, therefore, to expand the size of the mental health sector primarily by adding the less expensive personnel. An encapsulation of this benign view would be that there has been replacement because mental health personnel are substitutable in that services of comparable quality could be provided by less costly, more available personnel.

Most discussion of problems in mental health manpower, however, seem to disagree at least partly with this hopeful view and are far more skeptical of the value of the massive substitution that has occurred. The PCMH, for example, takes the view that the replacement of psychiatrists by other mental health personnel, though not entirely unwelcome, has gone too far. The primary problem in mental health manpower, if the literature is to be believed, is a "shortage" of psychiatrists. According to this view, there are too few psychiatrists in many areas of the United States. Public hospitals, CMHCs, and other settings for organized care have a chronic difficulty filling psychiatrists' positions (Bass and Craven 1978). Under this less benign view of what has happened in the past thirty years, much of the replacement that has occurred has been forced upon a reluctant society by the general shortage of psychiatric personnel. Instead of receiving comparable service from the lower cost personnel that has been substituted, we have sacrificed the quality and appropriateness of treatment.

In practice, the work roles of the professions are governed by state regulations, third-party reimbursement provisions, and rules set out by professional quasi-regulatory committees for the operation of health facilities. The diversity of approaches among the states confirms the absence of consensus about who should be allowed to do what. (See McGuire 1980 for a review of these practices.) Presently the primary way states differ in their regulation of psychotherapy regards "direct recognition" legislation for psychologists, requiring third-party payers, if they cover psychotherapy, to pay for psychologists' services billed independently of a physician. Thirty-one states with 80 percent of the U.S. population have enacted some form of direct recognition legislation. In the nineteen states without such laws, third-party payers may require psychologists to be supervised by a physician and to bill for services through a physician. Payment under most federal health programs (with the exception of Medicare) may go directly to psychologists.

Psychotherapy in the General Health Sector

Physicians other than psychiatrists see patients with mental disturbances and treat these patients with drugs and rudimentary psychotherapy. As we have already seen in Table 2-2, the vast majority of persons treated for mental disorders are treated in the general health sector. Darrel Regier of NIMH has repeatedly stressed the importance of the nonpsychiatrist physician in the delivery of mental health services. According to Regier and Goldberg,

> of 645 million visits to physicians in 1973, 4.6% resulted in a principle diagnosis of mental disorder which was classifiable under Section V of the ICDA, [Eighth Edition of the International Classification of Disease Adapted for use in the United States], and this percentage increased to 6.0% if all visits were included in which any one of three coexisting diagnoses, principle or otherwise, was found to be a diagnosis of mental disorder (1978: 5)

Regier and Goldberg argue that the percentage of patients with mental disorders in general practice "would undoubtedly be increased considerably if additional psychophysiological conditions and psychosomatic related symptoms classified elsewhere in the ICDA were included" (Regier and Goldberg 1978: 5).

Although only a fraction of the patients of nonpsychiatric physicians have a classifiable mental disorder, with so many more nonpsychiatric physicians than psychiatric physicians, more than half of physician visits in which there is a classifiable mental disorder are accounted for by nonpsychiatric physicians. Nonpsychiatric physicians do almost one-half of all the psychotherapy conducted by physicians, accounting for "fully 46% of all visits in which a psychotherapy/therapeutic listening treatment was provided" (Regier and Goldberg 1978: 6).

Although there can be no question that many mental disorders are treated in the general health sector, there is serious question whether they are treated appropriately. When nonpsychiatric physicians engage in psychotherapy, the treatment typically is brief, infrequent, and relatively inexpensive when compared to psychotherapy administered by a psychiatrist, and at least in this limited sense is economical. Nonpsychiatric physicians receive only limited training in psychotherapy. Danger arises when they treat mental disorders with the tools they are trained to use: drugs and surgery. One argument for including coverage for outpatient psychotherapy in an NHI package is to lure patients with emotional problems away from the general medical sector where they have been treated expensively and dangerously with somatic techniques. It is alleged that treating mental health problems appropriately will more than pay for itself by reducing treatment in the general medical sector (Chapter 3 will review some of the effects). A recurrent theme in mental health policy discussions is that the general medical and the specialized mental health sectors should work together more effectively to be sure the right people receive the right treatment (see PCMH 1978: 8).

Community Mental Health Centers

In response to perceived shortcomings in the supply of mental health services, the federal government, in 1963, established the community mental health center (CMHC) program. The purposes were to create organizations to care for chronic mental patients in the community and to improve the geographic and demographic distribution of mental health services. As of October 1, 1978, NIMH had funded 745 CMHCs. These handle one-third of all outpatient episodes in the mental health sector (Regier, Taube, and Goldberg 1978), making the CMHCs the major institution providing outpatient mental health services.

CMHCs have come under fire for their high cost per unit of service and for failure to orient adequately their care to the needs of the chronic population (GAO 1977). However, the program has a number of significant accomplishments. A very large number of people have been served. Although the cost per unit of service at a CMHC is high, the cost per episode is low (Sharfstein, Taube, and Goldberg 1977). And while CMHCs may not have reached the chronic patients they have reached the poor. Surveys show that over one-half of all people served at CMHCs fall below the official poverty line (Edwards et al. 1979). There is conflicting evidence as to whether, once taken into treatment at a CMHC, a poor person is treated with the same level and type of services as someone from the middle class. (See

Edwards et al. 1979 and Mollica, Redlich and Blum 1979 for two viewpoints.) Nevertheless, the CMHC program has been successful in providing services to low-income clients.

CMHCs have provided the organizational vehicle for massive substitution of other personnel for psychiatrists in the provision of mental health services. Less than 10 percent of the personnel in CMHCs are psychiatrists and psychologists (holding an MA degree or higher), those generally qualified to provide psychotherapy in private practice. Within the CMHC, most therapy is provided by social workers, nurses, and other mental health workers who, without the supervision and authentication provided by employment in CMHCs, would not generally have been eligible to provide psychotherapy. (For a review of the problems and accomplishments of the CMHC program see Dorris and McGuire 1980.)

Federal funding as seed money for CMHCs is declining. Some states provide substantial direct support, but CMHCs are relying more and more on third-party payments, as was intended in the original legislation. Terms of coverage for psychotherapy under third-party payment plans, especially national health insurance, will have a powerful impact on the viability and the orientation of this innovative form of mental health care delivery.

Diverse settings and numerous professionals offering psychotherapy represent choices to users. Someone seeking psychotherapy must choose from whom to seek care, and once that is settled, participate in the decision of the form and extent of services. Decisions by the users of care can be referred to as "demand decisions." Demand will be subject to numerous influences, among these insurance coverage, discussed in the next section.

FACTORS INFLUENCING DEMAND
FOR PSYCHOTHERAPY

It may not be obvious to anyone but the most dedicated economist that demand analysis has much to do with mental health services. But the movement of psychotherapy into arenas where users have significant choices about whether, from whom, and how much has made demand analysis crucial to policy in mental health services. Demand analysis traditionally emphasizes the effect of economic factors such as income, prices, and availability of services because they are often the most convenient "handles" for policy. It is hard to change the outcome of a user's decision about whether to seek mental health care, for instance, by changing someone's perception of a problem. It may be much easier to change a decision by changing the price, location, or type of service available.

Illness and Demand

Based on a review of the epidemiological literature of the past twenty-five years, Regier, Goldberg, and Taube (1978) estimate that about 10 percent of the U.S. population is mentally ill at any one time and that about 15 percent of the population is mentally ill over the course of a year. The number of people classified as being mentally ill varies depending on the definition of mental illness. Regier, Goldberg, and Taube believe their estimates are conservative. The appearance of mental illness in the population by major category of disease during a year has been estimated for the President's Commission on Mental Health (1978 II: 16) as follows:

Schizophrenia	.5−3 percent of the population
Manic-depressive psychosis	.3 percent
Neurosis (including the other depressive disorders)	8−13 percent
Personality disorder	7 percent

There is no strict connection between disease and demand. Not all who are mentally ill (by any definition) seek and receive care, and all those who seek care are not necessarily mentally ill. Compiling the results of eleven studies, a task panel of the President's Commission on Mental Health reports that "only about one-fourth of those suffering from a clinically significant disorder have been in treatment" (1978 II: 16). (However, persons with more serious diagnoses, psychoses, and schizophrenia, are much more likely to have been treated than those with less serious illness.) Much the same picture emerges from Regier, Goldberg, and Taube's (1978) study of the type of treatment received by the mentally ill in the United States. In 1975, only about 7 million people were treated in what they call the "specialized mental health sector"—about 3.5 percent of the U.S. population. If 15 percent of the population is mentally ill at some time during a year, this makes clear that most mentally ill are untreated or treated by someone other than a mental health professional.

The mismatch between services and problems is worsened by recognition that so many of those who do receive treatment may have problems of a lower order of severity. Increasingly, psychiatrists and other psychotherapists are being asked to deal with conditions more appropriately labeled "problems of living" than "mental illness." Figures are scarce and boundaries are fuzzy, but the general problem is expressed by another task panel of the President's Commission on Mental Health.

> The boundaries of the psychosocial therapies . . . seem to be expanding without limit. Psychotherapies are expected to do more than treat mental disorders; positive mental health is the new cry, presumably marked by "self-actualization," growth, and even spiritual oneness with the universe. The problems brought to the therapist are no longer simply individual internal conflicts, but problems of interpersonal and family relationships and recently even problems with society and its institutions. (1978 IV: 1,747).

If demand for private psychiatric care were neatly related to illness, if who gets what treatment were a strictly technological problem, there would be no reason to study demand. It is in part the weakness of this connection that makes the influence of other factors on users' decisions important to study.

Insurance and Demand

Insurance coverage reduces the price of care to the user, the third party paying part of expenses. The actual arrangement may be quite complicated, involving deductibles, limits, exclusions, and copayments, but the basic effect of insurance is simple: By forcing the user to sacrifice less of other goods for purchase of services, insurance stimulates demand. Insurance coverage may make it more likely that someone seeks care, that the patient wishes to stay longer in treatment, or that the provider recommends longer treatment.

It is obviously necessary to know how many more services will be demanded in response to insurance in order to predict the cost of national health insurance or similar policies. The response to insurance is also important in assessing the economic efficiency of national health insurance. Popular belief, based partly on the history of costs under private insurance plans and partly on the fear that demand for psychotherapy, once opened up, would be unlimited, is that people would be highly responsive to insurance coverage. There are few facts available on which to base a forecast of demand under national health insurance. Some of these are reviewed in Chapter 3. The study reported in Part II of this book is in fact the first true study of demand for psychotherapy, attempting to assess the effect of price on utilization while controlling for other factors.

The Interaction of Insurance and Other Factors

There are many factors influencing demand for psychotherapy in addition to the patient's illness and insurance coverage, such as income, attitudes toward mental health services, and the influence of the provider. Financing policy may directly change the insurance coverage people carry for psychotherapy. The effect of insurance may interact with other influences on demand. Some of the important issues (to be discussed later in Chapter 5) are as follows:

• *Insurance and income.* Outside of psychotherapy provided free or nearly free in clinics (predominantly community mental health centers), psychotherapy is a luxury good, enjoyed by the upper middle- and upper-income groups. We have a two-class system of care. National health insurance may change that through the interaction of income and insurance. If the poor are more responsive to price reductions on services than the rich, psychotherapeutic services will be redistributed in favor of the poor. If the richer groups are more price responsive than the poor, the distribution of psychotherapy may swing even further in favor of upper-income groups.

• *Insurance and influence of the provider.* Once a patient has chosen the source of care, one of the powerful influences on how much and what form of care to seek is the provider. How much of this influence is exerted in the interest of the patient and how much in the self-interest of the provider is controversial. In the general health literature, some investigations have found that physicians seem to influence patients' decisions in part in their own (the physician's) self-interest (Monsma 1970, Evans 1974, Fuchs 1978), but other careful investigations have failed to turn up such an effect (Green 1978).

Insurance may interact with a provider's influence in a number of ways. When a patient has insurance the therapist may feel free to recommend more extensive psychotherapy (GAP 1975). This behavior may or may not be in the patient's best interest, and in any case is very difficult to distinguish from a patient's choices in an empirical investigation. A therapist's recommendations to a patient about the extent of treatment may depend on the therapist's overall workload. A therapist with "slack" in a practice may extend the number of visits longer than necessary. Recommendations for intensive treatment with such motivations are clearly not in the patient's interest. National health insurance may affect the situation by increasing the practices of all therapists; with a general boost in demand there will be, at least in the short run, less slack in therapists' practices and may shorten the recommended treatment for some patients. The interaction of insurance and influence is empirically checked in Chapter 5.

• *Insurance and social attitudes.* Social and cultural factors clearly condition demand for psychotherapy. "Prejudice" against treatment for mental illness has been widely noted (NIMH 1976). This is in fact one reason some advocate national health insurance for psychotherapy, in essence to bribe people to ignore their (allegedly) false preconceptions. In any case, despite the increase in social acceptance of mental illness and treatment since the 1950s, there is still room for improvement. One factor that may affect a potential patient's acceptance of the idea of mental illness and treatment is others' willingness to undergo treatment and the consequent higher visibility of mental health services. National health insurance for psychotherapy would validate mental health services for some people. As a result of this change in attitudes, many people with emotional problems might be willing to seek treatment or to undergo more extensive treatment. An economist would call this a "bandwagon effect" (following Leibenstein 1950). Validation effects of national health insurance will be hard to determine, but bandwagon effects make up part of the empirical investigation described in Chapter 5.

There is a market for psychotherapy, but it is far from perfect. Governments already intervene to maintain the quality of care and to improve access to care for some disadvantaged groups. Compulsory insurance for psychotherapy is an intervention that could not be justified primarily on grounds of protection of quality or distributional concerns. The next chapter compares performance of the market for psychotherapy against standards for efficient resource use. In the process, a number of structural defects are discussed which serve as the basis for an argument for compulsory insurance for psychotherapy.

NOTES TO CHAPTER 2

1. Some readers may find useful the following brief definitions of some terms used to describe the major types of psychotherapy:

    Redlich and Freedman (1965) make a simple fundamental distinction between analytic and directive-supportive psychotherapy. Analytic psychotherapy includes classical *psychoanalysis*, pioneered by Freud. The fundamental aim of psychoanalysis, according to Nemiah, "is to bring into consciousness the unconscious elements of the psychological conflicts that underlie symptoms and character problems, and to trace these roots to their genesis in the childhood disturbances of the normal process of growth and development" (1976: 170). Psychoanalysis is never brief, may continue for years, and requires frequent meetings. "Anything less than four meetings per week, especially in the early stages of analysis, is generally thought to be incompatible with effective analysis (Nemiah 1976: 174).

    Psychoanalytic or *dynamic psychotherapy* describes a broad range of approaches to treatment, all of which rely on psychoanalytic theory but are generally less intensive and less insight-oriented than classical psychoanalysis. According to Offenkrantz (1975) the goal of psychoanalytic psychotherapy is alleviation of symptoms, a symptom being the stress for which the patient seeks help. Patients meet with the therapist generally once or twice a week. Treatment may extend beyond a year.

    Brief psychotherapy borders on the previous category in terms of goals and length of treatment but probably belongs more in Redlich and Freedman's class of "directive-supportive" therapies rather than "analytic." According to Castelnuovo (1975), brief psychotherapy tends to be "supportive or suppressive" as opposed to "insight-oriented" or "exploratory." Treatment is generally for from five to fifty meetings, spread over a period of up to a year. Clearly within the directive-supportive category are *crisis therapy* and *behavioral therapy*. Crisis therapy is very brief, dealing with a patient's acute emotional disturbance. Behavioral therapy stresses learning and conditioning, using concepts and techniques from experiential psychology.

    Other classifications of psychotherapy have been made. Karaso (1977) distinguishes dynamic, behavioral, and experiential psychotherapy. The task force on research for the President's Commission on Mental Health (1978) distinguishes psychodynamic, behavior, humanistic, and transpersonal psychotherapies. For description of somatic techniques used in psychiatric treatment, including drug therapies, see *The Handbook of Psychiatry*, vol. V, part 3.

2. Definition of mental illness and disorder is presently undergoing considerable change and is not subject to broad consensus among psychiatrists and other mental health professionals. Although these definitions may soon be officially outdated, common parlance defines the major categories of mental disorders as follows:

    1. The *psychoses* are severe disorders that result in highly idiosyncratic and impaired behavior. They are characterized by an extreme inability to give adequate regard to inner and outer reality and to organize socially adequate responses. Some psychoses are associated with brain disease; many are not; and about some we are in doubt.

    2. The *neuroses* are loose categories of ubiquitous disorders, primarily psychogenic. Ironically, they are called minor disorders, although they may cause extreme suffering. They are characterized by an inability to perform optimally and by evidence of internal and external conflict.

    3. The *psychosomatic diseases* are a group of organic dysfunctions of unknown etiology in which psychogenic factors play a prominent role.

    4. The *mental deficiencies* (or mental subnormality) are disorders with primary disturbance of intellectual functions; they are innate or acquired early in life.

(The definitions were taken from Redlich and Freedman 1965: 2-3.) A task force of the American Psychiatric Association has recently reclassified all mental illness in the Diagnostic and Statistical Manual of Mental Disorders, DSM-III. Manifestations of disease rather than cause are stressed in the new classification. Neurosis for example, is dropped as a separate category. The new manual reflects the tension about defining the boundaries of mental illness, including smoking tobacco as a form of drug dependency and not including homosexuality as a form of psychosexual dysfunction.

3 MARKET FAILURE AND INSURANCE FOR PSYCHOTHERAPY

Thinking back to our school days, many of us remember a failure as an extraordinarily poor, probably negligent performance. When a market "fails" as this term is used in economics, however, it is not necessarily an indication of so severe a problem. A market is said to fail if it does not attain standards of *perfect* resource use. It is as if on a math test, anyone who did not answer 100 percent correctly were given an F. Market failure is thus a harsh term for what can be a minor infraction of performance standards.

Standards for markets derive from goals of *efficiency* and *fairness*. Full, complete efficiency, achieved when an allocation of resources is such that no one can be made better off without making someone else worse off, is by itself a very exacting standard, rarely if ever met by real markets. "Fairness" has many definitions. Adding the requirement that a market be "fair" as well as "efficient" means that virtually all markets "fail" to some degree. In terms of a math test again perfection might require that not only all answers be correct but that the amount written for each answer be the same. The first is an efficiency requirement, the second a fairness requirement.

As a system for grading, the market failure approach is not very interesting since there are only two grades, pass and fail, and all markets fail. Rather, the market failure approach is useful as a guide to the most serious weaknesses of markets. Economists have spelled out criteria for efficiency and have contributed to the framework for study of fairness in markets. Economic theory and experience with the market failure approach combine to help suggest, from among all the possible "failures" in a market, where a particular market is likely to be going most seriously wrong. This, in turn, can guide policy in dealing with breakdowns in a market.

There are two markets most relevant to financing policy toward psychotherapy, the market for the services and the market for insurance to pay for the services. The market failures that make up the case for compulsory insurance for psychotherapy are the following:

1. Efficiency problems in the market for insurance
    a. adverse selection
    b. moral hazard
2. Efficiency problems in the market for psychotherapy
    a. patients' ignorance
    b. benefits external to the patient

Each possible market failure provides a possible justification for government intervention into the market for insurance for psychotherapy. In what follows these failures are taken up one at a time, the nature of market failure is explained, the seriousness of the failure assessed, and the role of government to remedy the problem considered. This chapter is concerned with efficiency problems. Issues of fairness and distribution are considered in Chapter 6.

EFFICIENCY PROBLEMS IN THE MARKET FOR INSURANCE

The mechanics of insurance are simple and familiar. Policyholders contribute premiums regularly and independently of illness, and receive benefits irregularly dependent upon designated events (such as receipt of medical care) related to illness. Insurance *markets*, however, are not simple. A pair of terms coming out of the insurance trade literature describe the causes of failure endemic to insurance markets: adverse selection and moral hazard. The nature of insurance, the problems caused by adverse selection and moral hazard, and the relation of these to the case for compulsory insurance, are sufficiently complex so that broad generalizations would serve the general reader poorly.

In order to make these ideas accessible to the nonspecialist, a simple example of a ten-person society is developed here to show how insurance works. It begins with a demonstration of insurance at its best, improving everyone's welfare by spreading risk. It uses the miniature society to show how the traditional difficulties besetting insurance markets, adverse selection and moral hazard, can interfere with the benefits of insurance, and in some cases, destroy the marketability of insurance entirely. Citizens of the imaginary society will be endowed with utility functions, demands for psychotherapy, and probabilities of becoming mentally ill, as needed to demonstrate the nature and effects of insurance.[1]

Risk Spreading—The Insurance Paradigm

Medical expenses, though infrequent, may loom large in a family budget. Health insurance reduces or eliminates the financial risk of illness by substituting for direct payment of medical expenses, payment of a constant premium sufficient to cover the average or expected expense plus the insurer's administrative cost. If payment of a dollar when disposable income is high (as when one is well) is less subjectively painful then payment of a dollar when disposable income is low (as when one is ill), spreading payments across time with insurance premiums may be a helpful course.[2] Insurance does not, however, eliminate or reduce the financial cost of illness, but actually increases it because premiums must pay expenses of the insurer as well as direct medical costs. The advantage of insurance is that it makes payment more convenient.

To emphasize benefits from spreading risk, consider an example of insurance at its best. Rule out moral hazard by assuming that neither the occurrence nor expense of illness are at the discretion of the policyholder. Rule out adverse selection by assuming that all ten persons in the society are identical.[3] The only illness is "mental illness," which strikes each person with probability of one in ten each year. Mentally ill persons are cured by making 100 visits to a psychiatrist. A visit costs $50, so the total expense of illness is $5,000. Each citizen earns $10,000 per year. This is disposable income (y), which the individual may spend freely, except if he is ill, when $5,000 spent on treatment reduces disposable income to $5,000.

Assume each person's welfare depends on his disposable income according to a utility function which, for simplicity, we assume takes the following form:

$$u = \ln(y) \, ,$$

where "ln" indicates natural logarithm and y is disposable income. This utility function is graphed in Figure 3-1. The functional form of the utility function, u, is arbitrary except for two plausible properties:

1. As disposable income increases, the individual is (subjectively) better off. The slope of the utility function is positive.
2. At higher levels of disposable income, an extra dollar increases utility less than an extra dollar at lower levels of disposable income. The slope of the utility function is decreasing.

The second property makes insurance attractive.[4]

Figure 3-1.   Utility of Income.

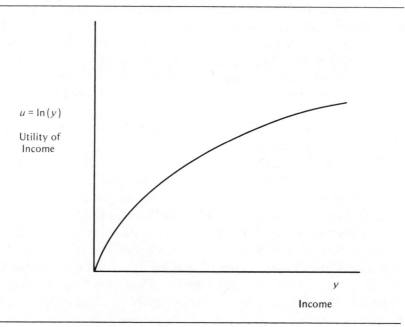

$u = \ln(y)$

Utility of Income

y

Income

In deciding to buy insurance, someone would ask, "Is the increase in disposable income when I am sick worth the reduction in disposable income when I am well?" *Expected* utility is a way to gauge these benefits and costs of insurance. If *on average* one is better off in utility terms with insurance, then paying the premiums to obtain extra income when one is sick will be worthwhile.[5]

Without insurance, if someone is well, disposable income is $10,000 and utility is ln(10,000), or 9.21. If someone is mentally ill, disposable income shrinks to $5,000 after payment of medical expenses and utility falls to ln(5,000), or 8.52. Consequently, without insurance, each person expects, nine times in ten, to have utility 9.21, and one time in ten to have utility of 8.52. Average or expected utility $E(u)$ is the utility in the two health contingencies weighted by the probability that each contingency occurs.

$$E(u) = 0.9\,(\ln(10,000)) + 0.1\,(\ln(5,000))$$
$$= 0.9\,(9.21) + 0.1\,(8.52)$$
$$= 9.14$$

With full insurance, if someone is ill, all $5,000 of treatment expense is paid by the insurer.[6] The premium the insurer must charge for this coverage is equal to the expected payout plus a "loading charge" to pay the expenses of administering the policy.[7] The insurance carrier's expected payout per person covered is simply one-tenth (the probability the person will be ill) times $5,000 (expense if the person is ill), or $500. Loading charges by insurers vary by type of policy, but average about 15 percent of benefits paid out (Rosett and Huang 1973). Adding 15 percent to $500 yields a premium per year of $575 for full coverage of medical expenses associated with mental illness. The insuree paying $575 per year has disposable income reduced to $9,425. Since the individual is fully insured, none of this is used for medical expenses and utility is always ln (9,425) or 9.15. The insurance policy is thus a good buy since expected (and actual) utility with insurance (9.15) is greater than expected utility without insurance (9.14).

It is interesting to note that expected disposable income with insurance ($9,425) is less than expected disposable income without insurance ($9,500). It is not income, as such, that the individual cares about but the benefits or utility from that income. So even when the premium exceeds expected benefits, as it must to pay the insurer's expenses, insurance may be a worthwhile purchase. Each person in our miniature society is made better off in terms of expected utility by purchase of insurance including the 15 percent loading charge.

Adverse Selection

The Market Failure. Adverse selection threatens the viability of insurance markets. Its cause is the insurer's ignorance of the degree of risk presented by individual policyholders.

An insurer is subject to adverse selection when it sets premiums for a group and a disproportionate number of "bad risks" in the group choose to buy insurance coverage. It is a fact of life in the insurance industry that premiums must be set according to the characteristics of groups: residents of New York State, members of Building Trade Local #114, males aged 45-50. The residents of New York State may be classified by age, sex, occupation, or health at the time the policy is issued; yet each person is grouped with thousands of others, some of whom are quite different in the degree of risk they present to the insurer. Expense prohibits insurers from grading each policyholder on his degree of risk. For any group that is not perfectly homogeneous, some members will have greater risk, some less, than the average, all paying the same premium.

For those who present less than the average amount of risk, the insurance premium is "too high." Some of these "good risks" may be willing to buy insurance at a fair premium (acturial cost plus administrative charges) but be unwilling to buy at the premium appropriate to the average member of the group in which they are classified. This is a market failure. In a perfect market, where insurers have full information about individuals' risks, each person would be offered insurance at the premium reflecting the cost of insuring that individual, and would not be inappropriately discouraged from buying insurance by the insurer's classifications. In the extreme, adverse selection may so severely handicap the marketing of insurance that even with a large group of eager consumers beset by distasteful risk, insurance may not be sold at all.

It is inefficient for people who would have been willing to pay a fair premium to decline coverage, but the damage caused by a group classification system for setting rates does not stop there. Those who decline coverage will often be the good risks; those who elect coverage will frequently be the bad risks. This gives adverse selection its name: The insurer is subject to an adverse selection of policyholders. The original calculation of the premium for the group is now wrong since many of the good risks (who kept the premium down) are out of the insurance pool. To cover the liability represented by the average member of the group that *chooses insurance*, the insurer must raise rates. But raising rates will cause others in the pool to drop coverage, and those who drop it will in general be the best risks of those who originally chose insurance. The premium will have to be raised again, leading to further deterioration in the risk of the insurance pool. There is clearly a vicious circle in the relation between the insurance premium and the degree of risk of the average member of the insurance pool. The premium may cover expenses for those who buy insurance at that premium, but fewer people would buy insurance than would do so at individually tailored fair rates. But there may be no premium that can cover cost, so that no insurance would be sold and the market failure would be complete.

As an example of how adverse selection can interfere with the marketability of insurance, suppose in our ten-person society, individuals faced different risks of mental illness but the insurance company could not distinguish the good from the bad risks. Suppose again that expenses for treatment of mental illness amount to $5,000. The key difference is that people vary in their probability of becoming mentally ill (see Table 3-1). The range is between a probability of 1.00 for person 1 (who is thus certain to be mentally ill each year) and a probability of 0.05 for persons 7-10. Individuals have the same utility function as before, $u = \ln(y)$, where y is disposable income, or income after medical expenses. The third column of Table 3-1 shows the individuals' expected utility without insurance. Those with a greater chance of becoming ill are more likely to incur medical expenses and so have a lower expected utility. The insurer's calculations for premiums are shown in the lower part of the table. Initially, the insurer expects to draw from the entire group of ten people, and calculates the premium necessary to cover expected benefits paid out plus administrative costs on this basis.

The insurer is assumed to know that the probability of illness for the average member of the group is 0.27, but not to know each person's probability. Premiums are initially set to cover costs of the

Table 3-1. Adverse Selection and Insurance Markets: An Illustration.

| | | Round 1 | | |
| | | Premium = $1,522.50 | | |

Person	Probability of Illness	Expected Utility without Insurance[a]	Expected Utility with Insurance[b]	Buys Insurance?
1	1.0	8.52	9.04	Yes
2	.5	8.87	9.04	Yes
3	.4	8.93	9.04	Yes
4	.3	9.00	9.04	Yes
5	.2	9.07	9.04	No
6	.1	9.14	9.04	No
7	.05	9.18	9.04	No
8	.05	9.18	9.04	No
9	.05	9.18	9.04	No
10	.05	9.18	9.04	No

Insurance Carrier's Income Statement

		1-10	
Anticipated	Group		
	Cost of claim	5,000.00	
	Expected claims/person	0.27	
	Expected payout/person	1,350.00	
	15% administration expense[c]	202.50	
	Total expected cost/person	1,552.50	
	Premium per person	1,552.50	
	Members	4	
	Total revenue	6,210.00	6,210.00
Actual	Cost of claim	5,000.00	
	Expected claims	2.2	
	Expected payout	11,000.00	
	15% administrative expense[c]	1,650.00	
	Total cost	12,650.00	12,650.00
	Expected net revenue		-6,440.00

a. Expected utility without insurance = probability of illness $\cdot \ln(10,000 - 5,000) + (1 - $ probability of illness$) \cdot \ln(10,000)$.

b. Expected utility with insurance = $\ln(10,000 - $ insurance premium$)$.

c. Administrative expense is assumed to be 15 percent of payout, independent of premium income.

Table 3-1. continued

Round 2 Premium = $3,162.50		Round 3 Premium = $5,750.00	
Expected Utility with Insurance[b]	*Buys Insurance?*	*Expected Utility with Insurance*[b]	*Buys Insurance?*
8.83	Yes	8.35	No
8.83	No	8.35	No
8.83	No	8.35	No
8.83	No	8.35	No
8.83	No	8.35	No
8.83	No	8.35	No
8.83	No	8.35	No
8.83	No	8.35	No
8.83	No	8.35	No
8.83	No	8.35	No

1–4		1	
5,000.00		5,000.00	
0.55		1	
2,750.00		5,000.00	
412.50		750.00	
3,162.50		5,750.00	
3,162.50		5,750.00	
1		0.0	0.00
3,162.50	3,162.50	0.00	
5,000.00		5,000.00	
1.0		0.0	
5,000.00		0.00	
750.00		0.00	
5,750.00	5,750.00	0.00	
	−2,587.50		0.00

average member of the group. Expected payout per person is $1,350 per year. Adding the 15 percent loading charge, the expected cost per person to the insurer totals $1,552.50. The insurance company sets this premium and expects to break even. It *would* break even, *if* it drew all ten members of the pool, or even representative members of the pool (who average 0.27 episodes of illness per year). But this is not what happens. The premium is only fair for the hypothetical average person in the group; it is too high for persons 5-10 and too low for persons 1-4. Only persons 1-4 enjoy higher expected utility with insurance at this premium. Persons 5-10 decline coverage. (If some person among the 5 to 10 were even more adverse to risk than we have assumed by choice of a utility function, that individual might buy insurance even at this "unfair" premium.) Consequences of adverse selection show up in the insurer's income statement at the bottom of the table. Total revenue is $6,210 from selling four policies. Expected total cost is over $12,000 since the four who chose insurance are the most likely to use it. In a typical year the insurer loses over $6,000 at the premium set to cover costs of the average group member.

An insurance company that continues to offer coverage for mental illness at a premium of $1,552.50 will not be in business very long. In a review of its claims experience, the carrier might decide to raise its premiums to cover the expected expenses of the people from the original group who chose insurance, that is, persons 1-4. Again the insurer is assumed not to be able to distinguish the risk of individuals within this group but only to know the group average.[8] We move into round 2 in Table 3-1. The average person among persons 1-4 has a probability of 0.55 of becoming mentally ill each year. Calculating premiums on this basis, the insurance company charges $3,162.50 per year. The expected utility of this new policy is less than the expected utility without insurance for everyone but person 1. Adverse selection again victimizes the insurer at this new higher premium by pushing persons 2-4 out of the market. The insurer, with only one person buying the policy, loses $2,587.50 each year.

Another revision of premiums, in round 3, reduces the insurer's losses only by eliminating the purchase of insurance altogether. Serving the trivial group of person 1, the insurance group must charge a premium of $5,750 per year to cover the yearly payment of $5,000.

But person 1 is obviously better off paying costs directly and avoiding the loading charge of the insurance carrier.

The short-sightedness of the insurer, naively thinking that it would attract policyholders at random from the group, has nothing to do with the final outcome. The far-sighted insurer simply would not have offered insurance in this market in the first place. In this example, there is *no premium* the insurer could set that would cover the expected expenses of the people the premium would attract.[9]

This is a market failure because in a well-functioning market each person (except person 1) would have been offered insurance at a fair premium (fair for each individual), would have purchased insurance, and would have had an expected utility greater than that with no insurance. Even though everyone is willing to buy insurance at fair rates, the insurer's ignorance of individuals' risks, and adverse selection, prevents any insurance from being purchased.

The Evidence on Adverse Selection.   Adverse selection is evident only when people have choices. For example, people who choose to buy insurance coverage are more frequently mentally ill than those who do not buy coverage. Absence of choice can also be evidence of adverse selection; as just pointed out, adverse selection can eliminate choice. Most people are probably risk-averse and would insure, at fair premiums, against unusual and large expenses such as expenses of mental illness. When that insurance is unavailable or available only at premiums that would cover expenses of very high risk individuals, adverse selection may be at work.[10]

There are a few circumstances when individuals have choice regarding insurance coverage for psychotherapy and when adverse selection can be observed more directly. Federal employees, as we have already noted, have choice of health insurance benefits. One of their choices is coverage by Aetna Life and Casualty, which was a victim of adverse selection.

In a review of their claims experience for mental and nervous conditions for 1973, Aetna reported:

> Mental and nervous expenditures are seemingly quite easy to predict (by the insured) as evidenced by the fact that most such expenditures commence within a few days of the effective date of the individual's coverage. The Indemnity Benefit Plan [of Aetna] apparently has the most liberal mental and nervous benefit [of any plan offered to federal employees], as evidenced

by the fact that persons who joined the plan in 1972 consituted 14% of the total lives insured as of May 1973; yet they incurred 21% of the mental and nervous expenses. In view of this high degree of antiselection [our term is "adverse selection"] it would seem that some action should be taken to reduce the plan's mental and nervous benefits. (1974: 1)

Aetna did take action, putting a limit of twenty visits per year on its outpatient coverage for mental and nervous disorders. Many of the heaviest users among federal employees apparently migrated to the Blue Cross/Blue Shield high-option plan. In the year after Aetna's cut in benefits, Blue Cross/Blue Shield saw its percentage of total benefits going for psychiatric care jump significantly for the first time in four years.[11] In the classic competitive response in the presence of adverse selection, the Blue Cross/Blue Shield plan for federal employees reduced its coverage for psychotherapy by increasing the coinsurance rate for this benefit.

Federal employees' choice between the Blue Cross/Blue Shield High- and Low-option plans provides further evidence of adverse selection. Even though the coverage was only slightly better in the high-option plan (deductible $100 versus $250, coinsurance 20 percent versus 25 percent, limit of $250,000 versus $100,000), the per capita average charge for supplemental benefits for mental conditions (psychiatric outpatient) in the high-option plan were over twice those in the low-option plan in 1973. The heaviest users chose the better coverage (Reed 1975: 5–7).

The Case for Compulsory Insurance. When adverse selection destroys the marketability of insurance by private organizations, there is a clear-cut case for compulsory insurance to correct this market failure. In a market we rely on prices, in this case insurance premiums, to guide individuals' choices. When the premiums are set inappropriately in a market, as when sellers of insurance inadequately distinguish the good risks from the bad risks, citizens will be led by the improper prices to make the wrong decisions about insurance purchase. In general, with insurers setting high prices to protect themselves against adverse selection, too few people buy insurance. In the example above everyone would have bought insurance at actuarily fair prices, but the market failed to convince anyone to buy insurance voluntarily.

There is a direct and simple solution to this market failure: Compel everyone to have insurance, as through a national health insurance plan or state mandate. This seemingly forces people to purchase insurance, but what it may actually do is give people the insurance coverage they would have purchased on a competitive market had insurers been able to price properly. Putting this solution in its most favorable perspective: *Compulsory or full insurance mimics the result of a perfect market.* An assumption necessary to reach this happy conclusion is that full insurance is optimal, in the sense that if faced with actuarily fair prices, people would choose in their own interests to buy full insurance. This assumption is questionable but hardly far-fetched. In the face of national health insurance, people who now complain they do not want coverage for psychotherapy care might properly be understood as saying, "I don't want that coverage at the price I am forced to pay for it through taxes." If for those who might rarely use psychotherapy the appropriate price could be calculated, the price might be quite low. At this "fair" price, the risk-averse person would choose to buy the insurance. The notion that most people are risk-averse when it comes to medical expenses is easy to accept.

In the presence of risk aversion, compulsory insurance is a *complete solution to the problem of efficient insurance coverage.* It is important to understand that because taxes are not collected from people for this program according to what a perfect market would charge in premiums, there will be many, for whom the tax price exceeds the actuarily fair premium, who would prefer not to have compulsory insurance. This does not negate the efficiency of full coverage. It is incidental from an efficiency standpoint what tax price people are actually charged, so long as they are insured. Apart from any inefficiencies introduced by the process of tax collection, who pays taxes (or mandatory premiums) is a *distributional* issue only.

Moral Hazard

The Market Failure. The hazard is called moral because insurance tempts policyholders to be careless in controlling insured losses. Someone with insurance may be more likely to initiate psychiatric care, and once in care, be more likely to opt for more extensive treatment. Either type of response to insurance coverage is referred to as moral hazard.[12] Insurers are constantly vigilant against moral hazard, checking its expression by coinsurance, deductibles, and limits on insurance policies. Their motivation is not to guard the morality of their policyholders but to sell insurance. Moral hazard can destroy the marketability of insurance by forcing people to pay through premiums for services they would not have found worthwhile to buy if payments were made out of pocket. If moral hazard is too severe, voluntary insurance will not be sold and compulsory insurance would impose more costs than benefits.

Moral hazard does not, as it may first appear, permit the policyholder to exploit the insurance carrier. Insurance carriers charge premiums based on the benefits they expect to pay out. If payouts are high because of moral hazard, premiums will also be high. With moral hazard, the original good deal of insurance—spreading the financial risk of payment for medical expense—is tied with a bad deal—paying through premiums for services not worth the cost. The result is a combined package deal less beneficial than the original insurance policy, and sometimes so much less attractive that no insurance is preferred to insurance tied up with moral hazard.

To see how moral hazard can destroy the marketability of insurance, return to our simple ten-person society where everyone is again identical, but bring in moral hazard by supposing that there is choice of how to treat mental illness. The choice is how many visits to make to the therapist. To illustrate how insurance spreads risk, we assumed everyone mentally ill had no choice and made 100 visits at $50 per visit. Now assume that 100 visits is the appropriate treatment such that visits up to and including 100 are worth the cost and visits beyond 100—although they may provide some benefit—are not worth the cost. A curve relating the benefits from visiting a therapist to the number of visits is plotted in Figure 3-2. The benefit from each visit declines with the number of visits but exceeds the cost for visits 1–100. Visits after this do not provide benefits of $50, but up to visit 200 there is some benefit from seeing the psychiatrist. One hundred is the number of visits that maximizes the benefits net of cost the patient receives from treatment. The benefits per visit curve graphed in Figure 3-2 expresses uniformly diminishing returns from treatment. Diminishing returns from treatment may not hold throughout the course of treatment—there may be "breakthroughs" when extra visits bring increasing benefits—but in the region of the optimal number of visits (A in Figure 3-2) there must be diminishing returns.[13]

Figure 3-2. Benefits of Visiting a Therapist.

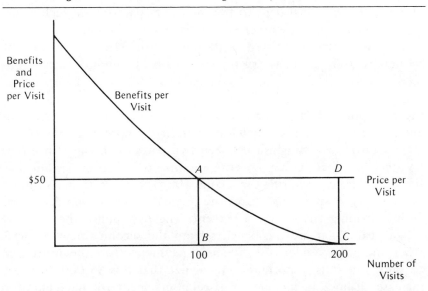

If the patient were fully informed about the benefits of treatment, the benefits curve in Figure 3-2 would also be the patient's demand curve, and 100 visits is the number the patient would choose at $50 per visit.[14] So without insurance illness costs $5,000, and because this expense is unpredictable there is a role for insurance to spread this risk.

Full insurance covers every visit to the therapist and so tempts the patient to visit the therapist more than 100 times. A visit is now "free" in that there is no out-of-pocket expense. Insurance premiums must go up to cover the extra expenses of coverage, but because the premiums are set by group characteristics and behavior, each member's premiums are virtually unaffected by the individual's behavior. The rational, self-interested policyholder continues to visit the therapist as long as there is any benefit at all from doing so since each visit is free. The rational policyholder makes 200 visits with full insurance. Everyone in the insurance pool faces the same temptation to expand utilization. As they all do so the average cost of the insurer goes up and the premiums must rise in turn. A single policyholder may recognize that all policyholders would be better off if all would stop making so many visits, but it would be irrational to cut back visits.[15] By cutting back, the policyholder would only be sacrificing some beneficial trips to the therapist (paid for through insurance) and have virtually no effect on his or others' premiums.

That expenses associated with illness are $10,000 instead of $5,000 is itself no difficulty for the insurer. Premiums can be doubled to cover the doubled expected expense. Although the premiums and the apparent benefits of the policy each go up by a factor of 2, the new policy in this changed situation, which includes discretion about treatment, will be *much less attractive* to potential buyers.

To illustrate, distinguish between two parts of the insurance policy, the "original" policy covering the first 100 visits or $5,000, and the "new" policy covering the second 100 visits or $5,000. As shown previously risk-spreading makes the original policy a good deal, even with a loading charge of 15 percent. The new policy, however, is a bad deal. What are the benefits from the second "new" policy? When the policyholder is ill, financial payments from the insurer are $5,000. But it is important to recognize that this $5,000 does not increase disposable income. It is reimbursement for payments for psychiatric care and is received only if the care is purchased. The benefits from the $5,000 are the benefits from what the money buys, the extra 100 visits. The benefits from visits 101–200 are shown in Figure 3–2 as the area under the benefit curve between visits 101 and 200. This area is *less than $5,000*. Figure 3–2 measures benefits in terms of disposable income. Five thousand dollars spent on psychiatric visits beyond those that the individual would have purchased at the going price is not worth $5,000 in terms of disposable income. According to the benefit curve in Figure 3–2, the benefits of visits 101–200 are less than one-half of $5,000.[16]

The benefits of the "original" policy were just $5,000 in terms of disposable income because the $5,000 payment from the insurer increased disposable income by $5,000. The individual in the initial example, without moral hazard, would have bought 100 visits to the psychiatrist with or without insurance. With no insurance, disposable income was $5,000; with insurance, disposable income was $10,000.

The policyholder pays $575 in premiums (a reduction in disposable income) for the "new" policy which returns benefits worth less than $2,500 one time in ten. The expected benefit for which the $575 is paid is thus less than $250, and the effective loading charge is more than 100 percent! As if this were not a serious enough handicap, no risk-spreading benefits compensate the policyholder for the whopping unfairness of the premium–benefit ratio of the new policy. The second $5,000 would not have been spent on psychiatric care were it not for insurance! If this new policy could be lopped off, leaving the original first $5,000 policy, the policyholder would endure no risk at all in disposable income. For the policyholder with nothing to gain in risk-spreading and paying $575 for expected benefits of less than $250, this "new" insurance policy is clearly a bad deal.

The actual policy that someone may buy combines the good deal and the bad, the original and the new policy. It is now problematic whether the package deal will be purchased at all by the citizens of our ten-person society. (An exact answer for this example could be found with further specification of individual preferences.) What is clear though is that the benefits from risk-spreading have been severely eroded by moral hazard. It is also clear why moral hazard haunts insurers making it much less likely they can sell policies. The bad deal involves an extraordinarily high effective loading charge to the policyholder, which is *not collected by the insurance carrier*. In this way moral hazard is as destructive to economic efficiency as a major tax on insurance purchases with the tax revenues shredded and discarded.

The Evidence for Moral Hazard. In the general medical literature, the empirical proposition that insurance encourages utilization of physician services is firmly established. Most studies show that a 1 percent decrease in price due to insurance coverage increases utilization by about .5 percent (Feldstein 1973, Rosett and Huang 1973, Newhouse 1978). There is no consensus about the impact of insurance on utilization of psychotherapy.

There are, of course, the horror stories of massive increases in utilization following expansion of insurance, such as the massive increase in claims to Blue Shield in Massachusetts after a mandatory $500 coverage for psychotherapy was enacted (Herrington 1979) and the "boom" in Washington psychiatry associated with better coverage for federal employees (Sharfstein and Dean 1977). It is hard to know what to make of these reports. The increase in Blue Shield claims in Massachusetts might have been associated not with increase in demand but with a shift in the locus of payment. Ten-year trends in the growth of psychiatry in Washington, D.C., might be caused by many things other than expanding usage by federal employees. Without research into demand behavior the influence of insurance on utilization cannot be isolated.

Most empirical work on the effects of insurance on demand and cost has not been concerned with the horror stories, but nevertheless has studied the aggregate behavior of large insured populations. Summary data from insurance carriers are relatively easy to collect, and the methodology of these studies is accessible to researchers with a wide variety of backgrounds. Utilization statistics are collected on a large population within an insurance pool. Depending on the detail of the insurer's claim data, the average utilization by type of person covered and by type of service is reported. From the experience of populations studied researchers seek to generalize to the effect of insurance on utilization by wider population groups. The primary problem with these studies is that since so many factors—population characteristics, coverage, and supply characteristics—come together to produce the observed outcomes, it is very difficult to know what would happen if any one circumstance changed. There is not space here to discuss all the studies, but a few have been selected to show the potential and problems with this type of research.

The most intensely studied group in the United States for utilization of mental health services is federal employees. Insurers carrying this coverage have been responsive to government-sponsored requests for information for research, and data have been easily accessible to researchers. With relatively liberal coverage, federal employees' policies are seen by many as a desirable model for national health insurance for mental health benefits. Federal employees' behavior has been followed closely from the late 1960s when federal employees were first given choice of health insurance with generous coverage for mental illness (Reed 1975, Husted and Sharfstein 1978). Mental health benefits did not impose unbearable financial burdens on insurance carriers. Extensive mental health benefits, including coverage for virtually unlimited psychiatric visits at 80 percent, were clearly insurable. Real costs for mental health coverage, however, have risen steadily over time. This has led to some question about the wisdom of including such generous coverage under national health insurance. As noted earlier, Aetna, which offers the second-largest among the plans available to federal employees, reacted to continued growth in costs of mental health benefits by placing a special limit of twenty visits per year on its outpatient mental health benefit.

John Krizay (1979) has examined the recent experience under the Federal Employees Benefit Program (FEHB) to investigate whether costs have continued to rise. Table 3-2 reports Krizay's basic data. Over the period 1973-77, inpatient costs of psychiatric care do not seem to have increased at all, while outpatient psychiatric costs appear to have mildly increased. On the basis of these figures, Krizay concludes that demand for psychiatric care by federal employees has leveled off.

It is difficult to interpret a relative constancy of psychiatric charges as a leveling off in demand, because other factors were changing during 1973-77 to hold back utilization. Aetna cut back psychiatric coverage in 1975. The effect of this may be showing up in the decreases in psychiatric costs, both inpatient and outpatient, in 1975. One natural interpretation of these figures is that demand has been steadily increasing over time and that it is the one-time cutback in benefits, quite evident in the table for 1975, that makes utilization for 1977 similar to 1973. In addition to the Aetna cutback, more employees are choosing HMOs of local plans with limited psychiatric benefits. In general, insurance coverage for psychiatric care for federal employees is less in 1977 than in 1973.

In sum, it is not possible to say that demand for mental health care has leveled off among federal employees. In spite of more employees choosing plans with lower coverage, the costs for psychiatric services have continued to creep upward for the period 1973-77. It is important to understand this trend. Is the cause a change in the

Table 3-2. Cost per Person for Psychiatric Benefit, Federal Employees Health Benefit Plan, 1973-77, at 1977 Prices.[a]

Year	Inpatient	Outpatient
1973	$14.18	$6.54
1974	14.40	7.02
1975	13.00	6.36
1976	14.58	7.29
1977	14.11	7.22

a. Nine plans covering approximately 70 percent of employees. Deflator for outpatient services in psychiatric office visit component of the U.S. Bureau of Labor Statistics CPI general medical index. Inpatient services are deflated by the hospital room and board component.

Source: Krizay (1979, p. 10).

mix of federal employees? Increasing real income? Slow learning about benefits? Changing attitudes toward mental health care?

Liptzin, Regier, and Goldberg (1979) recently examined the 1975 claims experience of the 2.3 million subscribers to Blue Cross/Blue Shield of Michigan and their dependents who were covered by the Comprehensive Hospital and Michigan Variable Fee–2 (MVF–2) benefits during 1975. The MVF–2 insurance plan has generous initial coverage for outpatient psychotherapy by psychiatrists or other physicians, including no copayment for the first five visits, but a total limit of $400 per year for outpatient psychiatric benefits.[17] In 1975 the Michigan population incurred per capita charges of $4.89 for outpatient and $16.18 for inpatient psychiatric care. Outpatient charges are noticeably low and inpatient charges high for a program designed to encourage early detection of mental problems through fully insured initial visits to a psychiatrist. Comparing these figures to those reported in Table 3–2 for federal employees, it can be noted that in spite of the generally lower socioeconomic status of the Michigan population and in spite of less generous coverage in important ways under MVF–2 (particularly exclusion of coverage for long-term outpatient care that represents a high proportion of the charges for federal empliyees), the Michigan population ran up a larger total cost for treatment of mental disorders.

There are a few possible explanations for this. Socioeconomic factors may not be as important in demand as many suspect when groups are nearly fully insured. Demand may be very sensitive to elimination of deductibles and early copayments for psychiatric care. (There is some support for this in the Michigan data: over 4 percent of the total population used some mental health benefit in 1975, compared to about 1 percent for the federal employees group.) Or possibly the MVF–2 plan is exactly the wrong thing for purposes of cost control. No initial barriers may bring the disturbed into the mental health care system, but with limited outpatient coverage the only way for the more seriously ill to be treated would be on an inpatient basis.

A number of studies have reported the cost of mental health benefits within prepaid group practices, or HMOs (Jones and Vischi 1979). In general, the findings show that mental health benefits can be provided to a population enrolled at a prepaid group, or HMO, at much less cost than comparable benefits to a population in a conventional insurance plan. The policy implications of this depend very much on just why it is prepaid groups achieve lower costs. Again, existing research has not been able to discriminate among some important possibilities: (1) Professional staff in a prepaid group generally receive a salary rather than collect a fee-for-service and may have less financial interest in extending treatment. (2) By hiring a limited number of mental health professionals, the prepaid group's management may force professionals to ration care by nonprice means. Staffing policy by management may effectively determine cost per member. (3) Treatment goals in a prepaid group are typically much more oriented to "return to function" than "personality reconstruction." (4) Prepaid groups make extensive use of non–MD staff. (5) Treatment is more frequently conducted in group settings. (6) Members of prepaid groups may differ systematically from those choosing other insurance plans.

It is hard to generalize from studies of utilization of mental health services by a large, insured population. They are incapable of providing information about how demand and utilization would vary with changes in coverage, population characteristics, or supply conditions. Too many circumstances differ among studies for one to attribute confidently differences in their results to specific factors.

The general health economics literature progressed rapidly from exploratory work on demand using aggregate data of the type just described to formulation and estimation of demand models of consumer or patient behavior based on household or individual survey data.[18] The advantage of disaggregated data is when key factors such as income or insurance coverage vary within the sample so their effect on demand can be assessed. Individual data on people in different circumstances are typically expensive to collect, however. In the mental health sphere, where illness and its treatment are particularly sensitive topics, collection of information about patients and their use of services presents special difficulties. One survey suitable for use as a bases for estimation of demand for mental health services was fortunately done very well, making it one of the most interesting sets of data ever assembled on patients and physicians. The survey, conducted by the Joint Information Service (JIS) of the American Psychiatric Association and the National Association for Mental Health, provided the data for the empirical work in this book.

In the first write-up of these survey results Marmor (1975) discussed a series of one- and two-variable breakdowns of descriptive material prepared from the survey data. One of the most interesting comparisons was utilization by insured and uninsured patients. On average, in the twelve months preceding the survey, uninsured patients made forty-nine visits to their psychiatrist, while insured patients made an average of only forty-four visits. This surprising and potentially important finding led Marmor to conclude: "The figures strongly indicate that the existence of insurance coverage does not lead to increased frequency of visits . . ." (1975: 137).

Two-variable simple associations can be misleading. Unless the insured and the uninsured patients are otherwise the same, comparing the whole group of uninsured with the whole group of insured in the sample is not a reliable way to test for the effect on insurance. On the basis of the multivariate analysis in the next chapter, this conclusion is reversed, illustrating that insurance does encourage utilization of psychotherapy and that the stimulus is at least as strong as the stimulus for physicians' services generally.

The Case for Compulsory Insurance.   Compulsory insurance carries the danger of *exacerbating* the problem of moral hazard. A natural check on the extent of moral hazard in private markets is absent with compulsory insurance. As observed earlier, if the package deal of an insurance policy combines the original risk-spreading benefits with the bad deal associated with moral hazard and is *overall* a bad deal, *the consumer need not buy it.* The chance to opt out if the costs exceed the benefits is, of course, lost in a compulsory insurance scheme. Benefits from risk-spreading for the average citizen may be more than offset by inefficiencies of moral hazard, but the citizen would be powerless to escape from this burden.

EFFICIENCY PROBLEMS IN THE MARKET FOR PSYCHOTHERAPY

Compulsory insurance for private psychiatric care might not only solve or create problems in insurance markets, but it would obviously also affect the provision of psychotherapy. Insurance subsidizes the purchase of psychotherapy. If, without insurance, patients would make too few visits, the insurance subsidy might correct for their mistakes. Let us consider why patients might, on their own, make too little use of psychotherapy and hence would benefit from a subsidy. Moral hazard, the increase in utilization due to insurance, may have benefits as well.

Patient Ignorance

The Market Failure.   Informed, rational patients, constrained by their ability to pay, choose the correct number of visits to make to a therapist without insurance, just as informed rational consumers choose the correct quantity of any good or service. But users of mental health care might not always make decisions in their own best interests. Mental health professionals, among others, have charged that many people are prejudiced against treatment because of fear and ignorance (Brown 1976, Hall 1974). By undervaluing the benefits of psychotherapy, these people make the mistake of buying too few services. Insurance, by allowing people to make more visits, may remedy this failure.

Consumers' ignorance is an outstanding characteristic of health markets. In a classic article Arrow (1963) recast the speciality of health economics by arguing that virtually all of the special features of health markets derived from patient (and to a lesser extent, physician) uncertainty. Consumer or patient ignorance justified wholesale interference with consumer sovereignty in medical markets: regulation of physician training, hospital facilities and personnel, drug efficiency, and so on. Even if lay people could be educated about medical techniques and consequences, though, it is not obvious that they would want to make choices for treatment without outside, objective counsel. This concern for rationality is one reason why medical ethics suggest that even the most informed patients—physicians—do not treat themselves or their own families.

The decision whether to initiate treatment and the choice of length and type of treatment for emotional disturbance do not rest solely with the consumer. Patients are often guided to a psychiatrist by a series of outsiders, such as police, clergy, family, or family physician. Sometimes the consumer's sovereignty is violated completely and he is ordered by a court to undergo psychiatric treatment. Once the patient is under care, the therapist takes an active, perhaps dominant, role in the decision for treatment. As Berwick and Zeckhauser (1975) point out, because the mentally ill person is judged incompetent, such coercion is permitted.

To say that patients are not always rational and informed in their choice of visits to a therapist is to admit that patients, possibly in conjunction with advisors, sometimes make mistakes in choice of treatment. Patients' mistakes and the corrections by insurance are conceptually illustrated in Figure 3-3, which modifies the apparatus presented in Figure 3-2. To simplify discussion, the word "consumer" is used to refer to the person or persons who decide the number of visits. Line *EAC* describes, as before, how the consumer believes he will benefit from psychiatric treatment. Visits up to and including 100 are believed to be worth the cost; those beyond are not. Without insurance the consumer would buy 100 visits, the efficient number if his beliefs are correct. But if he undervalues benefits, the true benefits may look like line *FGH*, everywhere above *EAC*, signifying that each visit is really worth more than the consumer thinks it is. With *FGH* as true benefits, 200 is the efficient number of visits. The consumer would make 200 visits if he could be convinced that true benefits are described by *FGH*. Alternatively, he would make 200 visits if the price of a visit were reduced sufficiently so that, holding to his old beliefs, he would buy 200 visits. Insurance reduces the apparent price and in this way can correct for undervaluation. (Figure 3-3 has been drawn so that full insurance just achieves the goal of 200 visits.)

Consumers may, of course, make mistakes of both kinds, overvaluing or undervaluing benefits from psychotherapy. If consumers

Figure 3-3. Perceived and True Benefits of Visiting a Therapist.

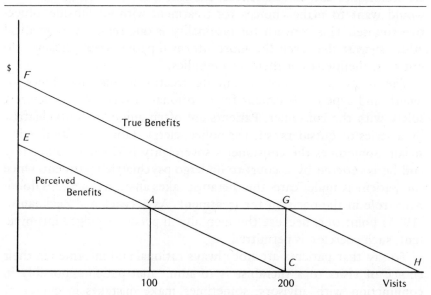

overvalue visits to a psychiatrist, as others have suggested, "insuring" (subsidizing) those visits is exactly the wrong thing to do. A consistent pursuit of efficiency would in this case require support of anti–NHI legislation for psychotherapy, imposing an excise tax on visits (the antisubsidy) as well as reducing the personal income tax (the antipremium). The idea of taxing psychiatric visits like alcohol or cigarettes may seem farfetched, but it illustrates the hazards of discussion of the effectiveness of psychotherapy. It is an argument that can cut both ways. As readers familiar with this debate know, "effectiveness of psychotherapy" is a battlefront along which the advocates of public financing for psychotherapy are on the defensive. They desperately defend a defensive position, that psychotherapy has *some* beneficial effect, rather than taking the offensive by arguing that psychotherapy does more good than people think it does.

The Evidence of the Effectiveness of Psychotherapy. It would be impossible in a limited space to review the accomplishments of the many forms of psychotherapy. Instead the focus here is on the general class of therapies falling under the name "dynamic psychotherapy" and practiced by a large majority of psychiatrists, psychologists, and other therapists. (See note 1 of Chapter 2 for definition of dynamic psychotherapy.)

To elucidate the evidence for the effectiveness of psychotherapy and the relation of this evidence to the case for compulsory insurance, three hypotheses are presented:

H_0. Dynamic psychotherapy has no beneficial effect.

H_1. Dynamic psychotherapy has some beneficial effect.

H_2. Dynamic psychotherapy has more beneficial effect than patients generally believe.

In these terms an important point can be made immediately: H_2 must be established if there is to be a case for insuring treatment of psychotherapy resulting from patients' mistakes. H_2 has not as yet entered the debate. The current struggle is between H_0 and H_1. It is not possible to argue, after a review of the literature on effectiveness, that people *generally underestimate* the value of psychotherapy, thereby adding to the case for coverage by compulsory insurance. That is not to say, however, that failure to demonstrate an underestimation should be interpreted as evidence *against* compulsory insurance. The perspective emphasized here is that researchers are simply *highly uncertain* about the effectiveness of psychotherapy.

One comprehensive review of the literature on effectiveness of psychotherapy has been done by Parloff et al. (1978) on behalf of the President's Commission on Mental Health. In a disease-by-disease summary Parloff et al. find no study that demonstrates the effectiveness of psychotherapy to scientific standards. In his presidential address to the 1978 meetings of the Society for Psychotherapy Research, Parloff summarized this work:

> In short, according to the research summaries prepared by the President's Commission on Mental Health, evidence regarding the effectiveness of psychotherapy suggests that with patients who present some of the most severe social and public health problems, psychotherapy appears to play but a supportive, habilitative and rehabilitative role rather than a primary treatment role; psychotherapy does not alone appear to be an effective treatment for the symptoms of schizophrenia, manic-depression, autism, alcoholism, or drug abuse. Further, psychotherapy has not yet been shown to be particularly effective in the treatment of severe obsessive compulsive behaviors in adults nor in the treatment of children with hyperactivity, anxiety, depressive problems, or learning disabilities. The disorders with which psychotherapy may be particularly useful are anxiety states—e.g. fears and phobias—and some nonpsychotic forms of depression. Note, however, that here the reviewers refer primarily to the effectiveness of behavior therapy rather than the usual psychotherapies (1978: 15).

Other, more recent reviews have come to more positive, but still guarded conclusions. The Office of Technology Assessment's Background Paper, "The Efficacy and Cost-Effectiveness of Psychotherapy" concluded:

> The available research, some of which meets rigorous methodological standards, seems to indicate that psychotherapy treatment is clearly better than no treatment. However, while the literature supports a generally positive conclusion with respect to the effectiveness of psychotherapy, there is a lack of specific information about the conditions under which psychotherapy is effective (1980: 4).

VandenBos and Pino (1980) note the trend in research on the effectiveness of psychotherapy. As research methods have improved and treatment and outcomes have been measured with greater precision, favorable effects of psychotherapy have emerged with more clarity.

It needs to be kept in mind, however, that these reviews are only asserting that psychotherapy has some beneficial effect, not that it is cost-effective, or that it is more effective than most people believe it to be.

It must be stressed that lack of evidence in support of the cost-effectiveness of psychotherapy should not lead to a conclusion that psychotherapy is not cost-effective, or less effective than people believe it to be. This is due to the extreme dangers of bias in research on psychotherapy. Although the nature of these biases is well known to statisticians, their importance in this debate has not been adequately appreciated. It is worthwhile to digress to show that even when the answer to whether psychotherapy *has been shown* to be effective is "no," the true answer can nevertheless be "yes."

Measurement error (sometimes called "error in variables") refers to the investigator's inability to measure accurately variables in an experiment. In research on the effectiveness of psychotherapy, mental health (the dependent variable) and therapy (the independent variable) are each measured with error. *Measurement error biases all research against the hypothesis that psychotherapy is effective*. After explaining the nature of the bias, this will be illustrated by means of an example of a clinical experiment.

No one thinks mental health is measured very well. According to Malan, a major stumbling block to worthwhile evaluative research on psychotherapy is the "failure to design outcome criteria that do justice to the complexity of the human personality" (1973: 128). Panzetta extends this criticism to measures of treatment: "If all we can say about psychotherapy in a *standardized* way, is that it is talk between a patient and a therapist, then we have failed to *differentiate* sufficiently" (1973: 452). Attempts to quantify dimensions of treatment and outcome are very new and as yet of unproven usefulness. (For the best example of use of quantitative methods see Yates 1980.) Imprecise measures of the effects of treatment (changes in mental health) and of the level of treatment (psychotherapy) bias research against finding psychotherapy effective.

Research on the effectiveness of psychotherapy proceeds by setting up the null hypothesis that psychotherapy has no effect on mental health, and then looking for evidence to contradict this hypothesis. Such evidence would be a statistically significant measure of beneficial effect of treatment. Even with a flawless measure of mental health, a certain amount of natural variance in mental health exists due to differences among individuals. To pass tests of statistical significance, the measure of the beneficial effect of treatment must be large in relation to this natural variance to provide evidence, beyond a reasonable doubt, that the improvement was not an accident. The value of a ratio of the measured effect of treatment to the natural variance in mental health (a t-statistic) indicates the significance of the effect of treatment. If the t-ratio falls below a certain conventional value, the effect of treatment is judged to be insignificant. Measurement error reduces the value of the ratio in two ways. Measuring mental health with error increases the denominator of the ratio by increasing the variance of mental health among individuals. Measuring treatment with error reduces the numerator by reducing the measured effect of treatment.

The fictitious experiment compares the mental health of twenty patients treated with psychotherapy with the mental health of a control group of twenty untreated patients. The fictional nature of the experiment allows us to know, by the way the data are generated, that psychotherapy is effective. We can then check to see if statistical tests lead to the conclusion that psychotherapy is effective. Constructing a data set based on the assumption that psychotherapy is effective is the correct way to proceed here because our interest is not in testing the effectiveness of psychotherapy but in checking the statistical methods used to evaluate the evidence for the effectiveness of psychotherapy.

To generate the data for the experiment, assume for mental patients otherwise identical:

1. That those untreated have a mean mental health score of 100 with a standard deviation of 10,
2. That those treated with psychotherapy have a mean mental health score of 110 with a standard deviation of 10.

These two assumptions imply that psychotherapy is effective, increasing the mental health score of patients by 10 points. This measure of mental health is the "true" measure, of course unknown in real experiments. With the aid of a table of random numbers, we draw two samples based on the two distributions described. These samples are the data for the experiment. The control group is twenty independent draws (patients) from a normal distribution of mean 100, standard deviation of 10. The treatment group is twenty independent draws (patients) from a normal distribution of mean 110 standard deviation of 10. These values are shown in Table 3-3.

The test of the effectiveness of psychotherapy using these data compares the mean level of mental health in the control group with the mean level in the treatment group. The mean for the control group $M_c = 103.05$; the mean for the treatment group $M_t = 112.13$. The estimated variances are $S_c^2 = 124.13$ and $S_t^2 = 155.34$.[19] A t-statistic tests whether the difference of 9.08 is statistically significant in

Table 3-3. Mental Health Scores with No Measurement Error.[a]

Patient	Control Group	Treatment Group
1	89.5	118.5
2	99.0	115.0
3	107.0	106.0
4	102.5	106.0
5	101.0	140.0
6	99.0	117.0
7	130.0	114.0
8	104.0	99.5
9	107.0	126.5
10	104.0	110.0
11	110.5	107.5
12	101.0	118.5
13	100.0	105.0
14	99.0	117.0
15	104.0	107.5
16	96.0	80.0
17	83.5	126.5
18	102.5	97.0
19	91.5	114.0
20	130.0	117.0
Sample mean	103.05	112.13
Sample variance	124.13	155.34

a. Sample mean = M.

Sample variance = S^2.

$$t = \frac{M_t - M_c}{\sqrt{\dfrac{(N_t - 1) S_t^2 + (N_c - 1) S_c^2}{N_t + N_c - 2}} \cdot \sqrt{\dfrac{1}{N_t} + \dfrac{1}{N_c}}} = 2.40$$

light of the estimated variance in mental health. The researcher does not know the true means and variances, but must use sample estimates. The value of the relevant t-statistic, computed to be 2.40 at the bottom of Table 3–3, is significant at the 0.01 level in a one-tailed test. The data in this experiment provide evidence that psychotherapy is effective. In the absence of measurement error, standard statistical tests lead us to reject the null hypothesis that psychotherapy is ineffective.[20]

True mental health of patients within the control and treatment groups varies because of individual differences, but we were nevertheless able to say in the last section that the mental health of the first patient in the control group was exactly 89.5. Now, more realistically, suppose the measure of mental health is not exact, that sometimes we overestimate and sometimes underestimate a patient's true mental health. The effect of this change is to increase the variance of the measure of mental health of patients within each group over the situation when we could measure mental health exactly.[21] Assume simply that measurement error increases the standard deviation of measured mental health from 10 to 15. The population mean of the control group remains 100 and of the treatment group remains 110, so that psychotherapy is just as effective as before. The researcher has no way of knowing this, of course, and can only work with what can be observed. Drawing the sample in the same way, now based on the new higher variance due to measurement error, the researcher would "see" the data listed in Table 3–4.

The measured difference in mental health between the treatment and control groups is now 9.85, but this is *not significant* at the 0.01 level in a one-tailed test. Measurement error increases the estimated variances of the two samples, S_c^2 and S_t^2, reducing the value of the t-statistic.[22] Misled by measurement error, based on these data, we would not reject the hypothesis that psychotherapy has no effect.

The problem can be partly overcome by increasing the size of the sample under study. An increased sample size reduces the "natural" variance of the dependent variable so that any given size of effect of psychotherapy is more likely to pass significance tests. This is the foundation of "meta-analysis" undertaken by Smith and Glass (1977) which, in effect, combines samples from separate investigations.

Treatment, as Panzetta stressed, is also a variable measured with error. Although it is obvious that control and treatment groups of

Table 3-4. Mental Health Scores Measuring Mental Health with Error.[a]

Patient	Control Group	Treatment Group
1	84.5	122.5
2	98.0	118.0
3	110.0	104.0
4	104.0	104.0
5	75.5	155.0
6	98.0	120.0
7	145.0	116.0
8	106.0	94.5
9	110.0	134.5
10	106.0	110.0
11	115.5	106.0
12	102.0	122.5
13	100.0	102.5
14	98.0	120.0
15	106.0	106.0
16	94.0	65.0
17	75.5	134.5
18	104.0	91.0
19	87.5	116.0
20	145.0	120.0
Sample mean	103.23	113.08
Sample variance	319.54	346.27

a. Sample mean = M.
Sample variance = S^2.
$t = 1.71$.

patients can be distinguished, it is not obvious that all patients in the control group receive exactly no treatment and those in the treatment group receive the same positive amount of treatment. Spending an hour with a therapist can involve varying amounts of treatment if treatment is defined in a meaningful way. In the fictional experiment, some patients in the treatment group may have received more treatment than others, and some in the control group may have been inadvertently "treated" in some way. When treatment is not simply a yes or no variable as it is in the experiment, the problem of measurement error is even more pronounced. It cannot always be supposed, for example, that someone seeing a therapist for ten hours has received twice the treatment of someone seeing a therapist for five

Table 3-5. Mental Health Scores Measuring Treatment with Error.[a]

Patient	Control Group	Treatment Group
1	89.5	104.0*
2	99.0	115.0
3	107.0	106.0
4	102.5	104.0*
5	101.0	140.0
6	99.0	117.0
7	130.0	114.0
8	118.5*	99.5
9	107.0	126.5
10	106.0*	110.0
11	110.5	107.5
12	118.5*	101.0*
13	100.0	105.0
14	99.0	117.0
15	80.0*	107.5
16	117.0*	104.0*
17	83.5	126.5
18	102.5	97.0
19	91.5	114.0
20	130.0	96.0*
Sample mean	104.60	110.58
Sample variance	182.41	121.61

a. Sample mean = M.

Sample variance = S^2.

$t = 1.53$.

Asterisks indicate values that were switched from Table 3-3. Random numbers to select switches were ten two-digit numbers in Freund (1977) divided by 5.

hours. The time spent in treatment is at best an imperfect proxy for the quantity of treatment that actually occurs.

In the presence of this sort of measurement error, differences in the mean measured mental health between the treated and control groups will be reduced, and estimates of the effect of treatment will be biased toward zero.[23] Suppose some of the patients in the control group, for whom treatment is measured to be zero, actually receive some treatment; and also suppose that some patients in the treatment group actually receive no meaningful treatment. The data in Table 3-5 simulate this problem. Five randomly selected patients from the control group were switched with five randomly selected patients from the treatment group. The researcher would not know which patients were improperly classified. We assume mental health is measured accurately.

The difference in the mean level of measured mental health between the two groups is reduced to 5.98 by this measurement error. This is not statistically significant. Measurement error on treatment leads the researcher not to reject the hypothesis that psychotherapy is ineffective.

It is unclear to what extent measurement error interferes with observation of true mental health and level of treatment in studies of effectiveness. What is clear is the direction of bias introduced by measurement error. Psychotherapy is highly likely to be more effective, and more cost-effective, than researchers have yet been able to establish in clinical experiments.

The Case for Compulsory Insurance. Insurance, by subsidizing purchase of care, may correct mistaken underevaluation of psychiatric services. People may not choose to buy insurance voluntarily, however, for the very same reason that they do not buy psychotherapy: they do not believe it worthwhile. Insurance changes the method of payment, but the reality of $50 per hour must be met either out of pocket or by insurance premiums. As shown in the section on moral hazard, an insurance policy covering services the consumer does not value at least at cost may appear to be a bad deal to the consumer and not be purchased. For this reason people cannot be relied upon to subsidize their own purchase of psychotherapy through voluntary insurance. The reliable way to induce more use is a *compulsory* insurance plan. By its nature a compulsory plan overrides some people's preferences, but when those preferences are misguided, it may be the appropriate thing to do.

It must be kept in mind that patients can make mistakes of both kinds, overvaluing as well as undervaluing services. If they overvalue services, insuring them is the wrong course, encouraging overuse. With little convincing evidence on either side of this issue, this part of the case for compulsory public financing of insurance is likely to remain unresolved for some time.

Benefits External to the Patient

The Market Failure. Seeing a therapist may benefit not only the person receiving treatment but that person's family, friends, or others in the community. The patient is not paid for providing these benefits; they are external to the price system. To present the patient with the socially correct incentives for use of psychotherapy it may be necessary to subsidize the activity—seeing the therapist—that generates external benefits. Sloan makes the same point, "without some appropriate government action, such as adopting policies for service price reduction, patients and potential patients will not consume enough mental health care, because they fail to consider the pay off to others arising from their consumption of their services" (1971: 12). Insurance is one way to accomplish a reduction in the price of service.

In a market economy with a highly developed division of labor, an individual depends on many others to sell what is needed and to buy what is available to sell. Prices guide the terms of this interdependence. If one's wage is $5 per hour, the benefits conferred on the employer are $5 for each hour of an employee's work; if the price of a 2-pound package of rice is $0.65, the total cost incurred by the farmer, processor, wholesaler, and retailer to bring that rice to the shelf is $0.65.[24] When the price of what is sold is how much it benefits the buyer and the price of what is bought is how much it costs the seller to provide, decisions to buy and sell in one's own interest are consistent with the broader social interest. One buys rice if it is worth more than $0.65; if this price is equal to the cost of the rice, then self-interested choice effects the social goal of distributing rice to all those for whom the benefits exceed the cost.

An *externality* exists if the price of something indicates *incorrectly* one's interdependence with others. For example, a manufacturer pays a price of zero to put smoke into the air (to use clean air). The use of clean air imposes on others costs of avoiding or enduring the smoke. The price of zero fails to indicate to the manufacturer the cost of using air. Thinking air is free, the manufacturer may put out too much smoke. The smoke is an externality because the cost it imposes on others is not accounted for through, or is external to, the price system. A tax on pollution, substituting for a market price, forces the smoke-producer to take account of the cost of using clean air. Externalities can benefit as well as annoy. Just as it is appropriate to tax the smoke-producing manufacturer, it may be appropriate to *subsidize* the patient's purchase of psychotherapy, an activity that generates external benefits to others.

External benefits from a patient seeking therapy go to two groups. First, it goes to those who care about the patient and benefit from his feeling of emotional well-being—primarily family and friends. There is no doubt that family and friends are vitally affected by mental illness and would benefit from its alleviation. Weisbrod (1979) in a study of mentally ill treated in a hospital and an experimental outpatient clinic in Madison, Wisconsin, found that 48 percent of the hospitalized patients' families reported some emotional disturbance and 25 percent reported some physical illness they attributed to the patient's mental illness. Curing mental illness would help them by removing the cause of their difficulties. Technically, such benefits qualify as an externality. Although these benefits to others for which the patient is not paid are external, these benefits are not external to the patient's decision for treatment. Prices do not lead him to take them into account, but direct contact with family and friends probably does. Family and friends are insiders to the decision for treatment, often encouraging the mentally disturbed person to seek care. It would be a wasteful duplication for the government to intervene with a subsidy on behalf of those already well-represented in decision-making.

The other group of people who may benefit from a patient's treatment do not care about the patient personally, but because of the way medical and social services are paid for in this society, are financially involved in the patient's decision for treatment. In 1975, 789,000 mentally ill were treated in mental hospitals; 927,000 in general hospitals; 351,000 in VA hospitals; 207,000 in nursing homes; and 13,000,000 by physicians other than psychiatrists. Mental illness is dealt with by means other than treatment by health personnel, including by police, welfare, and other social agencies. Taxes support social services and VA hospitals; taxes and insurance premiums together pay for 90 percent of hospital expenses and almost 70 percent of physicians' charges. This collective method of payment for services for mental illness *builds in* financial externalities. Each of us has a financial stake in treatment of everyone's mental illness. If psychotherapy deals effectively with mental illness, society may be interested in subsidizing psychotherapy, not out of an altruistic concern for the patient, but to save money on other social and medical services.

The Evidence.   The plausibility of offset effects is based on the well-recognized interrelationships between mental health and general health, and mental health and other social problems. Mechanic, for example, has observed, "[Mental health] problems are common and are often associated with physical symptoms and discomforts. . . . The distress associated with these patients' problems triggers a demand for medical services, and such patients are often recipients of intensive medical and surgical care that achieves little value" (1978: 494). Epidemiological data reported in the President's Commission on Mental Health (PCMH) show that at least 6 percent of the people who see a doctor other than a psychiatrist have primarily a psychological problem, and many more of the rest have psychological problems contributing to their feeling of ill health. Sometimes these people are treated appropriately by their physician, sometimes they are not. People seek help and physicians try to give it to them in the form of drugs and surgery—the kind of treatment doctors are trained to give. Direct treatment of the psychological problem and the psychological opponent of illness may lead to less demands on the rest of the health system. While offset effects seem highly plausible, the quantitative magnitude of any offset effect has not been established through empirical research. Indeed, in spite of the established interrelation between health and mental health, the research literature has failed even to unambiguously establish the *existence* of an offset. In a thorough discussion of the literature, Jones and Vischi (1979) found evidence for offset effects in 24 of 25 studies of alcohol, drug-abuse and mental health treatment, ranging in magnitude from 5 to 80 percent reduction in medical utilization. Near unanimity is rare in a research literature. The existence of an offset effect would be regarded as well-established, but for the deficiencies in the research designs of these studies. The most serious problem had to do with the nature of the control group, as Jones and Vischi emphasize. Some studies used a "before-and-after" design, comparing medical utilization of the same people before and after psychotherapy. This design can be confounded by the "peaking" of all kinds of utilization in times of physical and emotional distress. Observed declines in medical utilization may well have occurred in the absence of psychotherapy. Other studies compared medical utilization of a group after psychotherapy with a matched population who did not choose psychotherapy. The problem with this design is that the groups are not really the same since the treatment group freely chose psychotherapy, and the control group did not. Differences among members of the groups, rather than the psychotherapy itself, may account for differences in subsequent medical utilization.

Another limitation of this research is that the settings in which offsets have been investigated have by and large been confined to Health Maintenance Organizations, Community Mental Health Centers or clinics in industry. It may be that the response of medical utilization would be different to psychotherapy provided in the fee-for-service section, where most treatment occurs.

When interpreting this evidence for offsets, it is important to keep in mind the different perspective the scientist and the policy maker or legislator must bring to the question of evidence. Science is very conservative. For evidence to convincingly support a new idea, such as that treatment for mental conditions reduces other health costs, the researcher is required to rule out other possible explanations for the effect by the use of "controls" in the study and to reduce the possibility that the effect could have been the result of chance to less than 5 percent. If these criteria are not met, scientists remain skeptical of the hypothesis. This is appropriate when the activity in question is "hypothesis testing."

Legislatures, for their part, should not be interested in hypothesis testing. They need to know if an idea *likely* to be correct, rather than whether the idea has been proven correct to standards of scientific evidence. It would be a far too conservative approach to legislative action to require that all policies be demonstrated to be effective to the usual standards of scientific proof. What proof do we have that compulsory car inspections makes cars safer? What proof is there that compulsory education benefits society? People familiar with these matters can give some evidence on behalf of these but this evidence is unlikely to satisfy the usual scientific criteria for acceptability.

Adopting the perspective of the law-maker, how likely is it that offset effects exist? First of all, before any explicit empirical tests of offset are performed, there are powerful reasons related to the nature of physical and mental illness and the reasons people seek medical care to *expect* offsets to exist. Secondly, although no one study fully meets scientific standards for research design, as a body of work, the offset studies should probably be given considerable weight. Design flaws in these studies generally had the effect of biasing findings in favor of finding an effect. However, other problems in research on the effects of psychotherapy, notably problems due to measurement error, tend to bias the results against a finding of offset. Efforts to improve research methodology should certainly proceed, but in the meantime, it appears reasonable to conclude that some medical offset exists.

Not all evidence suggests that there is some substitutability between outpatient psychotherapy and other services. In one study, after one year of coverage for outpatient psychiatric services, hospitalization for emotional problems did not decrease (Glasser and Dugan 1976). Adding to the skepticism is the finding in the general health sector that outpatient and inpatient services are complements, not substitutes. There is a body of research that supports the finding that decreasing the price of physician services *increases* the use of hospital care (Davis and Russel 1972, Freiberg and Scutchfield 1976, Hill and Veney 1970, Lewis and Keairnes 1970).

Evidence on the effect of mental health services on other costs comes from what is not happening as well as what is. If early ambulatory treatment could prevent more serious mental illness or physical illness or control some mental illness more effectively than expensive hospital care and this fact was well known, insurers should be *eager* to cover outpatient psychotherapy. Health insurance carriers are in a position to capture many of the offset effects of psychotherapy. Eagerness would not aptly describe the attitude of most carriers toward psychotherapy. In spite of numerous experiments in progress, most insurers severely restrict such coverage. This negative attitude, built on the experience of those whose business it is to know the extra costs of additional coverage, is evidence against the proposition that insurance for ambulatory psychiatric treatment affords substantial savings in other services. Insurers may certainly make mistakes, but their general reluctance to offer insurance for private psychiatric care should give policymakers pause.

The Case for Compulsory Insurance. Offset effects of psychotherapy appear in other health costs, other social costs, and in productivity. Insurance carriers are not in a position to recoup the full savings from police, welfare, or other social agencies or the increased productivity that may derive from provision of outpatient psychotherapy. The government on behalf of its citizens should take these savings into account and should therefore not necessarily be guided by insurers' reluctance to underwrite outpatient psychotherapy. The apparent offset effects of psychotherapy must weigh significantly in the case for compulsory insurance for psychotherapy. The evidence so far is mostly in treatment settings where the insurer is directly involved with treatment decisions.

Although these studies indicate fairly persuasively that providing psychotherapy can sometimes produce savings elsewhere, it is not at all clear what they imply for compulsory insurance for psychotherapy. Most proposals for compulsory insurance for psychotherapy would, in fact, *eliminate the incentives private groups have had to set up the kinds of programs for which offset effects have been demonstrated.* Why would any firm pay for an employee assistance program if it must already pay through payroll deduction for insurance for psychotherapy? Why would any provider or employee group be interested in controlling utilization? The offset studies pose a dilemma—they demonstrate reasonably clearly the external benefits of psychotherapy, but in support of programs that would be undermined by most compulsory insurance schemes.

SUMMARY

Identification of the deficiencies in private markets for insurance for psychotherapy (and through empirical research measurement of the magnitude of those deficiencies) is the first step in arguing the case for an alternative system, such as compulsory public insurance. From the review in this chapter, two reasons to support compulsory insurance are clear. The first is the argument that private insurers, because of difficulty in correctly pricing insurance for psychotherapy, would be beset by an adverse selection of insurance risks and be forced to withdraw from offering coverage. The second is the external or offset effects of psychotherapy.

The difficulties in evaluating the benefits of psychotherapy have led to controversy about whether patients generally overvalue or undervalue psychotherapy. Systematic undervaluation would contribute to the case for compulsory insurance, but the existence of undervaluation is far from established. Overvaluation, which would argue against compulsory insurance for psychotherapy, has not been established either.

When third parties pay part of the price for service, people use more psychotherapy. Private markets have some advantage over the government in dealing with moral hazard. The more serious the problem of moral hazard, the less attractive is compulsory insurance for psychotherapy. The major risk with respect to insurance for psychotherapy is that it would lead to large increases in demand and utilization. As yet there has been no true study of demand for psychotherapy, isolating the effect of insurance from other factors, to assess this risk. The next part of this book is a report of the first study of demand for psychotherapy.

NOTES TO CHAPTER 3

1. The theoretical literature on insurance is well developed. The interested reader is referred particularly to Arrow (1963, 1974), Pauly (1968, 1974), Akerlof (1970), Spence and Zeckhauser (1971), Zeckhauser (1970), and Rosett (ed.) (1976). The "contingent commodity" framework offers a powerful approach to the theory of insurance (for example, Arrow 1974), though most important lessons about insurance fall out of the less general approach adopted here. Essentially, to simplify, I assume the individual's utility function is independent of the "state of nature."

2. Spreading payments over time, rather than among individuals, is emphasized in this section since with actuarily fair insurance, policyholders pay premiums just equal to what they receive in benefits, on average, plus associated administrative expenses. A large number of people in the insurance pool (with independently distributed risks) allows the insurance carrier to accept the risk transferred to it by the policyholder. So long as premiums are actuarily fair, no policyholder imposes net expected benefits or costs on the other policyholders. Insurance premiums are, of course, rarely actuarily fair person by person, so that some policyholders (the good risks) typically subsidize others (the bad risks). This is the cause of adverse selection (to be discussed). Cross-subsidization, as for example between the generally healthy and generally sick, may sometimes be desirable for reasons of equity.

3. Thus there is no cross-subsidization. When everyone is identical there is no point to having a society larger than one for the purpose of example. When adverse selection is considered people face different probabilities of becoming ill.

4. Diminishing marginal utility of income is not *necessary* in order for an individual to demand insurance at an actuarily fair price. What is necessary is that the marginal utility of income in times of illness be higher than the marginal utility of income when well. This could be so with constant or even increasing marginal utility of income if the utility function itself depended on the individual's health.

5. Under certain assumptions about how individuals make decisions, it is rational to choose insurance if and only if expected utility is higher with insurance. One of these assumptions is that the utility function is independent of the person's health. This is satisfied in the example but is probably not generally true. For discussion of this see Arrow (1974).

6. This is optimal coverage in this example since it equalizes the marginal utility of income whether the individual is sick or well.

7. In a well-working market, this premium would be enforced by competition among insurance companies.

8. After losing money on persons 1–4 for a year or two, the insurer has gathered some information that could be used to set premiums for individuals. Experience rating for individuals is rare in practice, however, even in cases where it is possible. Part of the reason may be that many people view insurance as a way for the well to help pay for the expenses of the sick. It would be "unfair" to charge the less healthy higher premiums.

9. There is a demand or average revenue curve for insurance coverage in this example that is downward-sloping because as the premium falls more buy insurance. There is an average cost curve of coverage that is also downward-sloping because the cost of covering "marginal" policies falls as reduction in premiums bring in better and better risks. In this example, the average cost curve is everywhere above the average revenue curve, so there is no premium the insurer may set for which average revenue meets average costs.

10. Moral hazard can cause similar manifestations of market failure. Brown (1976), Hall (1974), and others have attributed the "weak demand" for insurance for private psychiatric care to the stigma attached to mental illness.

11. Guillette (1976: 3–8) compares the Blue Cross and Blue Shield high option with Aetna's experience.

	1972	1973	Mental Health Benefits as Percent of Total 1974	1975
Aetna	8.6	12.4	11.1	7.3
Blue Cross/ Blue Shield	7.1	7.3	7.2	7.5

20-visit limit imposed by Aetna

12. Nordquist and Wu define moral hazard as follows: "Moral hazard refers to the phenomena whereby the method of insurance and the form of insurance policy affect the behavior of the insured and, therefore, the probabilities on which the insurance company has relied" (1976: 43).

13. Sharfstein makes this point: "The phenomena of resistance, regression and negative transference lead to a wave curve of treatment progress. An increment of treatment could lead to a decrement of mental health over the short term; only much later will the progress towards health resume" (1976: 1186-87).

    This observation makes it less likely that patients will have the foresight necessary to make intelligent choices about treatment.

14. This assumption of the informed, intelligent buyer is obviously open to question. This will be considered further.

15. It would be rational for an individual to cut back visits as part of a binding agreement with other policyholders. There is no way an individual can forge such an agreement. Use of insurance benefits is thus similar to a "prisoner's dilemma" game.

16. The area of ABC defines the benefits of visits 101 through 200. The area of ABC is less than one-half of rectangle $ABCD$. The area of rectangle $ABCD$ is height ($50 per visit) times base (100 visits), or $5,000.

17. The copayment schedule is as follows:

    | visits 1-5: | none | visits 11-15: | 30% |
    | visits 6-10: | 15% | visits 16-n: | 45% |

18. Compare the early work of Feldstein (1970), Newhouse (1970), or Scitovsky and Snyder (1973) with Newhouse and Phelps (1976) or the description of the ongoing *Rand* experiment in demand for medical care, described in Newhouse (1974).

19. Sample means and variances diverge from population values, of course.

20. There is a small chance that a random sample of patients drawn from the distributions specified would be consistent with the null hypothesis.

21. In the last section, the control group, for example, had measured mental health = X, where X was "true" mental health and was normally distributed with mean 100 and standard deviation of 10. Now, with measurement error, measured mental health = $X + V$, where V is an error term, independent of X and normally distributed with mean 0. The standard deviation of $X + V$ is larger than the standard deviation of X alone.

22. In linear regression, the t-statistic is also inversely related to the estimated residual variance of the independent variable. See Johnston (1972: 144).

23. See Johnston (1972: 280-83) for a demonstration of this in the general regression framework, of which the example is a special case.

24. Prices equal marginal cost; wages equal marginal revenue produced in perfectly competitive markets. This is a textbook paradigm but a useful approximation to the way many prices are set.

AN EMPIRICAL STUDY OF DEMAND FOR PSYCHOTHERAPY

4 THE DATA AND THE APPROACH

Two issues critical to policy for financing psychotherapy are the extent of added demand that would result from insurance and the impact compulsory insurance would have on the distribution of psychotherapeutic services and income among types of users. At present there are few reliable estimates on these concerns. There is no consensus about whether compulsory insurance would lead to large increases in demand for psychotherapy or would represent a massive resource transfer to upper income groups—which many view as a serious danger of this policy. The next three chapters address these issues by close examination of the experience of over 4,000 persons seeking care from private psychiatrists. The approach is to formulate and empirically estimate, based on the behavior of this group, the relation between characteristics of the patient, insurance coverage, characteristics of the psychiatrists, and the number of visits by the patient in the course of treatment. A demand curve is estimated with particular attention to the way insurance may influence the quantity demanded.

The results of this investigation, concerning the responsiveness of demand for psychotherapy to insurance coverage, are reported in Chapter 5. Since the sample of patients is classified by income, the effect of insurance by income group is also reported. This has important consequences for how compulsory insurance would affect the distribution of services. Distributional issues, of which income is but one dimension, are handled in Chapter 6.

The data open a number of interesting channels for research but bear some serious limitations. These are each discussed in the present chapter.

A SURVEY OF PSYCHIATRISTS
AND THEIR PATIENTS

Social scientists are given infrequent opportunity to study in detail the interaction between health provider and patient. Understandable concern for patients' privacy and reluctance of physicians and other providers to reveal clinical and financial information about themselves and their patients often impede investigation. Broad-based surveys of patient populations, such as the National Ambulatory Medical Care Survey, have relied on the very imperfect device of patients' recall. Patients often misunderstand health problems and are reluctant to report or unable to recall accurately treatment experience. Particularly when questions involve mental illness, serious self-reporting problems can be expected. Surveys taken from the patient's side of the exchange are thus likely to be weakest in the very areas of data the survey was designed to collect. Meanwhile, surveys of physicians, such as those conducted by the AMA or by *Medical Economics*, have typically been concerned with the physician's practice—hours, income, prices, patient load, use of auxiliary personnel—without exploring in any detail the personal, socioeconomic, and medical characteristics of the physician's patients.

Viewed in this context, the survey of psychiatrists in private practice conducted by the Joint Information Service (JIS) of the American Psychiatric Association (APA) and the National Association for Mental Health (NAMH) is a particularly noteworthy effort.[1] Although psychiatrists actually completed the entire questionnaire, the survey covers both sides of the medical encounter, providing a large data set without parallel in the richness of financial, clinical, and socioeconomic information about physicians, in this case psychiatrists, and their patients.

After pretesting, in February 1973, the JIS distributed the survey to a geographically representative 10 percent sample of psychiatrists who spent at least fifteen hours per week in private practice. Backed by the authority of the APA, and aided by repeated follow-ups by local chapters of the APA, the final response was 73 percent, for a total of 440 psychiatrists. A high response rate maintains the randomness of original sample.

Each psychiatrist filled out a questionnaire for himself or herself, and one each for his or her last ten patients in the most recent typical week of private practice. The sample of patients is thus over 4,000. The JIS guaranteed confidentiality by not collecting the names of patients and by eliminating identification of psychiatrists. Instead, psychiatrists are identified only by a three-digit number; patients by the three-digit number of their psychiatrist plus a number from one to ten. The survey provides the following information for each psychiatrist: age, location, subspecialty, size of practice, average length of treatment, and fee; for each patient: age, sex, race, marital status, inpatient history, office visits in the preceding twelve months, diagnosis and severity, recent types of treatment, alcohol and drug use history, expected future number of office visits, occupation, income, and extent of insurance coverage. A copy of the questionnaires filled out by psychiatrists for themselves and their patients is contained in Appendix A. A number of one- and two-variable breakdowns in these data are presented in Appendix B.

In order to set up an empirical model of the determination of the number of visits made by individual patients, data on the patient are linked to data on the psychiatrist with information on the *market conditions* in which psychiatrists practice. Various data were collected on market areas narrowly defined (counties) and defined broadly (states). In addition to providing measures of the atmosphere in which demand decisions are made, it could be foreseen at the early stages of this study that an instrumental variable estimate of insurance coverage would be necessary. Market data were collected to provide the exogenous variables for this part of the investigation.

With information on market conditions at the county and state level, there are four data sets: patients, psychiatrist, counties, and states. By adding a geographical code to the psychiatrist data for the state and county in which the psychiatrist practiced, the data sets were merged to one, associating each patient with his or her psychiatrist and then each psychiatrist with the market in which he or she practices.[2]

SPECIFYING THE MODEL OF DEMAND

Specifying the model of demand involves making the connection between the analytically ideal concepts—quantity demanded by a patient, the price paid, insurance coverage, a patient's diagnosis, a patient's family income, and so forth—and the information actually available for scrutiny. Often, information is missing entirely or appears only in an incomplete or imperfect form. This will dictate the way the existing data should be handled.

The Dependent Variable: Number of Visits Made by a Patient

Each patient in the sample was in treatment by a psychiatrist at the time of the survey. The patient had made a number of visits, reported by the psychiatrist, and would make additional visits, predicted by the psychiatrist. The dependent variable, total visits (the logarithm of total visits is used in the regressions) is the sum of the past and projected visits. For some patients, psychiatrists did not make precise predictions, responding to the question of how long the patient would be in treatment with the answers "Indefinitely" or "Don't know." These two responses are treated differently. Don't know is treated as revealing no information and these patients are dropped from our sample. Indefinitely is interpreted as meaning "a long time," a phrase that may mean different things to different psychiatrists. For patients with indefinitely long projected treatments, we substitute the length of treatment projected for the patient of any of the psychiatrists with the longest *definite* projected length of treatment. Along with projected future frequency of visits this allows the construction of a projection for the patients with indefinitely long predicted lengths of treatment. Because the procedure is arbitrary and somewhat conservative, "indefinitely" can be defined alternatively to mean twice the maximum definite prediction the patient's psychiatrist made for some other patient. This alternative proves to make virtually no difference in the estimates of the demand function, however.

Psychiatrists' predictions of the number of visits a patient will eventually make may be inaccurate, of course. Care was taken to guard against any bias this inaccuracy might introduce into the estimates. If psychiatrists were unbiased in their predictions, the total visit variable would be an unbiased measure of the patient's actual total visits. Psychiatrists may, however, systematically over- or underestimate the number of future visits. If some bias of this kind exists in prediction, the patient's *stage of treatment* should influence the measure of total visits. As Figure 4-1 illustrates, if psychiatrists are conservative in their predictions, systematically underestimating future visits, patients observed at earlier stages in treatment will have a lower total. Figure 4-2 illustrates the opposite case of the psychiatrist overestimating future visits. To control for this effect, a variable in the estimated demand function is entered equal to the share of projected visits in the total:

$$\text{PROSH} = \frac{\text{projected}}{\text{past} + \text{projected}} \cdot$$

The sign of the coefficient on PROSH will be negative if psychiatrists underestimate future visits (Figure 4-1); it will be positive if psychiatrists overestimate future visits (Figure 4-2). If psychiatrists are unbiased the estimated coefficient of PROSH will be close to zero.[3] (A variable interacting insurance and PROSH is entered to check whether psychiatrists especially over- or underestimate visits when a patient has insurance.)

Figure 4-1. Psychiatrists Underestimate: PROJ = a (true total – past), $0 < a < 1$.

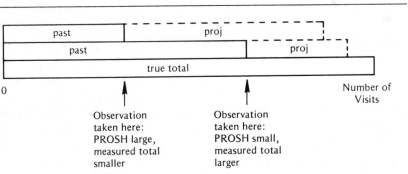

Figure 4-2. Psychiatrists Overestimate: PROJ = a (true total - past), $a > 1$.

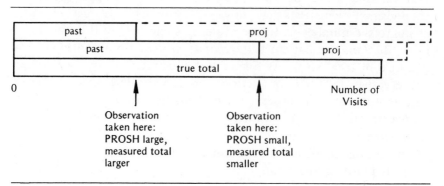

The Determinants of Demand

The determinants of a patient's utilization of services fall naturally into a series of categories. These are shown in Table 4-1 along with the specific variables in each category that are included in the study.

The Patient's Personal and Socioeconomic Characteristics

Personal characteristics include sex, race, age, marital status, and place of birth. Socioeconomic characteristics include income and occupation. Interpretation of these apparently simple variables is complicated by the psychiatrist's role in the decision for treatment. For example, suppose blacks make fewer visits than otherwise similar whites. In a "normal" market demand setting this finding would be interpreted as information about the tastes of persons of different races. Blacks with the same income, insurance coverage, and so on would be said to prefer to buy fewer services than whites. An alternative explanation may reflect the preferences of the psychiatrist rather than those of the patient. Psychiatrists may prefer to treat certain kinds of patients. Psychiatrists, who are generally white males, may prefer to talk with whites rather than blacks, women rather than

Table 4–1. Determinants of Demand.

Patient's Personal and Socioeconomic Characteristics	Mental Health	Psychiatrist's Characteristics	"Atmosphere"	Price or Insurance
Sex	Diagnosis	Age (experience)	Area demand (bandwagon effects)	Price
Age	Severity	Subspeciality		Insurance
Race	Inpatient history	Slack in practice	Average education in area	
Place of birth				
Income			Urbanization	
Occupation			Geographic Region	

men, the younger rather than the old, or professionals and white collar workers rather than manual laborers.[4] Such preference, or perhaps prejudice, could explain the statistical effect of any one of the variables in the personal and socioeconomic categories of Table 4-1. In the estimates shown in this chapter it has not been possible to determine whether it is the preferences of the patients or of the psychiatrists that explain why older patients, for instance, make less intensive use of private psychiatrists.

In general, almost all the variables included in the demand model will be subject to a dual interpretation: either being connected with the decisions of the psychiatrist or with the decisions of the patient. Although it is interesting and important to distinguish whose preferences are causing differences in treatment, it is not usually crucial. In predictive models, the consequence is the same whether the patient decides to demand more or the psychiatrist prescribes more. It is more natural in discussion of a demand model to interpret the effects of variables as originating with the patient, lower income patients demanding less, patients with more insurance demanding more, and so on. The following discussions will be largely oriented to the patient's behavior, but the reader should heed the general caveat that these variables can originate with the psychiatrist's preferences as well.

The Patient's Mental Health

The next set of variables listed in Table 4-1 as determining a patient's utilization of psychotherapy has to do with the patient's mental health. These variables are the diagnosis, the severity of the patient's impairment at the time treatment began, and the patient's history as an inpatient for mental illness. It is unusual in a study of medical utilization to have so much information about the health of the patient. Yet it does not provide perfect measures. As is true for all the data in this study, these variables were supplied by the psychiatrist and all psychiatrists do not talk the same diagnostic language. As Redlich and Freedman have noted, "Common diagnostic terms . . . mean different things to different psychiatrists" (1965: 248). Moreover, the presence of insurance may distort diagnostic reportings for patients covered. Insurance carriers require that patients be "mentally ill" as indicated by the psychiatrist's diagnosis to qualify for payment. In order to permit patients to take advantage of their insurance coverage psychiatrists may provide them with a diagnostic label even if the patients are not really mentally ill but simply desire treatment. As Aetna's medical director put it, some psychiatrists are willing to "put an insurance acceptable diagnosis on a condition that is not considered a covered diagnosis" (Guillette 1976: 9).

A second problem arises in interpreting the diagnosis variable in the presence of insurance. When a patient has insurance his or her medical records may be subject to review by the insurer or possibly by the patient's employer if the insurance is partly paid for by the employer. To protect the patient the psychiatrist may inaccurately report diagnosis. The Group for the Advancement of Psychiatry (GAP) notes that in these circumstances, "Psychiatrists may adopt the strategy of putting down an 'irrelevant label,' e.g., 'depressive neurosis'" (1975: 515). Such labels are acceptable to the insurer and avoid revealing information the patient may prefer to keep confidential. The psychiatrist's reporting of the severity of the patient's impairment may also be distorted by the presence of insurance. If a patient is really mildly impaired, but is well-insured and would like to make many visits, the psychiatrist may be tempted to report severer impairment to justify the patient's treatment. Thus the estimated effect of insurance on utilization would be underestimated because some of the effect of insurance would be improperly attributed to the variable "degree of impairment."

The Psychiatrist's Characteristics

Some characteristics of the psychiatrist may influence patients' utilization, such as the psychiatrist's age (related to experience) or subspecialty. Patients look to psychiatrist for guidance, and the guidance offered may be influenced by the psychiatrist's own training and experience as well as the patient's condition. As GAP puts it, "The absence of clear cut, generally accepted criteria of suitability for various types of psychotherapy may influence the therapist to offer the kind of treatment he prefers and is trained to carry out rather than make his treatment decision on more objective grounds" (1975: 517). Of particular interest is the extent to which a psychoanalyst influences the length of the patient's treatment.

In the economist's standard model of demand, the choice of how much to buy rests entirely with the consumer. By contrast, in what might be called a medical model, the basic decision about treatment is made by the physician. The physician, in this case, the psychiatrist, examines the patient, makes a diagnosis, and *prescribes* treatment. The psychiatrist may take into account the personal circumstances of the patient in deciding the exact form and length of treatment to be recommended, but the decision in this medical model is predominantly a technological one—the physician prescribes the treatment medically appropriate for this patient's illness. These are obviously radically different models of how treatment is decided. Since a patient and a physician must both agree to continue treatment input is necessarily included from each extreme model.

Controversy about the role of the physician in influencing treatment for the patient concerns whether the physician prescribes treatment solely in the interest of the patient (as the physician sees it), or in his or her own financial interest. Evidence on whether physicians influence patients in their own (the physicians') interest is surprisingly ambiguous when subjected to close scrutiny. Two recent conferences have wrestled with the issues and the evidence (Greenberg 1978, Fuchs 1978), without coming to a resolution.

This study pursues investigation of psychiatrists' influence on their patients' demand.[5] The details on psychiatrists and patients discovered by the survey allow us to examine how and in what circumstances psychiatrists influence demand. Ideally, the decision to terminate a patient's psychiatric treatment should be made in the interests of the patient, not the psychiatrist. Offenkrantz and Tobin (1975) define professional integrity for the psychiatrist as not treating a patient for personal income, training goals, or self-gratification. Integrity is cheap when times are good, but more expensive if times are hard. During hard times, a psychiatrist might want to see many more private patients at the going price per hour of treatment and prolong the treatment of current patients. Were such a compromise with professional integrity to be made, a measure of slack in the psychiatrist's practice would be positively associated with patients' length of treatment. The empirical estimate of demand presented here includes a measure of the general slack or tightness in a market to check whether psychiatrists do indeed encourage more extensive utilization during slack markets.

A slack market by definition is a market where demand growth has been relatively slow. Whereas in the long run supply adjustments would tend to even out tightness across markets, in the short run relatively rapid recent increases in demand produce relatively tight markets. Recent demand growth in a market is measured in this study by the growth in the number of people less than sixty-five years of age who had coverage for regular medical expense insurance between 1970 and 1973 for each state. This variable combines both population growth and growth in extent of insurance coverage. It is used to test whether growth in insurance coverage is negatively related to the length of treatment of individual patients, as suggested by the idea that psychiatrists would recommend shorter treatments when markets are tight. Growth in regular medical expense insurance is far from the ideal variable to test the hypothesis of physicians' influence. It is a market-level measure of slack rather than a measure specific to the psychiatrist's practice. Further, coverage in regular medical insurance policies may or may not include private psychiatry.

"Atmosphere"

As mentioned earlier, demand for psychotherapy may depend on social and cultural factors, since these factors may vary in different parts of the United States. The demand equation includes a series of regional dummy variables and variables measuring the educational level and urbanization in the patient's county. These are meant to proxy for the attitudes toward mental illness and treatment that might be expected to be more permissive in big cities, in areas with higher average education, and in other areas of the country. Of special interest are atmospheric variables designed to reflect bandwagon effects in demand because these effects would be amplified by broad-based compulsory insurance for psychotherapy.

In simple demand theory, the bandwagon effect and its connection with compulsory insurance can be displayed as follows: In Figure 4-3, *AB* is an individual's demand curve for psychotherapy before compulsory insurance. Suppose for discussion the compulsory insurance takes the form of a NHI plan including coverage for psychotherapy. The individual pays $50 per visit and buys 30 visits per

Figure 4-3. Bandwagon and Price Effects of National Health Insurance.

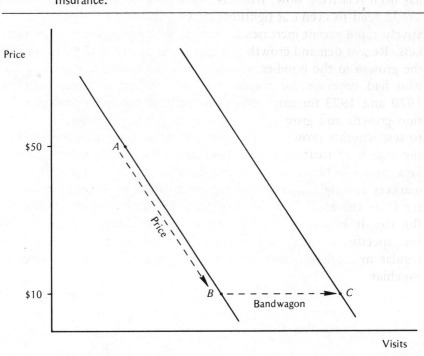

year (point A). Now impose national health insurance paying 80 percent of charges. If the only effect of national health insurance on this individual's demand is a price reduction, the individual would move to point B in the figure. But suppose also that this consumer's demand for psychotherapy depends on the social acceptability of treatment. After national health insurance, many more people may seek psychiatric help and more extensive care than before. If mental illness and treatment thereby become less odd or shameful, the individual's demand schedule may be affected by this bandwagon effect. In short, the individual would buy more services *at any price*.

It is possible to break down the effect of national health insurance on demand into a bandwagon and a price effect. If national health insurance took the peculiar form of insuring everyone but the individual whose demand is depicted in Figure 4-3, bandwagon effects would shift the entire demand curve as shown. The pure bandwagon effect is the move from B to C. The pure price effect of national health insurance, when insurance coverage to the individual only changes is, as noted, the move from A to B. Combining these two moves gives the total effect of national health insurance, the price plus the bandwagon effect, moving the individual from A to C.

As the shift in demand curves is drawn in Figure 4-3, the bandwagon effect is large. How large it is, and if it exists at all, is of course an empirical matter. The bandwagon effect is not a law of behavior, only a possibility. Since it may be an important determinant of the behavior of buyers of psychotherapy, this possibility is checked in the empirical study. Economic theory, based on the supposition that the individual's demand curve is fixed with respect to others' behavior, predisposes investigators to neglect bandwagon effects. This is the first attempt to incorporate bandwagon effects in a model of demand for medical services.

Price and Insurance

Interpretation of a price variable in a demand study is normally straightforward. Price is inversely related to quantity demanded along a demand curve. Changes in quantity demanded with changes in price indicate the slope or elasticity of the demand curve. Psychiatrists may engage in price discrimination, which complicates this simple interpretation.[6]

The percentage of charges paid by the insurer is the basic measure of insurance coverage used in this study. Slightly less than one-half of all patients surveyed had some insurance, ranging in coverage from less than 50 percent to 100 percent of all charges. Table 4-2 shows a breakdown of coverage.[7]

Table 4-2 also reports the average number of total visits (past and projected) for insured and uninsured patients. It is interesting that the uninsured patients make on average more visits than the insured patients. This sort of two variable comparison led Marmor in his original report of the JIS data to conclude, "The figures indicate strongly that the existence of insurance coverage does *not* lead to increased frequency of visits . . ." (1975: 137). This conclusion would be valid only if the insured and uninsured groups in Table 4-2 were alike in every other respect except insurance coverage and any difference between them could be attributed to differences in coverage. If the groups were not otherwise the same, an uncontrolled compari-

Table 4-2. Insurance Coverage and Visits (N = 3,001).

Coverage	Percentage of Patients	Average Total Visits
None	58.9	269
Insurance paying		
less than 50%	18.0	
50%	12.4	225
75–80%	9.4	
more than 80%	1.3	

son between insured and uninsured patients could give a misleading impression of the effect of insurance.

To illustrate this point further, consider Table 4-3a, a fictitious data set consisting of six patients. Table 4-3b makes the simple comparison of the mean number of visits of the insured and uninsured patients. Insurance apparently has no effect on visits. But because more low-income patients have insurance than high-income patients, and because high income leads to a high number of visits, the apparent conclusion from Table 4-3b is incorrect. Table 4-3c, which compares the insured and uninsured, controlling for income, shows clearly that insurance increases visits for both the rich and the poor. The JIS data share with this example the characteristic that the low-income patients are more likely to have insurance. Thirty-nine percent of patients with income over $20,000 had some insurance coverage, whereas 51 percent of patients with income less than $20,000 had some insurance coverage. In general, the other influences on utilization must be controlled for in order to attain an accurate estimate of the effect of insurance on utilization. Control can either be achieved by an "experiment" or by use of multivariate statistical methods.

The effect of insurance coverage on utilization is the key relation under investigation here. If insurance changes how much does utilization change? Other factors beside the "causal link" between the two can be confused in observation of their empirical association. If a positive association emerges from a regression analysis, an estimate of the effect a change in insurance would have on utilization may not have been isolated. People who are frequently mentally ill or desire mental health services may make heavy use of psychiatrists and choose the best coverage for mental conditions in anticipation of

Table 4-3. A Fictitious Data Set.

a. *Income, Insurance and Visits*

Patient	Income	Insurance	Number of Visits
1	Low	No	30
2	Low	Yes	40
3	Low	Yes	40
4	High	No	60
5	High	No	60
6	High	Yes	70

b. *Visits With and Without Insurance*

	No Insurance (Patients 1, 4, 5)	Insurance (Patients 2, 3, 6)
Average number of visits	50	50

c. *Insurance and Visits, Controlling for Income*

	No Insurance	Insurance
Low income	30 (Patient 1)	40 (Patients 2, 3)
High income	60 (Patients 4, 5)	70 (Patient 6)

this heavy use. If this were true, a patient might make the same use of psychiatrists with or without insurance. But those with insurance make more visits than those without in the sample, and, unable to "control" adequately for the variables "mental health" and "taste," this study would estimate a positive coefficient for an insurance variable. Interpreting this as the cause of higher utilization would then be incorrect. Although a positive association is observed, a change in insurance coverage alone would cause no change in utilization.

The standard correction for this bias problem is to substitute an instrumental variable estimate in the regression equation for insurance coverage rather than the actual variable itself. The effect of this is to eliminate the unwanted correlation of insurance and the disturbance term in regression because of incomplete observation of mental health and demand characteristics. This standard procedure is followed in the report of empirical findings in the next chapter.

The importance of any bias depends partly on how much choice patients have. A variety of coverages for psychiatric insurance is rare outside of federal employment. If patients have no choice about coverage, or the choice of coverage is made largely on grounds other than psychiatric benefits, insurance coverage will be unrelated to the unobserved variables, mental health and taste for treatment, and there will be no bias. Even if a bias is important, the effectiveness of an instrumental variable correction depends on the suitability of the instruments.[8]

The JIS survey presents a unique opportunity to study demand for psychotherapy. Rich observation of patients' characteristics, including mental health, furnishes excellent controls for isolating the effect of insurance on demand. Difficulties discussed in this chapter concerning measurement of utilization as the sum of past and projected visits, and interpretation of causality in the case of variables measuring insurance coverage and psychiatrist's specialty, will be reflected in the statistical techniques applied in Chapter 5. Probably the most interesting complication associated with using the JIS data has to do with the nonrandom sample of "last ten" patients seen during a week. The trouble this causes, and how it will be dealt with, is the first item of business in the next chapter.

NOTES TO CHAPTER 4

1. The questionnaire was developed by the staff of the JIS in cooperation with the American Psychiatric Association. The results of the survey were originally reported in Marmor (1975). See this reference for a description of the development of the questionnaire and its pretesting.

2. The data file produced by the merge contains nine card images for each patient. If the data had been punched on cards, the stacked cards would have been over thirty feet high.

3. This definition of the dependent variable may lead to heteroskedasticity, there being more variance in the number of visits when the value of PROJ is high than when it is low. Some checks, described in note 5 of Chapter 5, found no indication of heteroskedasticity, however.

4. A number of task panels on the President's Commission on Mental Health dealt with the needs of special populations: women, minorities, the poor, the aged, and the young. In their reports these panels discuss the degree to which these groups are underserved or inappropriately served and the possible explanations.

5. It is unnecessarily restrictive to suppose that in order to influence a patient's utilization a physician must shift the patient's demand curve. Most models of the market for physicians' services are based partly on a downward-sloping demand curve of a patient for the services of a single physician. Since the physician sells a nonretradable service, the physician may influence utilization by "forcing" the patient to consume outside his demand curve. The physician interested in influencing a patient need not permit the patient to be a "price-taker" and equate marginal benefit to price. For simplicity we will follow usual terminology in this area and refer to the physician as influencing the patient's demand.

6. Because of the possibility discussed in the previous note that a patient may be pushed by a psychiatrist's influence "outside" the patient's demand curve, there is the possibility that in a cross-sectional analysis of patients, price may not be inversely related to quantity demand. This is discussed further in note 4 of Chapter 5.

7. Psychiatrists reported that 1.5 percent of patients either declined to use their coverage or had exhausted their coverage at the time of the survey. As Taylor (1975) has pointed out in the context of demand for electricity, when marginal and average prices to the consumer differ, a measure of average price belongs in a demand equation to pick up income effects. An attempt here to control for "exhausted" patients was unsuccessful. The information that someone had exhausted coverage seemed to indicate that the patient was undergoing lengthy treatment, and the sign of the estimated coefficient of an "exhaust" variable turned out to be positive. A regression resetting the value of insurance coverage equal to zero (the no-insurance value) for patients who had exhausted or declined coverage reduced the estimated effect of insurance for the lowest income group only in the regressions reported below. If the information that some patients measured as having insurance really do not, is, in essence, ignored, the empirical estimates understate the true impact of insurance coverage.

8. Newhouse and Phelps (1976) treat the net price of hospital care to patients as endogenous in a model of hospital use. Their two-stage least-squares estimates of the effect of insurance on utilization were disappointing, the estimated price elasticity being insignificantly different from zero. In his comment on their paper, Eli Ginsberg argues that two-stage least squares is an inappropriate procedure since the bias from self-selection will be small where people have little choice about their insurance coverage. For other estimates of demand for insurance equations, see Feldstein (1971), Phelps (1976), and Sloan (1976).

5 EMPIRICAL RESULTS
Insurance and Demand
for Psychotherapy

In filling out questionnaires for this study, psychiatrists did not include a random sample of their patients. Instead they were instructed to choose the last ten patients seen in a week. Since the object is to generalize from the behavior of these last ten to the whole user population, any way in which the last ten might be atypical of the total group of patients must be taken into account. One thing is obvious: A patient who sees a psychiatrist more frequently is more likely to be among the last ten patients seen during a week than a patient who sees a psychiatrist less frequently. Heavy users of psychiatric services are overrepresented in the sample. The consequence is that sample means, such as average number of visits per patient, overstate the true average.

Some factors that influence the number of visits a patient makes may also influence whether the patient appears in the sample. For example, it is reasonable to expect that income influences the decision to see a psychiatrist, the frequency of visits, and the length of treatment.

If income lowers the threshold of how sick one must perceive oneself to be to desire a high frequency of visits, the average sickness of those who see a psychiatrist frequently with high income will be less than those with low income. Or, in terms of desire for treatment, those with high income who make frequent visits may have on average a lower desire for services than those who make frequent visits with low income. Because "sickness" and "desire" are measured imperfectly, the comparisons between the utilization of the high- and low-income groups will be obscured by the inability to control for these differences. The way the sample was selected may fill the high-income group with those who are not as sick or who have less desire for services. In the comparison of the rates of utilization by income, the estimate of the effect of income may be biased downward unless these differences are somehow taken into account.

The problem extends beyond income. Similar cases concern how other independent variables, such as occupation, insurance, age, or race or sex, affect both the probability that some user appears in the last ten as well as the length of treatment. In technical terms, the problem is that the expected value of the stochastic term in a regression model, because of incomplete observation of all factors that influence visits (we are thinking again of "mental health" and "desire" for treatment) is associated with some of the independent variables. This violates an assumption necessary for ordinary least squares (OLS) to yield unbiased estimates.[1]

Heckman (1976) has suggested a straightforward correction for this bias.[2] Our model for a number of visits can be written as follows:

$$V = X\beta + u \quad , \tag{5-1}$$

where V is visits, X is a vector of explanatory variables, β a vector of coefficients, and u a disturbance term. From this we can write the expected value of V given values of the regressors as

$$E(V) = X\beta + E(u|X, \text{sample-selection rule}) \quad . \tag{5-2}$$

Ideally, the sample-selection rule is random sampling so $E(u|X, \text{sample-selection rule}) = 0$, and (5-1) may be estimated by OLS. When the sample-selection rule is not random sampling, as in this case, $E(u|X, \text{sample-selection rule}) \neq 0$, and OLS estimates will be biased.

Now consider the following model, an adaptation of (5-1) recognizing the sample-selection problem:

$$V = X\beta + \alpha\lambda + u^* \quad , \tag{5-3}$$

where α is a parameter, λ a variable closely related to the probability that an observation appears in the sample, and u^* a disturbance term. The formulation reflects the fact that this is a two-equation model, the first equation determining whether an observation appears, the second determining how many visits are made, given some visits are being made. The parameter α is the ratio of the covariance of the stochastic terms in the two equations to the square root of the variance of the equation determining visits. The variable λ can be expressed as follows:

$$\lambda = \frac{f(\phi)}{1 - f(\phi)} \tag{5-4}$$

where $-\phi$ is a probit index for the "first equation" and f and F are the density and cumulative distribution functions of the standard normal.

Heckman shows that $\lambda = E(u|X$, sample-selection rule), making u^* the "pure" component of u unrelated to the regressors. Basically, Heckman's method is to treat sample selection as a misspecification or an omitted variable problem.[3] All the researcher must do is come up with an estimate of the ϕ function to be able to construct the new independent variable, Heckman's λ.

Heckman illustrates how this may be done for a "censored" sample, which in this study would correspond to a sample including observations on people who made no visits to a psychiatrist in 1973. If such a sample existed, the probability that someone with certain characteristics appeared in the sample could be estimated, and the probit index to construct λ could be used. However, in the current problem there is not access to a censored sample but only to what Heckman calls a truncated sample. There is no observation for anyone but those in treatment. The method I propose for estimating λ in our truncated sample is as follows:

We need to know the probability that someone appears in our sample given his personal and financial characteristics. We need to know $P(\text{last ten}|X)$. This probability cannot be estimated directly from a truncated sample. However, we know from the formula for conditional probability that $P(\text{last ten}|X)$ is related to another set of probabilities:

$$P(\text{last ten}|X) = \frac{P(X|\text{last ten})}{P(X)} \cdot P(\text{last ten}) \tag{5-5}$$

Consider each of these right-hand-side probabilities. $P(X|\text{last ten})$ can be estimated directly from the data. This is the probability that someone has a certain set of values for the X variables, given that person is a patient; for example, the probability that an observation is a married white woman, aged 35–45, unemployed, with a family income of between \$20,000 and \$30,000. To estimate this, take the relative frequencies of this set of values in the sample. The other two probabilities are unconditional. $P(X)$ is the probability that the set of X characteristics appears in the population, available from the Census Bureau. P(last ten) is only a factor of proportionality. Substitute for it the probability of seeing a psychiatrist in 1973, estimated from national medical care surveys. With these three right-hand-side probabilities, take observations on P(last ten$|X$) and estimate the functional relation between seeing a psychiatrist and certain X characteristics. Details on the method and construction of Heckman's λ are presented in Appendix C.

The seriousness of a bias from nonrandom sampling of this nature depends on how well diagnosis, level of impairment, inpatient history, and personal characteristics control for mental health and taste for treatment. If these controls do a good job, Heckman's omitted variable may be of little consequence for the estimates. There is no way of knowing in advance the consequences of neglecting this possible bias.

ESTIMATION RESULTS

The dependent variable of the demand function is the logarithm of the total number of visits (past and projected) a patient makes to a psychiatrist. A very long list of controls, or shift parameters of the demand function, includes predominantly personal, socioeconomic and medical characteristics of the patient. A variable equal to the percentage of charges paid by a third party, COINRATE, measures movement down the patient's demand curve. COINRATE interacts with income to allow for different responses among income classes to insurance coverage. After entering Heckman's "omitted variable" to correct for bias random sampling, demand equations are estimated by OLS, with the exception of regression (2), which substitutes an instrumental estimate called COINHAT for the insurance variable.

Many independent variables are entered in the demand function in dummy variable form: sex, race, place of birth, marital status, income, diagnosis, and others. The coefficient of a (0, 1) dummy variable is an estimate of the difference between the category indicated by the dummy variable and the omitted category. A coefficient of 0.077 on the dummy variable male, for instance, means that males have a log of total visits 0.077 higher than do females (the omitted category for sex). Because the dependent variable is the log of total visits, coefficients on dummy variables may be interpreted as percentage differences: thus a coefficient of 0.077 means that males make 7.7 percent more visits, controlling for the other variables in the regression. The statistical significance of each point estimate in Table 5-1 is indicated by the t-statistic in parentheses beneath each coefficient. A t-statistic of about 2 indicates significance by conventional tests; the estimated difference of 7.7 percent between males and females is not statistically significant by this standard. Where psychiatrists did not fill out questionnaires fully, the values of variables are not indicated. Rather than drop partially complete observations from the sample, a separate category "Not indicated" was created. (The definitions of variables are indicated in the table, except for the capitalized variables, COINRATE, COINHAT, and PROSH, which have been defined in the text.)

Let us begin with the first column in Table 5-1, regression (1), moving down the column to take up each set of variables in turn. Although many of the estimates of coefficients for personal, socioeconomic, and medical variables may be of considerable general interest, we will pass over discussion of these rather quickly to get to the variables most relevant to our inquiry. After moving down the first column, we move across the table. Regressions (2) and (3) represent changes in specification of (1). Regressions (4)-(7) break down the effect of insurance into a choice of therapist (psychoanalyst or nonpsychoanalyst) and to the number of visits given the choice of therapist. Variables to measure bandwagon effects are added to the basic regression in a separate section.

The Basic Demand Equation

The basic demand equation is regression (1). According to these initial estimates, blacks make 20 percent fewer visits than whites, but this difference is not statistically significant. Married people make 24 percent fewer visits than singles. The negative coefficients on all the dummy variables in the marital status group indicate that all

Table 5-1. Regression Results.

Independent Variable	(1)	(2)	(3)
Sex (female omitted)			
Not indicated	.2648	.2340	.2591
	(1.61)	(1.42)	(1.57)
Male	.07683	.07364	-.08215
	(1.30)	(1.24)	(1.67)
Race (white omitted)			
Not indicated	.09012	.09942	.1027
	(0.47)	(0.51)	(0.53)
Black	-.2085	-.2341	-.4070
	(1.30)	(1.38)	(2.61)
Latin	.3121	.3740	.2001
	(1.43)	(1.70)	(0.92)
Other	.01998	.02640	.01229
	(0.09)	(0.12)	(0.05)
Place of birth (U.S. omitted)			
Not indicated	-.02526	-.04083	-.02870
	(0.29)	(0.46)	(0.32)
Outside U.S.	.2571	.2730	.2666
	(2.63)	(2.77)	(2.72)
Don't know	-.1207	-.1318	-.1237
	(1.07)	(1.12)	(1.09)
Marital status (single omitted)			
Not indicated	-.4139	-.3790	-.4152
	(1.42)	(1.30)	(1.42)
Married	-.2399	-.2490	-.2262
	(4.31)	(4.25)	(4.06)
Widowed	-.1160	-.1332	-.03124
	(0.80)	(0.91)	(0.21)
Divorced	-.08983	-.09750	.07455
	(1.13)	(1.21)	(1.03)
Separated	-.4134	-.4208	-.2576
	(3.76)	(3.78)	(2.44)
Don't know	-1.074	-1.027	-1.109
	(2.09)	(1.97)	(2.15)

Table 5-1. continued

(4)	(5)	(6)	(7)
.2318	.02292	.1991	.2119
(1.54)	(0.33)	(0.98)	(0.94)
.04917	.03744	-.06480	.06580
(0.91)	(1.50)	(0.87)	(0.80)
.1828	-.6974	.2364	.4174
(1.04)	(0.86)	(1.16)	(1.13)
-.3776	.1280	-.5625	-.1446
(2.56)	(1.88)	(2.99)	(0.59)
.1799	.1087	.07908	.2411
(0.90)	(1.18)	(0.31)	(0.76)
-.1366	.1601	-.1112	-.2000
(0.66)	(1.67)	(0.36)	(0.73)
-.1036	.09041	-.03446	-.2206
(1.29)	(2.54)	(0.33)	(1.74)
.1878	.1003	.08100	.2367
(.209)	(2.42)	(0.64)	(1.86)
-.1418	.03903	-.1103	-.1099
(1.38)	(0.82)	(0.82)	(0.69)
-.3413	-.1009	.001294	-1.505
(1.28)	(0.82)	(0.00)	(2.49)
-.2334	-.2051	-.2915	-.08102
(4.58)	(0.87)	(4.39)	(1.01)
-.1279	-.001927	-.2469	.1026
(0.96)	(0.03)	(1.59)	(0.40)
-.04431	-.06985	-.01643	-.2988
(0.61)	(2.08)	(0.17)	(0.26)
-.3354	-.1046	-.2953	-.3939
(3.33)	(2.25)	(2.24)	(2.51)
-.9130	-.1968	-.9257	-1.461
(1.94)	(0.91)	(1.73)	(1.40)

(Table 5-1. continued overleaf)

Table 5-1. continued

Independent Variable	(1)	(2)	(3)
Occupation (unskilled omitted)			
Not indicated	-.9904	-1.080	-.7233
	(2.76)	(2.99)	(2.03)
Professional (non MD)	.01510	.03168	.3151
	(0.13)	(0.28)	(3.35)
MD (nonpsychiatrist)	-.2504	-.007379	.3636
	(0.17)	(0.04)	(2.86)
Psychologist	.7927	.7982	1.083
	(3.28)	(3.28)	(4.61)
Semiprofessional	-.1326	-.1381	.1657
	(1.36)	(1.41)	(2.21)
Skilled labor and lower white collar	-.01888	-.02742	-.02349
	(0.22)	(0.31)	(0.27)
Homemaker	.09408	.09253	-.0005370
	(1.06)	(1.03)	(0.00)
Unemployed	.1188	.1389	.07758
	(0.83)	(0.96)	(0.29)
Retired	-.006575	-.01014	-.0009072
	(0.03)	(0.04)	(0.00)
None or unknown	-.1176	-.1324	-.1907
	(0.85)	(0.93)	(1.38)
Religious	.2157	.2394	.1683
	(1.06)	(1.16)	(0.83)
Disabled	.2013	.2021	.1728
	(0.78)	(0.72)	(0.67)
Income (less than $10,000 omitted)			
Not indicated	.6675	.5768	.6793
	(2.49)	(1.61)	(2.53)
$10,000-19,999	.3205	.3189	.3327
	(4.66)	(2.50)	(4.82)
$20,000-29,999	.5474	.4676	.5968
	(6.77)	(3.23)	(7.41)
$30,000+	.8241	.6568	1.028
	(9.47)	(4.77)	(13.51)

Table 5-1. continued

(4)	(5)	(6)	(7)
-.7474	-.2245	-.6983	
(2.25)	(1.50)	(2.07)	
.06209	-.05621	.3586	-.1537
(0.60)	(1.18)	(2.42)	(1.07)
.03536	-.001484	.07874	-.2099
(0.26)	(0.03)	(0.35)	(1.17)
.7534	.06143	.8076	.5249
(3.40)	(0.60)	(2.33)	(1.77)
-.01867	-.1252	.1859	-.1618
(0.21)	(3.06)	(1.46)	(1.28)
.1034	-.1430	.2105	-.1256
(1.30)	(3.92)	(2.19)	(0.81)
.1417	-.05630	.1601	.04330
(1.75)	(1.50)	(1.58)	(0.32)
.2096	-.1223	.1345	.5506
(1.59)	(2.02)	(0.88)	(2.08)
-.02239	-.01925	.1850	.3643
(0.12)	(0.23)	(0.87)	(0.94)
-.1088	-.03565	-.1154	-.1120
(0.86)	(0.61)	(0.73)	(0.50)
.2627	-.01165	.1917	.7586
(1.41)	(0.13)	(0.88)	(2.04)
.2924	-.06292	.3807	-.5962
(1.24)	(0.58)	(1.51)	(0.85)
.7447	-.08666	.6704	1.075
(3.03)	(0.76)	(2.50)	(1.69)
.2333	.09018	.2474	.1102
(3.70)	(3.10)	(3.43)	(0.81)
.3872	.1823	.4080	.1748
(5.21)	(5.34)	(4.48)	(1.22)
.6390	.2244	.8225	.3315
(7.98)	(6.14)	(7.81)	(2.29)

(Table 5-1. continued overleaf)

Table 5-1.   continued

Independent Variable	(1)	(2)	(3)
Don't know	-.0848	-.3676	-.06967
	(0.41)	(0.82)	(0.34)
Age in years	-.007332	-.006861	-.01342
	(2.99)	(2.79)	(6.36)
Primary diagnosis (depressive neurosis omitted)			
Not Indicated	-.9147	-.09366	-.07562
	(0.27)	(0.27)	(0.22)
Psychotic, organic brain syndrome	-.007977	-.06164	-.006239
	(0.03)	(0.29)	(0.03)
Nonpsychotic organic brain syndrome	-.05735	-.07748	-.02503
	(0.18)	(0.25)	(0.08)
Schizophrenic	.1685	.1697	.1612
	(2.38)	(2.39)	(2.27)
Affective psychosis	-.1804	-.1939	-.1867
	(2.09)	(2.24)	(2.15)
Other psychosis	.2950	.3005	.3062
	(1.71)	(1.74)	(1.77)
Other neurosis	.4895	.4912	.4927
	(9.14)	(9.14)	(9.16)
Alcoholism (not otherwise diagnosed)	-.1088	-.08914	-.1270
	(0.58)	(0.48)	(0.68)
Drug abuse (not otherwise diagnosed)	.8166	.8251	.7929
	(2.38)	(2.40)	(2.30)
Personality disorder	.4360	.4427	.4434
	(7.52)	(7.58)	(7.61)
Psychophysiologic disorder	-.0943	-.1037	-.1014
	(0.72)	(0.79)	(0.77)
Mental retardation	.7650	.8822	.7326
	(0.75)	(0.86)	(0.72)

Table 5-1. continued

(4)	(5)	(6)	(7)
-.09046	.0002371	-.1476	.3282
(0.48)	(0.00)	(0.74)	(0.58)
-.006679	-.001594	-.007941	-.008540
(2.97)	(1.59)	(2.82)	(2.19)
.08578		-.1260	1.103
(0.28)		(0.36)	(1.69)
-.1286		.05655	-.4765
(0.67)		(0.24)	(1.39)
-.003587		.1440	.4734
(0.00)		(0.48)	(0.52)
.1979		.2807	-.003374
(3.05)		(3.79)	(0.03)
-.1044		-.07629	-.2241
(1.32)		(0.88)	(1.13)
.2659		.3316	.1098
(1.69)		(1.64)	(0.43)
.3837		.3172	.3398
(7.79)		(4.93)	(4.38)
-.08329		.1062	-.8827
(0.49)		(0.55)	(2.48)
.6824		.6706	.3248
(2.17)		(1.44)	(0.76)
.3986		.4322	.3037
(7.50)		(6.37)	(3.54)
-.05508		.1255	-.3702
(0.14)		(0.88)	(1.71)
.9946		1.093	
(1.07)		(1.18)	

(Table 5-1. continued overleaf)

Table 5-1. continued

Independent Variable	(1)	(2)	(3)
Transient situational disturbance	-.9145	-.8898	-.9320
	(5.85)	(5.76)	(5.93)
Other	.2043	.1752	.2175
	(0.99)	(0.85)	(1.05)
Impairment when treatment began (very mild omitted)			
Not indicated	.3986	.3817	.3951
	(2.37)	(2.27)	(2.34)
Mild	.02157	.01942	.01370
	(0.20)	(0.18)	(0.13)
Moderate	.3973	.3966	.3877
	(3.96)	(3.94)	(3.85)
Severe	.5693	.5614	.5608
	(5.33)	(5.24)	(5.23)
Patient admitted to hospital by respondent? (no omitted)			
Not indicated	.4525	.3778	.4820
	(1.10)	(0.94)	(1.24)
Yes, for 10 days or less	-.1173	-.1261	-.1298
	(1.23)	(1.32)	(1.36)
Yes, for 11-20 days	-.2153	-.2115	-.2258
	(2.21)	(2.16)	(2.31)
Yes, for 21-30 days	.04833	.02514	.03631
	(0.47)	(0.24)	(0.35)
Yes, for more than 30 days	.2962	.3039	.2977
	(2.84)	(2.90)	(2.84)
Patient first contacted (private office omitted)			
Not indicated	-.07162	-.04906	-.05370
	(0.38)	(0.26)	(0.28)
Inpatient	-.5327	-.5278	-.5347
	(6.40)	(6.32)	(6.40)
Clinic	.1624	.1986	.1745
	(1.06)	(1.29)	(1.13)

Table 5-1. continued

(4)	(5)	(6)	(7)
-.8633		-.7087	-1.169
(6.03)		(4.29)	(4.08)
.2070		.5732	-.6045
(1.09)		(2.46)	(1.76)
.2238		.01899	.4449
(1.45)		(0.09)	(1.83)
-.02855		.07225	-.1233
(0.29)		(0.62)	(0.71)
.2369		.3156	.1305
(2.57)		(2.82)	(0.80)
.3916		.4863	.2607
(3.99)		(4.09)	(1.50)
.5474		.6072	.9610
(1.54)		(1.00)	(0.98)
-.03786		-.1250	.2779
(0.43)		(1.30)	(1.32)
-.08099		-.06100	-.4510
(0.90)		(0.65)	(1.48)
.1279		.1252	.2872
(1.36)		(1.22)	(1.19)
.3733		.3745	.3118
(3.89)		(3.45)	(1.53)
-.09067		-.2380	-.1430
(0.53)		(0.95)	(0.60)
-.4670		-.3911	-.9099
(6.12)		(4.81)	(3.78)
.2214		.1986	.3138
(1.57)		(1.18)	(1.22)

(Table 5-1. continued overleaf)

Table 5-1. continued

Independent Variable	(1)	(2)	(3)
Other	-.3929 (2.27)	-.3515 (2.02)	-.3480 (2.00)
Psychiatrist's age in years	-.0005951 (0.27)	-.0007459 (0.34)	-.0003223 (0.15)
PROSH	-.8778 (9.94)	-.6021 (3.20)	-.8860 (10.00)
Insurance (0, 1) * PROSH	-.1831 (1.81)		-.1841 (1.81)
Growth insurance in state 70-73	-.06784 (-.41)	-.05421 (0.31)	-.05206 (0.32)
Price in dollars	.01246 (4.16)	.01310 (4.34)	.01308 (4.35)
COINRATE	.5693 (4.09)		.5951 (4.27)
Heckman's λ	.2398 (4.79)	.2436 (4.85)	
Insurance + Income interactions			
COINRATE * NI	-.9654 (1.27)		-1.001 (1.31)
COINRATE * 10-19	-.1635 (1.01)		-.1920 (1.19)
COINRATE * 20-29	-.3515 (1.89)		-.4044 (2.16)
COINRATE * 30+	-.7119 (3.35)		-.7373 (3.45)
COINRATE * DK	-.005063 (0.00)		-.04706 (0.09)
Region (middle and mountain states omitted)			
South	-.1908 (2.56)	-.1639 (2.18)	-.1857 (2.48)
Northeast	.02399 (0.42)	.01758 (0.30)	.02002 (0.35)

Table 5-1. continued

(4)	(5)	(6)	(7)
-.2913		-.3693	-.1067
(1.83)		(2.02)	(0.34)
-.001104		-.006100	.004971
(0.55)		(2.43)	(1.46)
-.8229		-.9486	-.7130
(10.18)		(9.29)	(5.44)
-.1818		-.2353	-.07577
(1.96)		(2.08)	(0.47)
-.1407		.02494	.5223
(0.93)		(0.14)	(1.64)
.007184		.004839	.002546
(2.60)		(1.49)	(0.43)
.4873	.07913	.6539	.05386
(3.83)	(1.49)	(4.53)	(0.19)
.1484	.1059	.009082	.2537
(3.23)	(5.00)	(0.14)	(3.79)
-.8443	-.05553	-.9348	-1.552
(1.21)	(0.17)	(1.29)	(0.67)
-.09978	-.04105	-.1992	.05507
(0.68)	(0.60)	(1.18)	(0.18)
-.2594	-.07418	-.1611	-.08993
(1.52)	(0.94)	(0.76)	(0.28)
-.5458	-.1691	-.5976	-.2967
(2.80)	(1.87)	(2.31)	(0.87)
-.07953	.1258	-.1660	-1.008
(0.18)	(0.60)	(0.03)	(0.80)
-.05669	-.1012	-.01654	.06104
(0.83)	(3.51)	(0.22)	(0.35)
-.0279	.04453	.08130	-.2074
(0.24)	(1.87)	(1.29)	(2.16)

(Table 5-1. continued overleaf)

Table 5-1. continued

Independent Variable	(1)	(2)	(3)
D.C.	.2052 (1.68)	.1659 (1.29)	.2301 (1.87)
West Coast	.2794 (4.33)	.2637 (4.01)	.2775 (4.29)
Percent of county with 4+ higher education	.01305 (3.32)	.01323 (3.32)	.01312 (3.32)
County pop/mi^2	.000006707 (5.77)	.000006608 (5.61)	.000006842 (5.87)
COINHAT		.8765 (2.04)	
COINHAT * PROSH		-.7232 (1.98)	
Estimated insurance and income interactions			
COINHAT * NI		-.6733 (0.30)	
COINHAT * 10-19		-.1122 (0.25)	
COINHAT * 20-29		-.02308 (0.04)	
COINHAT * 30+		.4977 (0.75)	
COINHAT * DK		1.323 (0.71)	
Psychiatrists' subspecialty (none or general omitted) Psychoanalysis			
Child			
Other			
Constant	3.502	3.532	3.952
Adj R^2	.3659	.3619	.3610

Table 5-1. continued

(4)	(5)	(6)	(7)
.4691 (0.42)	.2446 (5.34)	.005844 (0.03)	.2983 (1.84)
.2677 (4.53)	.006408 (0.25)	.3253 (4.53)	.3084 (0.29)
.006685 (1.85)	.008502 (5.33)	.01962 (4.09)	-.003558 (0.60)
.000003389 (3.15)	.000003211 (7.28)	.000008536 (5.39)	-.0000001404 (0.08)
.9610 (22.70)			
.1671 (1.98)			
-.2545 (2.64)			
4.012	.04109	4.023	5.925
.4637	.2032	.3124	.2268

those who have been married make fewer visits than singles. Age is measured continuously. An increase of thirty years in a patient's age decreases visits by about 20 percent. If the effects of income and other variables are controlled, a patient's occupation seems to have little to do with the number of visits made. Only psychologists make significantly more (80 percent) visits than do unskilled workers, after the effects of income are controlled.

Patients with higher income make on average more frequent visits. In the top category of patient's family income of $30,000 minimum, patients make 82 percent more visits than a comparable patient with a family income of less than $10,000.

Patients diagnosed with schizophrenia (+17 percent), other neuroses (+49 percent), drug abuse not otherwise diagnosed (+82 percent), and personality disorder (+44 percent) make significantly more visits than patients diagnosed with depressive neurosis. Diagnoses for which patients make significantly fewer visits are affective psychosis (−18 percent) and transient situational disturbance (−91 percent). Whereas there was no difference in the number of visits made by the "very mildly" and the "mildly" impaired, patients judged moderately and severely impaired make significantly more visits. The severely impaired make 57 percent more visits than patients with a very mild impairment.

Patients' hospitalization reveals a curious relationship. Patients who were hospitalized for a short time make fewer visits than those who were not hospitalized, but patients with long hospitalization make more visits. Patients first contacted by their physician in an inpatient setting make 53 percent fewer visits than patients first contacted in the physician's private office. The location of first contact might indicate a willingness of patients to undergo private psychiatric treatment. The psychiatrist's age seems to be an unimportant factor in explaining visits.

Psychiatrists appear to underestimate seriously the number of visits their patients will eventually make, as indicated by the large negative and highly significant coefficient on PROSH, the share of projected visits in the total. (Refer again to discussion surrounding Figure 4–1.) A patient with a PROSH of 50 percent would have a measured total of visits about 22 percent less than an otherwise similar patient with a PROSH of 25 percent. The negative coefficient on a variable equal to the product of an insurance dummy (1, 0) and PROSH indicates that psychiatrist's underestimation is even more serious for their patients who have insurance.

A set of regional dummy variables indicates that patients in the West make significantly more (28 percent) and patients in the South significantly fewer (–19 percent) visits than patients in the rest of the United States. It has been suggested that the District of Columbia, with a high concentration of federal employment, might have demand characteristics different than the rest of the United States. A dummy variable for the District of Columbia however, although positive, is not statistically significant. (The District of Columbia was also included in the Northeast group, so the coefficient is interpreted as the estimated difference between the two.)

Social factors, particularly social acceptance of mental illness and treatment may obviously have an important influence on demand. Although such factors might be expected to effect the decision to initiate treatment rather than the decision about the extent of treatment, two county-level variables were nevertheless added (measured for the county in which the patient's psychiatrist had his or her practice) — percentage of the county population with four or more years of higher education, and county population density (population/ square mile), to proxy for social attitudes. In counties with a more highly educated populace and in more densely populated counties, patients made more extensive use of psychiatrists.

A test of a version of the physician's influence hypothesis fails to support the idea that in areas with rapidly growing demand psychiatrists would be less likely to "hang on" to their patients. The estimated coefficient of the insurance growth variable is positive, but insignificantly different from zero.

The positive coefficient on the price of care is puzzling. Price is unlikely to be picking up a regional effect since region and extent of urbanization in the area are explicitly controlled. A high price may be an indicator of quality of service. After controlling for the psychiatrist's subspecialty in regression (4) of Table 5–1 (a possible measure of quality), the coefficient on price falls toward zero, but remains positive and significant.[4]

The coefficient of COINRATE together with the interactions between COINRATE and the income classes reveal that the demand elasticity (loosely interpreted) is greatest for patients with the lowest income. The estimated demand elasticity for patients with family income of less than $10,000 is about 0.57. The estimated demand elasticity falls steadily through the income classes, to 0.40, to 0.22, to a small negative number for the persons with income above $30,000. That the elasticity of demand is inversely proportional to income bodes well for the distributional effects of compulsory insurance for psychotherapy. The implications of this are set out in the next chapter.

The coefficient of Heckman's λ is statistically significant and of the expected sign, possibly indicating that some unobserved common factor influences the decision to seek treatment as well as the decision of how many visits to make. The importance of λ is indicated not by the magnitude of the coefficient but by what happens to the estimated coefficients for other variables when this correction for sampling bias is removed. This is discussed in regression (3).[5]

Instrumental Insurance Variables

To avoid a possible simultaneity bias, regression (2) is a reestimate of regression (1) with actual levels of insurance coverage replaced by estimated levels. (The equations for estimating insurance coverage are reported in Appendix D.) COINHAT replaces COINRATE directly and in the interaction terms. The estimated coefficients on COINHAT and the income and insurance interaction terms in regression (2) indicate more powerful effects of insurance on utilization for every income class than were estimated in regression (1). There appears to be no danger that the estimates in regression (1) overstate the effect of insurance due to the simultaneous choice of coverage and visits. Estimates of the interaction appear to be particularly sensitive to the loss of information caused by substitution of a highly imperfect instrument for the true value of insurance coverage.

Dropping Heckman's λ

Without correction for sampling heavy users, the estimate of income or another variable effecting utilization should in general be biased toward zero (Hausman and Wise 1977). Dropping λ should lead to reduced estimates of the coefficient of income, occupation, age, and other variables. In fact, as regression (3) makes clear, the effect is just the opposite. Dropping λ, the estimated effects of income, race, age, sex, and occupation become more powerful. This suggests that the bias due to oversampling heavy users is not serious in the sample, and that Heckman's λ should be interpreted not as an omitted variable equal to the expected value of the disturbance term given the Xs, but simply as a nonlinear combination of some of the independent variables. After all, λ is a function of five of the independent variables in the basic equation, and may be picking up the nonlinear effects of these variables on utilization. If this is so, the variables making up λ may truly have a more powerful effect on utilization than indicated by the single coefficients in the basic equation. In any case, the estimated effects of variables having to do with insurance coverage are basically undisturbed by the presence or absence of λ.

That neither a simultaneity bias nor a bias from nonrandom sampling appears to trouble the estimates in regression (1) may be due to the extensive control variables in this study. Mental health is measured by diagnosis, severity of treatment, and inpatient history. Taste is measured by income, occupation, and many other variables. If mental health and tastes are adequately controlled, and are not taken up in the disturbance term, neither type of bias would be expected to be a serious problem.

Psychiatrist's Subspecialty and the Extent of Treatment

It has been widely noted that patients of psychiatrists who are psychoanalysts make many more visits than patients of psychiatrists who are not psychoanalysts. It is not obvious, though, that psychoanalysts "cause" patients to make more visits. The model of how the number of visits is decided underlying regression (1) and its modifications is that patients choose the type of psychiatrist they believe will accomplish their own goals. A patient interested in long-term psychotherapy would choose a psychiatrist, possibly a psychoanalyst, who would give him this.

If patients are unsure what they want or need and do not choose a psychiatrist on the basis of the length of treatment likely to be recommended, the therapist's theoretical predisposition may have an important independent influence on the number of visits. Under this alternative model of the way treatment is decided, the psychiatrist's subspecialty does not belong in the demand equation. Regression (4) estimates an equation consistent with this alternative model by including the subspecialty of the psychiatrist, if any, in the list of control variables. Before evaluating the results, it should be noted that this is a risky procedure.

For example, suppose there were just two types of treatment, long and short, provided by the psychoanalysts and the nonpsychoanalysts, repectively. Suppose insurance caused patients to be more likely to choose a psychoanalyst, but that the psychiatrist had no independent influence on the patient's length of treatment. A regression of visits on insurance would reveal the true cause and its importance. But if subspecialty were included, subspecialty would "explain" everything, being perfectly correlated with length of treatment, and destroy the evidence of the true cause, insurance.

Fortunately, this form of statistical lightning did not strike here. The psychiatrist's subspecialty makes up a powerful set of dummy variables, particularly the variable indicating whether the psychiatrist is a psychoanalyst. In regression (4), interpreting coefficients as indicating the strength of causal relationships, with all else equal, if a patient walks into the office of a psychiatrist who is a psychoanalyst, he makes about twice as many visits than if he walks into the office of a psychiatrist with no subspecialty. Although extremely powerful in this sense, inclusion of the psychiatrist's subspecialty did not change the estimates of the effects of the other independent variables to any significant degree. Even if a psychiatrist's subspecialty does have an independent influence on the number of visits, this does not change the magnitude of the estimate of the effect of insurance and income on the number of visits. It is possible that the psychiatrist's subspecialty is serving as a proxy for some unobserved characteristics of the patient. However, the strength of the subspecialty variable and the fairly full set of patient characteristics available strongly suggest that the psychoanalyst's theoretical predisposition is at least partly responsible for the higher utilization.

Having established the robustness of the estimates in this respect the role of choice of type of psychiatrist will be explored in more detail. This is done by dividing the patient's choice of visits into a choice of type of psychiatrist and then a choice of number of visits. Regression (5) is a linear probability model for the likelihood a patient sees a psychoanalyst, given that the patient sees a psychiatrist. The dependent variable is (0, 1) and the sample is the same as for the previous regressions. Regression (5) relates the choice of psychoanalyst to the socioeconomic and personal characteristics of the patient and to the patient's insurance coverage. It is clear from regression (5) that the choice of a psychoanalyst can be explained at least partly by the demand characteristics of the patient. Income is a particularly powerful variable. A prospective patient in the highest income class has a probability 0.22 higher of seeing a psychoanalyst than someone from the lowest income class. (The true effect may be larger in magnitude depending on the interpretation of the role of λ.) The estimated effect of insurance is positive but with a low significance level.

The next step is to reestimate regression (1) separately for the patients of nonpsychoanalysts and the patients of psychoanalysts. These are regressions (6) and (7). The behavior of the nonanalysts' patients ($N = 1,857$), given that they are seeing a nonanalyst, closely parallels the behavior of the entire original sample.

Regression (7), estimated for the patients of psychoanalysts ($N = 1,074$), sees many of the key variables become insignificantly different from zero. Income matters much less than in the other regressions, and insurance appears not to matter at all. A possible explanation is that psychoanalysts basically provide one form of treatment, long-term psychotherapy. Economic variables play a role in the decision to seek analysis (regression 5), but once in analysis, choice about length of treatment is dictated by other factors.

Exploring the Bandwagon Effect

The bandwagon effect is that others' demand increases the patient's demand. Who are the others relevant to a patient, and how is their demand measured? Ideally, a reference group is defined for each patient or perhaps even a hierarchy of reference groups and a demand index for each group is developed. This study limits reference groups geographically, at the coutny or state level, although the ideal study would certainly include reference groups other than a patient's neighbors.

A number of different demand indices for these geographically defined reference groups are considered. A problem shared by all the measures is that as in any nonexperimental setting the question of just what is being measured by an independent variable always remains. Even a straightforward variable such as income may indicate something else, such as social class; if so, interpreting the estimated coefficient of income as an income effect would be wrong. Increasing someone's income might not change his or her social class and might not have the predicted effect on behavior. Similarly, the indices of

local demand may indicate some other characteristic of the county
or state that is not sensitive to change with broad-based insurance, as
demand would be. The literature that seeks to find evidence of wage
discrimination by sex and race is particularly beset by this problem
(Goldfarb and Hosek 1976). Large and significant coefficients of sex
or race variables in a wage equation are not convincing evidence of
discrimination unless other possible explanations of the coefficients
(such as higher quit rates) have been eliminated by suitable controls.
Including in the regressions regional dummies and variables for local
education levels and urbanization help to control for the major alternative explanations for what a bandwagon variable may be picking
up. The proposed measures of local demand are as follows:

1. Probability the "average person" in the county sees a psychiatrist.

Estimated in Appendix C is the probability that a person sees a psychiatrist (in 1973), based on personal and financial characteristics of
the individual. To estimate the probability that the "average" neigh-
bor of a patient sees a psychiatrist, simply apply (an abridged version
of) this formula to the "average" person in the county of the psychiatrist's practice.[6] The formula used to define this variable is as
follows:

$$\text{Probability the average person sees a psychiatrist} = \frac{1}{(1 + e^{-\text{index}})} \qquad (5-6)$$

where

index $= 4 \quad - 1.254 \text{ (percent male)}$

$\quad\quad\quad\quad - 1.693 \text{ (percent sixty-five years or older)}$

$\quad\quad\quad\quad + 1.455 \text{ (percent of families with income greater than \$25,000)}.$

This variable takes the form of a logistic probability density function with the index an abridged version, with proxies for some variables, of that estimated in Appendix C. Of the six classes of variables
in the logit index estimated in Table C-1, measures or proxies are
included for three of these in the logit index: sex, age, and income.
Education could have proxied for occupation, but education was
already entered in the equation independently. All variables are measured at county level from the census of population for 1970. There is

no good proxy for marital status of the average person in the county. Information about race of the average person was omitted from the index since the sample is overwhelmingly white and on the judgment that the reference group for whites would be other whites. The constant term in this measure was taken from Table C-1.[7]

The next three measures of the bandwagon effect are indices of insurance coverage (demand) for private psychiatric care for persons in the patient's state.

2. Percentage of the population under sixty-five covered by regular medical insurance in 1973[8]
3. Percentage of (sampled) patients of private psychiatrists with some third-party coverage

This may be a more direct measure of the insurance for private psychiatric care held by a patient's neighbors.

4. Percentage of (sampled) patients of private psychiatrists with third-party coverage at 50 percent of charges or better

This is an indicator of the percent of neighbors with "good coverage."

5. Office-based psychiatrists to population ratio in the state in 1970

This is a supply measure, but on the presumption that demand equals supply, it is an index of demand at the state level. A special difficulty with this variable is that psychiatrists may be more willing to locate in certain areas of the country apart from demand considerations. A positive estimated effect of this variable may then be indicating a lower nonmonetary price of services because of better "availability" of therapists.

It is important to establish that *area demand*, which would be sensitive to broad-based insurance, is a positive influence on an individual's extent of treatment. Other elements of the local "atmosphere," like average education or the California lifestyle, which would not be sensitive to insurance, are ruled out by including controls for such variables in the regressions along with the demand indices. Table 5-2 reports the estimated coefficients of the bandwagon variables entered singly into the basic regression (1) along with the coefficients of the

Table 5-2. Adding Measures of the Bandwagon Effect to the Basic Equation (1).

Variable	Basic Equation (1)	Estimated Coefficients (t-statistics in parentheses)				
		(2)	(3)	(4)	(5)	(6)
Regional dummies						
Northeast	.02399 (0.42)	.004256 (0.08)	.004507 (0.08)	.02364 (0.42)	.03645 (0.64)	.04756 (0.73)
D.C.	.2052 (1.68)	.1793 (1.46)	-.001909 (0.00)	.2234 (1.68)	-.02184 (0.15)	.3560 (1.50)
South	-.1908 (2.56)	-.2003 (2.69)	-.1896 (2.55)	-.1894 (2.54)	-.2077 (2.78)	-.1920 (2.57)
West	.2794 (4.33)	.3334 (4.99)	.2796 (4.34)	.2764 (4.25)	.2503 (3.85)	.2950 (4.35)
Percentage of population with 4+ years of higher education	.001305 (3.32)	-.00008615 (0.14)	.001459 (3.67)	.001315 (3.33)	.001207 (3.06)	.001347 (3.39)
Population/square mile	.000006707 (5.77)	.000008685 (6.52)	.000006163 (5.23)	.000006712 (5.78)	.000006701 (5.78)	.000006943 (5.76)

Bandwagon Variables

Probability "average person" in county sees psychiatrist	43.70 (3.02)
Percentage of state population with regular medical insurance, 1973	.5590 (2.69)
Percentage of patients in state with third-party coverage for private psychiatry	.06846 (0.35)
Percentage of patients in state with 50 percent or more coverage for private psychiatry	.6820 (3.10)
Office-based psychiatrists/state population	-.7151 (0.71)

other variables concerning the local atmosphere. (No coefficient of any other independent variable changed in an important way when the demand indices were added.) The proposed bandwagon measures met with mixed success. Three of the five estimated coefficients are positive and significant, supporting the hypothesis of bandwagon effects in demand. Two estimated coefficients are insignificantly different from zero.

Although these results are not conclusive evidence of the existence of bandwagon effects in demand for private psychiatric care, local demand indices, in the presence of controls for other aspects of atmosphere, appear to have some positive effect on the extent of treatment of individual patients. The magnitude of this effect is easy to interpret in the case of the second and fourth proposed measure. A 1 percent increase in the number of persons covered increases the extent of treatment by 0.5 to 0.7 percent. This increase in visits is of the same order of magnitude as would result from a 1 percent increase in the percent of changes paid by insurance (COINRATE).

IMPLICATIONS

Impact of Compulsory Insurance on Demand for Psychotherapy

The empirical research reveals that insurance increases the number of visits patients make to private psychiatrists. The responsiveness to insurance varies inversely with income class. Members of the lowest income group increase visits by about 0.6 percent for each 1 percent increase in coverage, whereas members of the uppermost income group are virtually insensitive to insurance coverage.

In predicting the total impact of a broad-based insurance plan, such as national health insurance, it must be recognized that national health insurance would encourage people to seek a therapist as well as encourage more visits if a therapist is being seen. The increase in the *total* expected number of visits a person makes with respect to a 1 percent change in insurance is the sum of the percentage change in the probability of seeing a therapist plus the percentage change in the number of visits made given that a therapist is being seen.[9] We have estimated the percentage increase in the number of visits to be about 0.4 for the average person in the United States.

This study cannot tell how much insurance coverage increases the likelihood someone seeks treatment in the first place. However, compare the rate of seeking treatment of one group in the population with insurance coverage similar to what might apply under national health insurance to the behavior of another group without much coverage. Two and one-half million federal employees and their adult dependents were covered by the Blue Cross/Blue Shield high-option plan in 1973, which paid (after a small deductible applicable to all medical expenses and up to a limit of $250,000) 80 percent of charges made in a psychiatrist's private office. These people saw private psychiatrists at the rate of 30 per 1,000 (Reed 1975). This rate is consistent with the behavior of other groups with coverage featuring low deductibles. Liptzin, Regier, and Goldberg (1979) for example, report that 4 percent of the 2.3 million subscribers covered by the Michigan Variable Fee–2 Plan of Blue Cross/Blue Shield made use of mental health benefits in 1975.

Compare this rate of treatment with the rate for the U.S. population not in the Blue Cross/Blue Shield high-option plan. Subtracting the 66,000 federal employees and their adult dependents in treatment in 1973 from the estimated U.S. total adults in treatment of 728,000, and subtracting the 2.5 million enrollees from the U.S. adult population, the cases per thousand of the over 130 million adults in the United States was about five cases per 1,000. Coverage for nonfederal employees varied, of course, but a reasonable guess is that the average coinsurance rate for adults in the United States not enrolled in the Blue Cross/Blue Shield high-option plan was about 15 percent. The average coinsurance rate in the 3,000-patient sample was 23 percent. Although Reed, Myers, and Sheidemandel (1972) quote no figure, they give evidence that in the early 1970s about one-third of Americans had some form of coverage for private psychiatry and that the average coinsurance rate was about 50 percent.

Fitting a curve with a constant percentage change in probability with a change in coinsurance to the two points (80 percent coverage, thirty cases per 1,000), (15 percent coverage, five cases per 1,000), gives an estimate of a 2.75 percent increase in the probability of seeing a psychiatrist with a 1 percent change in coinsurance. This is a rough estimate, neglecting as it does adverse selection into the high-option plan but the implication that the decision to see a psychiatrist is sensitive to insurance coverage could hardly be avoided. This estimate may include some bandwagon effects from coworkers' increase in utilization with insurance, but such effects would also apply to national health insurance.

This, along with our more precise estimates of how much the quantity of visits would increase for those in treatment, implies total demand would increase at least 1 percent in response to a 1 percent increase in insurance coverage. Demand for psychotherapy appears much more responsive to insurance than demand for other medical services even before taking any possible bandwagon effects into account. The measurement of bandwagon effects is tentative, but they appear to be of roughly the same magnitude as the moral hazard effect in their effect on the extent of treatment. A rock-bottom estimate of the overall percentage increase in demand with a 1 percent increase of insurance would be 1 percent. The tentative evidence on the bandwagon effect would push this to 1.5 percent or so. Better measures of bandwagon effects (in addition to their geographical dimension) could move this estimate higher still. Taken together, these findings about the bandwagon and moral hazard effects of insurance imply that the demand for psychotherapy is likely to increase substantially under a broad-based national health insurance plan.

The Importance of Bandwagon Effects

The results imply that bandwagon effects are clearly worthy of further investigation. If everyone is entitled to essentially free care, social attitudes toward use of all kinds of medical services might undergo significant shift. RAND's health insurance experiment is expected to produce the most definitive estimates of the price effects of insurance (Newhouse 1974). The RAND experiment ensures randomly selected families without changing the "atmosphere" in which medical services are demanded. If bandwagon effects create demand for general medical services, the RAND experiment is not a small-scale model of national health insurance. Predictions based on simple price elasticities may seriously underestimate demand increases under a broad-based insurance plan.

One of the most significant findings of this investigation is that the poor appear to be much more responsive to insurance than the rich. This means that compulsory insurance for psychotherapy would lead to a greater percentage increase in demand among lower income groups. Conventional wisdom holds that public financing for psycho-therapy would be distributionally harmful, collecting revenue from the average taxpayer and subsidizing consumption by the well-to-do. Our results indicate that the conventional wisdom needs reexamination. The next chapter, in consideration of the distributional impact of public financing for psychotherapy, estimates the impact of a prototypical NHI program covering psychotherapy on the distribution of income.

NOTES TO CHAPTER 5

1. Since so many independent variables may be involved, an instrumental variable correction is impractical.
2. See Hausman and Wise (1977) for application of maximum likelihood methods to a similar statistical problem.
3. Heckman (1976) demonstrates that this method produces estimates close to those obtained by maximum likelihood techniques.
4. An alternative explanation relates to price discrimination. Patients have different amounts of "trust" in their therapist. More "trusting" patients have greater demand for their therapists' services. If the therapist is practicing price discrimination, which many psychiatrists in the sample admitted doing, to maximize profit, price is set at the average benefit the patient receives from services. (This extracts all consumer surplus associated with "trust," which the therapist may do since psychotherapy is a nonretradable service.) Thus, more trusting patients may be asked to consume more service and pay a higher price, creating the positive correlation between price and visits. According to this interpretation a higher price would not be the cause of a higher number of visits. Price to an individual would be co-determined in the visits.
5. Equation (1) was checked for heteroskedasticity. The variance of visits may increase with the total number of visits. Also the definition of the independent variable here may lead to additional heteroskedasticity. If psychiatrists' projections are subject to error, the larger is PROSH, the larger will be the variance in our measure of total visits. To deal with this a regression of the square of the error terms for (1) on total visits and PROSH was estimated; surprisingly, neither estimated coefficient was significantly positive, so a generalized least squares estimate was not attempted.
6. I am grateful to Richard Frank for suggesting this measure of the bandwagon effect.
7. The index is not scaled, so that the average value of this variable is equal to the average probability that someone in the United States saw a psychiatrist

in 1973. The average value of the variable is about 0.4, whereas the average probability of seeing a private psychiatrist in 1973 was closer to 0.01 or 0.005. Although the variable is defined as a probability density function, in the range of "average persons in counties" it is essentially a linear index.

8. Regular medical insurance pays for services at a physician's private office, although not all plans cover psychiatrists on the same basis as other physicians.

9. The expected number of visits a person makes to a psychiatrist is equal to the product of the probability of seeing a psychiatrist, times the expected number of visits given that a psychiatrist is being seen. Thus, the percentage change in the expected number of visits is the sum of the percentage changes in the probability of seeing a psychiatrist and in the number of visits, given that a psychiatrist is being seen.

6 DISTRIBUTIONAL EFFECTS OF INSURANCE FOR PSYCHOTHERAPY

This chapter is about the equity of compulsory financing for psycho-therapy. For the most part concern will be for compulsory financing arising as part of an NHI plan, where benefits are financed by federal taxes. Fairness is a subjective concept, so it is not surprising to find disagreement about whether markets for psychotherapy are presently providing a fair distribution of service or about whether compulsory insurance for psychotherapy could improve the situation. If debate were simply over value judgments (such as "The rich and the poor ought to receive the same quality of care"), there would be little opportunity for research to advance policy discussion. But in addition to disagreement about value judgments, there is substantial dis-agreement about the objective effects of national health insurance on the delivery of mental health services.

The fairness of national health insurance for psychotherapy should be judged on several dimensions. One is its effect on the distribution of income between rich and poor, taking into account taxes paid to support the program. This question is answered by information from the JIS survey and the estimation of demand for psychotherapy. Two other main dimensions of fairness are then considered: the distribu-tion of benefits of national health insurance between providers and patients, and between the sick and the healthy.

EFFECTS ON THE DISTRIBUTION OF INCOME

National health insurance is redistributive, taking purchasing power from the temporarily healthy and putting it in the hands of the temporarily sick. There has not been substantial concern that redistribution from the healthy to the sick would worsen the distribution of *income* in the United States. Although higher income groups use more medical services than lower income groups, they do not use more in proportion to their income.[1] Combining this fact with a federal tax system roughly proportional to income leads to the result that the net incidence of national health insurance would be progressive; that is, would redistribute in favor of the poor.[2]

Distributional complacency does not pertain to all parts of proposed NHI packages. In particular, coverage for some mental health services has been criticized on the grounds that public insurance would redistribute income to upper income groups; insurance for most of the mental health service system is immune from this attack. Public inpatient facilities primarily serve the indigent. Despite debate about whether public outpatient facilities such as CMHCs serve the poor equally with the middle class (the rich avoid these settings altogether), there is absolutely no doubt that, taking into account taxes paid as well as benefits received, such programs transfer income toward the bottom of the income distribution. Well over one-half of all patients served at CMHCs fall below the official poverty line.

Criticism of the distributional impact of national health insurance centers around anticipated effects of public funding of psychotherapy provided by private therapists. Intensive individual therapy is and is widely anticipated to remain the nearly exclusive privilege of the well-to-do. Data from the JIS survey of psychiatrists in private practice support this widely held view. Forty-one percent of patients in the 1973 survey had family income above $20,000; in the United States overall only 14 percent of families had income that high. Only 2 percent of psychiatrists' private patients were black. Senator Edward Kennedy, among others, has cited these statistics and expressed concern about the distributional consequences of public financing for this service:

> If we were to implement a comprehensive national health insurance program tomorrow, and if we did not change in any way the geographical location or the patient loads of psychiatrists, we would be asking the 86 percent

of American families whose earnings are under $20,000 a year to pay the lion's share of the cost of a health care service which is rendered by and large to individuals in families whose incomes are over $20,000 a year.[3]

The consensus that national health insurance for mental health services provided in private practice would subsidize the rich needs serious reexamination. Data from the JIS survey when correctly interpreted do not support the view that national health insurance for psychiatrists in private practice—potentially the most controversial part of mental health services—would redistribute away from the poor.

A correct interpretation of the evidence involves three points. First, the method of sampling, drawing the last ten patients, oversamples heavy users. This method in effect takes a random sample of *visits* rather than of *patients*. Statistical inference to population values for patients requires a weighting of observations. Since the poor tend to use service with less frequency than the rich, the proportion of poor patients is understated when the sample of the last ten patients is treated as a random sample. Second, the mix of patients would change under national health insurance. With the poor more sensitive to price reductions brought about by insurance, the poor would increase their share of services under NHI. Third, the rich pay more taxes than the poor.

The Last Ten Problem (Again)

The data used to estimate the distribution of benefits from national health insurance for private psychiatry are from the JIS survey of private practice described in Chapter 4. As discussed in the last chapter, in the construction of an empirical model of demand, these data require special handling because the survey drew a sample of last ten patients seen, not a random sample of patients in private practice. In the last chapter the correction introduced for this problem, Heckman's "omitted variable," may not have been necessary, since bias in the estimation of the slope coefficients of the demand function was not a serious problem (possibly because of the extensive measures of mental health and taste for treatment). In this chapter, by contrast, it is crucial to correct for oversampling of heavy users. High-income patients tend to be the heavy users and, without correction, these patients appear to make up a larger percentage of the private psychiatrist's practice than they actually do. To illustrate the seriousness of the problem from nonrandom sampling and the nature of the necessary correction, a simple example is considered before proceeding to the more complex problem.

There are two classes of people in the example, rich and poor. Three thousand of the 100,000 rich see a psychiatrist each year, and 1,000 of the 100,000 poor. There are three frequencies of visits, 5/week, 1/week, and 0.25/week. The rich patients are equally distributed among the three frequencies. No poor person makes 5/week; one-half make 1/week, and one-half make 0.25/week. Thus, the average number of visits made by a rich patient is 2.0833 and by a poor patient 0.625. The average number of visits made by a rich person (patient or not) is 0.0625; by the average poor person 0.00625. In summary, the rich make ten times the use of psychiatrists as the poor. These numbers are all true values in this example, and are reported in Table 6-1.

The social scientist, of course, does not know the true values, but must infer from a sample survey the utilization of the rich and poor. Suppose (analogous to the JIS survey) the social scientist draws a sample of 4,000 last patients seen by a random sample of psychiatrists. Since each visit has an equal chance of being a last visit, the social scientist will draw observations from the five types of patients in proportion to the number of visits they contribute to the total made each week. The sample generated by this method is shown in Table 6-2, with the more frequent users being overrepresented. The rich, 5/week patients are truly only 25 percent of the patients, but because they account for a large portion of the visits, they make up 72.7 percent of the social scientist's sample.

If the social scientist erroneously treated the sample as if it were a random sample, he or she would make the following incorrect inferences:

1. The rich make up 90.9 percent (= 72.727 + 14.545 + 3.636) of the patients; the poor make up 9.1 percent (= 7.263 + 1.818). (*True values*: 75 percent, 25 percent)

2. The probability that a rich person sees a psychiatrist is 0.03636 (= 0.909 × 4,000 patients/100,000 rich); the probability that a poor person sees a psychiatrist is 0.00364 (= 0.091 × 4,000/ 100,000). (*True values*: 0.03, 0.01)

Table 6-1. Population Values in a Two-Class Society.

Class	Number of People	Number in Treatment	Probability of Being in Treatment	Frequency of Visits			Average Visits per Week per Patient	Average Visits per Week per Person
				5/wk	1/wk	.25/wk		
Rich	100,000	3,000	.03	1000	1000	1000	2.0833	.0625
Poor	100,000	1,000	.01	0	500	500	.625	.00625

Table 6-2. Expected Distribution of Observations in a Sample of Last Patients.

Type of Patient	Total Number of Patients	True Relative Frequency	Total Visits Made per Week by Group	Relative Frequency in a Sample of Last Patients[a]
Rich				
5/week	1,000	.25	5000	.72727
1/week	1,000	.25	1000	.14545
0.25/week	1,000	.25	250	.03636
Poor				
1/week	500	.125	500	.07273
0.25/week	500	.125	125	.01818

a. Assuming (1) each visit has equal chance to be "last," and (2) that sample is small relative to population so that the expected frequency is approximated by sampling from a distribution "with replacement."

3. The average rich patient makes 4.17 visits (a weighting of 5, 1, and 0.25 in proportion to their appearance among the sampled rich); the average poor patient makes 0.899 visits (a weighting of 1 and 0.25).
   (*True values*: 2.0833, 0.625)

4. The average utilization of a rich person (patient or not) is 0.1515 (= 0.0363 × 4.17); the average utilization of a poor person is 0.00327 (= 0.00364 × 0.899).
   (*True values*: 0.0625, 0.00625)

5. The rich use 46 times (= 0.1515/0.00327) more services than the poor.
   (*True value*: 10 times)

The social scientists would vastly overstate the relative consumption of the rich.

This is not an idle example. Senator Kennedy's remarks quoted earlier were based on published results of the JIS survey used here, which treated the sample of last tens as if it were a random sample of patients. As will be shown, Kennedy was misled into thinking the rich use a higher proportion of services than they actually do.

It can clearly be crucial to correct for a method of sampling that is nonrandom. In this example the correction is simple. The probability that an individual makes a last visit is proportional to his rate of visits. By weighting each observed patient by the inverse of frequency of visits, expected weighting of each individual in the sample for any sample statistic is equalized. A method analogous to this is applied to the last ten sample subsequently.

Responsiveness of Demand to Insurance Decreases with Income

At present, psychotherapy from providers in private practice is used disproportionately by upper income groups. There is precedent and hope that public financing can transform the distribution of services. In the last century policymakers questioned whether public financing for secondary education would be inequitable; at that time secondary education was a luxury for children of upper income groups. Had one argued then that public financing would simply substitute for the out-of-pocket expenses of the rich one would have been proved wrong. The reason is that public financing of secondary education changed the price of education for everyone, and the poor and middle classes were much more responsive to price reductions than were the rich. After public financing and the price change, the distribution of services was much more equitable than before.

According to the empirical results of the last chapter, public financing for psychotherapy may have distributional consequences similar to public financing for secondary education. Even for a privately purchased good consumed in quantities that increase more than proportionately with income, public financing may redistribute in favor of the poor, if they are more responsive to price reductions than the rich. It is the distribution of services after the price change rather than before that determines the distribution of benefits of public financing.

Greater price responsiveness of the poor implies that demand will have the general shape shown in Figure 6-1. At a high price such as $50 per visit, the rich demand many more visits than the poor. But because the poor are more responsive to price reductions, at a lower price such as would be brought about by national health insurance, the distribution of visits is more equitable. Whether it is enough to compensate for the head start of the rich will be examined here.

Figure 6-1. Demand Curves Illustrating Greater Price Responsiveness of Poor.

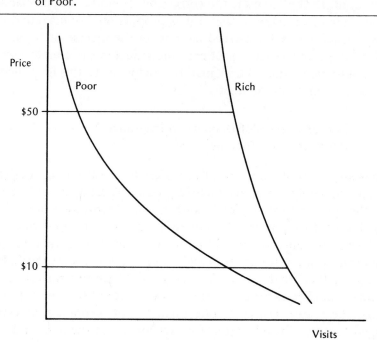

Imputation of Benefits from National Health Insurance for Psychotherapy from Psychiatrists in Private Practice

In order to predict on whose behalf expenditures under a NHI program for private psychiatry would be made it is necessary to predict the expected utilization of a member of each income class. This is based on three specific pieces of information for each income class: (1) how much is being used now, (2) how sensitive is utilization to insurance, and (3) how much insurance would increase under NHI? What is known about these is summarized in Table 6-3.

To determine how much is being used now, the present expected number of visits made to a private psychiatrist for someone in each income class is estimated. The form of the JIS questionnaire dictates use of the income classes set out in Table 6-3. The expected number of visits is equal to the probability that someone sees a psychiatrist during the year times the average number of visits they would make to the psychiatrist. Since the sample is not a random sample of the U.S. population but only includes patients in treatment, the formula

Table 6-3.   Utilization of Private Psychiatrists, by Family Income, 1973.

Family Income	(1) Probability of Seeing a Private Psychiatrist	(2) Average Visits per Patient in Last Year	(3) Average Visits per Person per Year	(4) Average Percentage of Bills Paid by Third Parties	(5) Percent Change of Visits by Patient With 1 Percent Change in Portion Paid by Third Party
Less than $10,000	.00403 (.00325)	27.3 (32.4)	.110 (.105)	.360	.569
$10,000–19,999	.00561 (.00475)	29.9 (46.5)	.168 (.221)	.287	.405
$20,000–29,999	.00633 (.00706)	34.5 (57.6)	.218 (.407)	.236	.247
$30+	.0177 (.0246)	37.4 (75.4)	.662 (1.85)	.106	.000[a]

a. In Chapter 5 this was actually estimated to be a small negative number, insignificantly different from zero.

for conditional probability must be applied to estimate the probability that someone in an income class sees a psychiatrist during the year.

$$\text{prob (sees} \mid \text{income)} = \frac{\text{prob (income} \mid \text{sees)}}{\text{prob (income)}} \cdot \text{prob (sees)} \qquad (6-1)$$

The probability on the left-hand side of Equation (6-1) is the answer. On the right-hand side, prob (income) is the unconditional probability that someone in the United States is from a certain income class; this is available from the Census Bureau.[4] The term prob (sees) is the unconditional probability that someone in the United States sees a psychiatrist during a year; this is available from national medical care surveys and has been estimated to be about 0.00545 for adults (Regier and Goldberg 1976).

The probability that someone is in a certain income class if he or she is seeing a psychiatrist—prob (income | sees)—can be estimated from the sample. Since the sample is of the last ten patients, this estimation is complex. Analogously to the weighting used to correct for nonrandom sampling in the simple example just discussed, the observations of patients are weighted by the inverse of the probability that they appear in the sample of last tens.[5] Information from the survey on the current frequency of visits for each patient and the total number of hours each psychiatrist devoted to private practice each week allows this to be done.[6] The probability that someone from each income class sees a psychiatrist during a year is reported in the first column of Table 6-3. The second column of Table 6-3 reports average visits per year for patients by income class, given that they see a psychiatrist. (This statistic also requires a weighting of the observations.) The expected number of visits for a person in each income class is then the product of columns (1) and (2), given in column (3) of Table 6-3.

In parentheses after these estimates are the unweighted estimates showing again how important it is to correct for the manner in which the sample was drawn. Uncorrected, the overrepresentation of high utilizers and high-income patients is quite misleading. The rich are not as disproportionately represented in psychiatrists' practices and they do not use as many more visits than the poor as would appear in the unweighted sample.

Still, column (3) explains the concern for the distributional consequences of financing private psychiatry from tax revenues. At present the rich are more likely to see a psychiatrist, and would use a psychiatrist more heavily if they did see one. Overall, as column (3) indicates, someone from the $30,000+ income category makes six times the use of private psychiatrists as someone from the lowest category. (This multiple would be eighteen times were the sample treated as a random sample.)

Column (4) shows the percentage of patients' bills paid by a third party. This would go up for everyone with national health insurance, but higher income patients with less present coverage (who are more likely to be professional), would enjoy the greatest increase in coverage.[7]

The last column in Table 6–3 reports regression results from the last chapter on the effect of insurance on the average number of visits per patient. These statistics—showing the inverse relation between income and response to insurance—provide the factor that offsets the present consumption patterns in favor of higher income patients. The poor will increase their visits more than the rich under national health insurance, moving the distribution of visits toward a more equal distribution.

The prototype NHI bill pays for 80 percent of private psychiatrists' charges. For simplicity, limits and deductibles are ignored. Supply is assumed to be perfectly elastic so that the price of private psychiatric care is unaffected by increases in demand brought about by insurance. This is unrealistic, but the shape of the supply curve primarily affects the distribution of benefits between buyers and sellers rather than among buyers. This issue is taken up in the next section.

A NHI plan paying 80 percent of psychiatrists' charges would have two effects on utilization: It would increase the number of visits made by patients in treatment and it would increase the probability that someone becomes a patient. Estimates in the last two columns of Table 6–3 reveal how visits of patients in treatment would increase when national health insurance paid 80 percent of charges. For patients with a family income less than $10,000, the prototype NHI plan would increase the percentage of the bill paid by a third party by 80 percent less 36 percent, or 44 percent. The increased coverage would increase visits by $44 \times 0.569 = 25.0$ percent. Adding 25 percent to the 27.3 visits per patient reported in column (2) of Table 6–3 gives an estimate of the average visits per patient in this income class under national health insurance of 34.1 visits. This is recorded in the second column of Table 6–4. The predicted average

Table 6-4. Utilization and Distribution of Benefits and Taxes under National Health Insurance.

Income Class (percentage of families)	(1) Probability of Seeing a Private Psychiatrist	(2) Average Visits per Patient	(3) Average Visits per Person ((1) × (2))	(4) Charges per Person at Price = $50 (NHI pays 80%)	(5) Taxes per Person to Finance Program	(6) Net Benefits Program ((4) – (5))
Less than $10,000 (38.9)	.00403	34.1	.137	$5.48	4.11	+1.37
$10,000–19,999 (41.2)	.00561	36.1	.203	$8.12	8.22	-0.10
$20,000–29,999 (14.2)	.00633	39.3	.249	$9.96	14.10	-4.14
$30,000+ (4.7)	.0177	37.4	.662	$26.48	23.50	+2.98

visits for each income class under national health insurance in Table 6-4 were constructed in similar fashion.

Unfortunately, corresponding information about how the initial decision to see a psychiatrist is affected by insurance is lacking. Although crude inferences are possible regarding the average effect for all income classes, there is no indication of how the effect of insurance on the decision to seek care varies by income class. A complete analysis of the distributional effects of national health insurance cannot be made at this time. On the basis of what is known, however, it is possible to make the following statement: *Assuming upper income groups are not more responsive than lower income groups in the decision to seek private psychiatric care, NHI for private psychiatry would not redistribute income against lower income families.* This is valuable information. The assumption that the rich are not more responsive in the decision to see a psychiatrist seems reasonable in that they are less responsive to insurance than the poor in terms of the extent of treatment.

Table 6-4 concerns utilization by income class with national health insurance and presents the basis of the distribution statement in the preceding paragraph. The probability of seeing a psychiatrist is unchanged from Table 6-3. (An equal proportional effect of insurance on this probability has no effect on the direction of redistributions, only on their magnitudes.) Expected visits per person in each class is shown in column (3). At a price of $50 per visit, national health insurance would pay $40. This generates expected visits per person shown in column (4). Expected benefits are equal to the amount the government would spend on behalf of the average person in each income group. The rich would still enjoy five times the benefits of the poor. But the fact that the rich pay more taxes to support the program must be taken into account. Estimated taxes per person are reported in column (5). It is assumed that the average income within each group is $7,000, $14,000, $24,000, and $40,000, respectively, and that federal taxes (a composite of income and payroll taxes) are proportional to income (Pechman and Okner 1974). Program costs are found by weighting utilization per person by the percentage of population in each class.

The distributional bottom line, the net benefits imputed to each income class, is shown in column (6). (Recall that these numbers are proportional to any increase national health insurance would have on the average probability that persons would see a private psychiatrist.)

According to column (6), the 80 percent of the families in the United States with incomes less than $20,000 would come out about even or slightly ahead under national health insurance for private psychiatry. The only significant redistribution would appear to be between the upper middle class and the upper class. By these estimates, in the upper 20 percent of the income distribution, demand for private psychiatry increases more than proportionately with income. Because there are more than three times as many upper middle class families as there are upper class families, the net positive position of the upper class would be more than compensated for by the net deficit of the upper middle class.

The key conclusion from this analysis is negative but important. The information currently available does not support the hypothesis that national health insurance for private psychiatry would redistribute income away from the lower and middle classes. Since private psychiatry is probably the most exclusive setting for psychotherapy, generalizing this finding to other settings would seem appropriate. From the analysis here the only major redistribution of income would be a transfer from the upper middle class to the upper class. There are many important considerations in deciding policy for psychotherapy in national health insurance, but clearly, coverage for psychotherapy does not deserve to be dismissed on distributional grounds.

DIVISION OF BENEFITS BETWEEN PROVIDERS AND PATIENTS

Psychotherapists are in a position to benefit financially from national health insurance for psychotherapy. National health insurance is intended to reduce the out-of-pocket price of psychotherapy to the patient and in some cases to stimulate demand. Depending on the nature of the "industry" supplying psychotherapy, response by providers to the demand increase from national health insurance may frustrate these intentions. Essentially, if supply of psychotherapy were elastic in response to price, the extra demand brought about by national health insurance would result in a large increase in supply of services. Market price would not rise much, quantity of services would rise, out-of-pocket price to users would fall. National health insurance would have its intended effects. If, on the other hand, supply were inelastic—not very responsive to price—the extra demand brought about by national health insurance would be choked by price rises. Market price would rise substantially, services provided would not increase much, out-of-pocket price to users would not fall much. The major effect of national health insurance would be to increase incomes of providers. The intended effects of national health insurance would be frustrated.

These points are illustrated in a simple demand and supply framework in Figure 6-2. Suppose demand before national health insurance is AB and market equilibrium is at point E_1 with V_1 visits provided at price P_1. National health insurance subsidizes demand increasing it to schedule AC. (This is the general impact of national health insurance paying a set percentage of charges—increasing patients' willingness to pay proportionately for all quantities.) If supply were elastic a large expansion of visits would be possible at little or no price increase and the new equilibrium would be at E_2. The impact of the higher demand would be to call forth an increase in services to patients, from V_1 to V_2. It is the increase in visits that provides benefits to patients. Patients also benefit from having the government pay part of the price of a visit. After national health insurance, the out-of-pocket price to the patient falls with perfectly elastic supply to P_2'. Although providers do more business at the new equilibrium, the supply price to them, P_2, is the same as the price before national health insurance. There is no increase in "providers' surplus" or profit associated with the increase in demand.[8] Patients receive all the benefits from national health insurance with perfectly elastic supply.

The division of benefits changes radically, however, if supply is inelastic; that is, increases in quantity supplied can be called forth only with relatively sharp increases in price. With an increase in demand brought about by national health insurance under this situation, there is a small increase in visits, V_1 to V_3. The major impact of the increased demand is to drive up the price paid to providers from P_1 to P_3. With such a large increase, the out-of-pocket price paid by the patient falls very little with national health insurance, from P_1 to P_3'. If supply were totally inelastic—the supply curve a vertical line— the out-of-pocket price to patients would not change at all with national health insurance and patients would receive absolutely no benefit. As it is drawn in Figure 6-2, patients enjoy a small price reduction. Most of the benefits of national health insurance for this

Figure 6-2. Division of Benefits Between Providers and Patients with Elastic and Inelastic Supply.

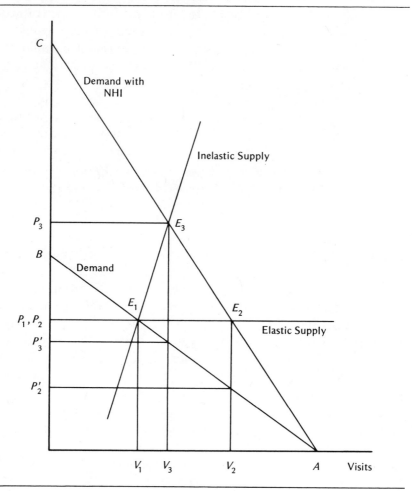

service are appropriated by the providers in the form of higher prices. Even though national health insurance spends money on behalf of patients, if supply is inelastic, benefits are shifted to providers by price increases. Increased profits to providers in Figure 6-2 are equal to the area of the trapezoid $P_3 E_3 E_1 P_1$.

Presuming national health insurance would be intended to benefit consumers of psychotherapy rather than the providers, one of the distributional concerns for policy should be that supply of psychotherapy is no more inelastic than is consistent with the social cost of services. There should be no "artificial" restrictions on supply that would vent demand increases into price increases rather than into increased services. Since national health insurance would raise demand for all medical services, it is unlikely psychiatry would draw out physicians from other specialities. Major increases in the supply of psychotherapy must come largely from nonmedical personnel.

How well clinical psychologists, psychiatric social workers, psychiatric nurses, or other groups can substitute for psychiatrists is an interesting, difficult, and important question. (See McGuire 1980 for discussion.) Putting aside issues of the quality of care, in the limited context of the division of benefits between providers and patients, it is clear that adding competition on the supply side would benefit consumers by making supply more elastic. Patients would have more visits at a lower price than if supply were restricted to just psychiatrists. Where the law allows, psychologists have eagerly entered into supply of psychotherapy. This competition would help to avoid the shifting of the benefits of national health insurance from the patients to the providers.

SICK AND HEALTHY

A major objective of all health policy is to provide fairly for the sick. In part, the role of compulsory insurance is to provide a way for the healthy to help the sick pay for their medical bills. A fair compulsory insurance plan would not pay people back (on average) what they paid in, but rather would redistribute purchasing power away from people who are generally healthy, toward those who are generally less healthy. The standard of fair prices for this insurance would not be a set of premiums perfectly experience-rated, person by person. It would be fairer for each person to pay the same premium (or a premium in proportion to income), while those who are sick more often would receive a larger share of the benefits. The rest are "lucky" and should not object to helping the sick.

An insurance plan benefits only a few each year. The distribution of benefits from fire, life, or hospitalization insurance is highly skewed. If benefits were distributed evenly, there would be no risk, and no reason to insure against the expense. Louis Reed's (1975: 19) study of federal employees enrolled in the Blue Cross/Blue Shield high-option plan for 1973 revealed that a few intensive users of private psychiatric care accounted for a large portion of the total charges. Over one-third of the charges were made by 3/10,000 of the persons covered. There is no question that charges under this plan were distributed unevenly, but was this uneven distribution inequitable?

Whether or not this is regarded as equitable depends on whether one regards persons in psychotherapy as sick and therefore worthy of financial help for paying for their illness. As GAP has recognized, collective payment for services forces society to confront these value judgments: "The effect of payment via health insurance is to expose to scrutiny the extent to which psychiatric patients are like other medical patients" (1975: 514).

Psychiatry may be the only specialty where ambulatory patients can run up expenses of $5,000, $10,000, $15,000, or more in a single year. Such large expenses are usually associated with a catastrophic illness. It will not be possible to settle here the question of whether most people regard patients in psychotherapy as worthy of help with their medical bills, but it is possible to help readers decide for themselves if they regard psychiatrists' patients as "worthy" as general medical patients.

Consider the "worthiness" of two fictitious patients with illnesses equally catastrophic in a financial sense. Patient A has been in a general hospital for forty days and has spent $10,000. Patient B has visited a psychiatrist 200 times and has spent $10,000. Which patient do you sympathize with more, and which do you think is more worthy of your financial support? (And probably most relevant, how do you think the "average voter" would answer that question?) You are not asked to judge if mental illness is as "real" as physical illness; you are not asked to judge if the typical catastrophically mentally ill person is as sick as the typical catastrophically physically ill person. You are asked to compare the typical *patient* of a private psychiatrist running up a $10,000 expense with the typical *patient* with a physical illness running up the same expense. Many people may suspect that the typical patient of the private psychiatrist (as contrasted to the typically mentally ill person) is "less sick" than the typical physically ill patient, and therefore less worthy of redistribution from the healthy.

Skepticism about the sickness and worthiness of psychiatrists' private patients has been widely expressed. Senator Kennedy has voiced concern that coverage for psychotherapy would disproportionately benefit patients "whose need is really not great," (in Marmor 1975: 152). Brown (1976) the former head of the National Institute of Mental Health, notes that psychiatrists often deal with "problems of living" and try to improve their patient's "quality of life." In a speech before psychiatrists, Aetna's medical director, Dr. William Guillette explained, "We can understand why a person would go to an analyst to get rid of unpleasant or unwanted human behavior, or to find themselves, but insurance was never intended to cover this type of 'non-psychiatric problem'" (1976: 10). These statements all express value judgments, but when the issue is "fairness," value judgments must be the center of concern.

This skepticism is opposed by those who argue for "equal treatment for the mentally ill" (American Psychiatric Association 1977, NIMH 1976) or those who oppose "discrimination on the basis of diagnosis" (Hall 1974). These are effective rallying cries, but to battles already largely won. It is doubtful that Kennedy, Brown, or Guillette would deny that the mentally ill are as sick and as worthy as the physically ill. What they question is whether patients in psychotherapy, especially in provider's private offices, are consistently mentally ill.

The results of the JIS survey are sometimes cited to show that private patients are genuinely mentally ill. As judged by the psychiatrists, 78 percent of the patients were either moderately or severely impaired by their illness at the time treatment began (Marmor 1975: 49). Psychiatrists had no incentive to answer the questionnaire falsely, but this statistic is not convincing evidence, as those with psychological training should best appreciate. The theory of cognitive dissonance strongly suggests that psychiatrists asked "Does this person paying almost $1 per minute to talk with you need your help?" would have difficulty admitting any answer other than "yes."

SUMMARY

Other distributional issues arise in connection with national health insurance for psychotherapy in addition to the three discussed here. An important one is the geographical distribution of services. NIMH (1976: 39) has acknowledged that psychiatry may be the most severely "maldistributed" of any major medical specialty. Psychiatrists are concentrated in rich suburbs. Other mental health professions in private practice follow a similar pattern. The reason for this uneven geographical distribution is that the willingness to pay for psychotherapy is unevenly distributed — concentrated in rich suburbs. National health insurance would increase the demand of the poor more than of the rich, which would tend to alleviate part of the geographical distribution problem. Distributional concern for the needs of special population groups, such as minorities, the aged, children, women, or others, are unlikely to be effectively addressed with a general policy such as NHI financing.

Distributional criteria should not be the exclusive criteria by which to judge national health insurance for psychotherapy, but they are given the most attention because efficiency criteria are so difficult to define. (The President's Commission on Mental Health is the best example of this.) In this analysis distributional criteria will be weighed, together with efficiency critera. To be clear about the value judgments adopted here, it is regarded as

1. Bad that national health insurance for psychotherapy would transfer income from the poor to the rich,
2. Bad that benefits from national health insurance for psychotherapy would be shifted to providers in the form of higher income, and
3. Good that national health insurance for psychotherapy would transfer income from the healthy to the sick.

How do the objective facts about national health insurance measure up along these lines? Regarding (1), no evidence was found that national health insurance for psychotherapy would redistribute away from the poor. Although more research should be done to confirm this conclusion, national health insurance for psychotherapy at present should not be regarded as detrimental to the distribution of income. Criterion (2) presents some dangers. If eligible providers are narrowly defined, price increases in the market for psychotherapy will shift benefits to providers. National health insurance for psychotherapy appears mildly favorable in terms of criterion (3), although difficulty in defining "need" for care makes this criterion less powerful for psychotherapy than for most physical illness.

This part of the book has been concerned with estimating the impact of broad-based insurance for psychotherapy on demand and utilization. Two conclusions have been reached. Insurance seems to lead to substantial increases in utilization. Compulsory insurance for psychotherapy is unlikely to be distributionally harmful. These findings, together with the arguments developed in Part One, form the basis of policy recommendations in Part Three.

NOTES TO CHAPTER 6

1. Newhouse and Phelps (1976) estimate income elasticities of demand for physicians' and hospital services to be less than 0.1. Partial income elasticities, with other variables controlled, are not relevant for distributional questions; it is the *uncontrolled* association of income and consumption that is important. Even if education were the true cause of higher utilization and the effect of income controlling for education were zero, the rich would still be consuming more medical services since they were better educated. Davis and Reynolds (1976) provide evidence that consumption of medical care rises less than proportionately with income.

2. See Feldstein, Friedman, and Luft (1976). Data limitations forced Feldstein et al. to assume an income elasticity of zero and income–price cross-elasticities of zero. These assumptions virtually guarantee that a federally financed program will be redistributive in favor of the poor.

3. Kennedy's remarks are in Marmor (1975).

4. *Statistical Abstract of U.S.* 1975: 390. Sixty percent of families in the $15,000-24,999 category were assigned to our $10,000-19,999 category, on the basis of the median income in the $15,000-24,999 category being $18,976 (*Statistical Abstract of U.S.* 1975: 391).

5. In deriving statistics from a random sample each observation is typically weighted equally since each observation is expected to be "representative" of as many similar nonsampled cases as every other observations. When observations have an unequal probability of being sampled, an observation is expected to be "representative" of other cases in inverse proportion to the probability the observation with those characteristics is drawn.

6. The probability that a patient appears in the sample of last tens is estimated as follows: Available from the survey is the number of hours the psychiatrist spends in private practice per week, T, and the current frequency of visits per week for each patient, V. Since a visit takes about one hour of a psychiatrist's time, the probability that a patient has the last visit is approximately V/T. The probability the patient has the next to last but not the last is $(1-V/T)(V/T-1))$. The sum of these two probabilities gives an estimate of the probability the patient made one of the last two visits per week. The probability that the patient with given characteristics is in the last ten is built up in an analogous way.

7. The average person in treatment probably had more insurance coverage than the average person in the income group. It is not known how many people had insurance for private psychiatric care in the United States in 1973. Reed, Myers, and Scheidemandel (1972) report that for 1970, slightly less than 40 percent of the population had some coverage and that the typical policy paid about 50 percent of charges. This suggests that the average person in the United States might have had between 15 and 20 percent of private psychiatrists' charges paid by insurance. Correcting the figures to bring the average coverage in line with this estimate would have very little effect on the results.

8. It is not obvious that simple demand and supply models can be applied to the market for psychotherapy. Many of the qualifications necessary upon recognition of possible provider influence have been discussed already in Chapter 2. Particularly important here is the possibility that therapists do not respond to competition in the standard way, by lowering price, but in order to meet a target income, raise price when they serve fewer patients. This "perverse" reaction would undermine many of the conclusions of this section. For discussion, see Reinhardt (1978).

PUBLIC POLICY

7 FOUNDATIONS FOR POLICY

Analysis of the issues and evidence to this point has not led to an unambiguous answer about the advisability of compulsory insurance for psychotherapy. The issues have been considered singly, and not all considerations point in the same direction. Before charting a course for policy that balances the pluses and minuses in the most beneficial way, it will be useful to summarize the point-by-point analysis. Table 7-1 presents the scorecard.

The key arguments against compulsory insurance for psychotherapy are issues (2), (7), and possibly (3). Moral hazard (issue 2) is an efficiency problem. In the presence of insurance coverage, people increase utilization beyond what they would use if paying full cost. This can lead to waste of services and high total program expenditures. There is strong evidence (primarily that reported in Part II but supported in other work) that demand for psychotherapy is much more responsive to insurance coverage than is demand for general health service. Policy toward financing psychotherapy must give serious attention to controls on moral hazard.

Compulsory financing for psychotherapy may have unfavorable distribution effects between provider and patient (issue 7). A large increase in demand running up a limited inelastic supply will manifest itself primarily in higher prices for service. The issue of patient ignorance and the effectiveness of treatment (issue 3) is the major

Table 7-1.   Issues for National Health Insurance and Psychotherapy.

Issue	Favorable to the Case for National Health Insurance for Psychotherapy?	Quality of Evidence
Efficiency problems in the market for insurance		
1. Adverse selection	Yes	Fair
2. Moral hazard	No	Good
Efficiency problems in the market for psychotherapy		
3. Patient ignorance (effectiveness)	?	Poor
4. Externalities (offset effects)	Yes	Fair to Good
Fairness in the distribution of burden and benefit		
5. Rich and poor	Neutral	Fair
6. Healthy and sick	Yes	Fair
7. Provider and patient	No	Good

wild card in all mental health policy, including financing. It has not been established that patients generally underestimate the effectiveness of treatment (to justify an insurance subsidy for care). Evidence for the simple effectiveness of treatment remains controversial and continues to undergo close scrutiny (Parloff et al. 1978, Office of Technology Assessment 1980). Severe problems in measuring treatment and mental health and the resulting appearance of ineffectiveness in interpreting the clinical research data, means that this important issue must be scored temporarily with a question mark. Decisions about what to pay for and whom to pay must of course be made nevertheless.

A perhaps surprising omission from the above list of opposing arguments is a concern for the distribution of services between rich and poor. There is no good evidence at present to suggest coverage for psychotherapy would be unfavorable for the poor.

Arguments in support of compulsory financing for psychotherapy originate with issues (1), (4), and (6). Adverse selection (issue 1) caused by the inability of private insurers to accurately "experience-rate" their policyholders, is an unambiguous part of the supporting case. The evidence for its importance is sketchy, however, and it is unclear how much weight can be placed on this argument. Sympathy for the sick (issue 6) argues for transferring income to those using psychotherapy.

The most powerful argument for compulsory insurance for psychotherapy has to do with the external or offset effects of psychotherapy (issue 4). It is a major opportunity for public policy to see that those offset effects, primarily on productivity, medical care costs, and other collectively financed social services take place.

Some general conclusions can be set out at this point. Compulsory insurance for psychotherapy, as part of national health insurance or a state mandate, should (1) effectively control moral hazard; (2) promote offset effects; (3) designate qualified providers to encourage efficiency in delivery and to avoid undesirable transfers of income. Each general foundation for policy is discussed in the remainder of this chapter.

CONTROLLING MORAL HAZARD

Controls on moral hazard—the increased utilization due to insurance subsidy—must be effective if compulsory insurance for psychotherapy is to be practical. Controls on moral hazard may take several forms depending to whom the controls are directed and how the controls work. They can be directed at providers or consumers or both and can work through incentives or rules. Table 7-2 is a list of major alternatives with a few summary comments.

Before elaborating upon each of these comments, it is important to make clear that with the probable exception of governmental regulation of treatment, each scheme has something to contribute to effective control of moral hazard. In a system for delivery of mental health services that allows for various organizational forms, the most appropriate and effective means of control should be applied in each case. Discussion of the list of possible controls does not necessitate choosing one form of control to the exclusion of others. In a mixed system of mental health service delivery, a mixed system of controls will be best.

Table 7-2. Controls on Moral Hazard.

Method of Control	Comments
Incentives to the patient through deductibles, coinsurance, or limits	Sure to work but defeat the purpose of insurance
Third-party regulation of form and length of treatment	
1. By government	Not likely to work; to be avoided if possible
2. By private insurers	More workable than governmental system; limited promise for effective control
Peer review	May sometimes be helpful; very limited effectiveness if providers have no incentive to make it work
Making providers or providers' organizations responsible for cost	Promising; seems naturally to call forth peer review and organizational control

Incentives to Patients through Deductibles, Coinsurance, or Limits

One way to eliminate the moral hazard associated with insurance is to take away coverage. This is not a solution to moral hazard, but only a way to avoid the problem entirely. Patients and society do not pay the price of overutilization, but neither do they get the benefits from insurance coverage. A limit to control utilization eliminates insurance protection for those who need it most—those with large expenses. A deductible would discourage "casual" utilization; but if offset effects are taken seriously, discouraging such casual utilization may be counterproductive. Coinsurance succeeds in making patients conscious of costs only by forcing them to pay those costs, the very thing that insurance is designed to avoid. Although restoring the per unit cost to the insured is somewhat self-defeating, if there is no other reliable way for dealing with moral hazard—a way that tries both to restrain excess usage and to maintain financial protection for necessary services—some form of control through deductibles, coinsurance, or limits, may be necessary.

Third-Party Regulation of Form and Length of Treatment

This form of control can be exercised by government and applied to a wide range of plans, or can be exercised by private organizations as conditions for membership in their plans. Both the government and private organizations will have difficulty making such controls work in restraining moral hazard. Given that controls are effective, the major problem would be inflexibility, the unavoidable arbitrariness in any set of treatment rules. A government-run system would be most offensive because its inflexibility would likely be universal. In a private system, patients and providers might have a choice of rules under which they could serve and receive services.

A rule under a system of a third-party regulation might take the form that a patient with a bipolar affective disorder and a moderate degree of impairment, for example, would be entitled to twenty covered visits during a benefit period. This type of rule offends providers and patients. It implies that a formula can relate a simple diagnostic category to the treatment a patient should receive. To the extent such a rule does in fact constrain utilization, it impinges on professional autonomy and may prematurely terminate payment for treatment.

It is sensible to apply a rule or a formula connecting diagnosis and covered service if diagnosis can and will be objectively made, and if an agreed-upon link between objective diagnosis and proper treatment exists. It is not obvious that mental illness and its treatment fulfill any of these conditions. As Reed, Myers, and Scheidemandel point out, mental illness is "illusive," with a "lack of objective manifestations such as X rays and laboratory findings that indicate pathology" (1972: 75). The American Psychiatric Association's latest Diagnostic and Statistical Manual of Mental Disorder (DSM–III) sets forth a recategorization of mental disorders with the hope of at least developing a common terminology for the labeling of problems. With competing theories seeking to explain disorders and disagreements within the profession about what constitutes disease (for example, in the new DSM, smoking tobacco is, and homosexuality is not, a symptom of mental disorder), general agreement on terms may not be possible at this time. And if other professions—with their own models of mental disturbance and treatment—are to provide psychotherapy in any way other than completely subservient to psychiatry, further controversy about labels and the connection between labels and treatment would result. Any set of rules imposed by third parties would be highly imperfect.

An unwanted side effect of such rules, perfect or imperfect in connecting labels to treatment, would be to retard innovation of new treatments for mental disorders. Auster has made his point in the context of the delivery of mental health services: "A particularly unfortunate consequence of efforts to devise appropriate controls is inherent in the very nature of controls—namely their institutionalization of the status quo" (1969: 707). The task panel on cost and financing of the President's Commission on Mental Health (1978) referred to the same problem by noting that the requirements set down by third parties may force application of out-of-date or inappropriate technology.

Experience with governmental regulation of the terms of service or technology in other sectors of the economy makes it almost certain that government regulation would retard innovation and protect those with financial interest in providing the current technology. Providers can put concentrated political pressure on regulators to exclude new competitors or competing technologies. This problem would apply with much less force to a system of controls implemented decentrally by private organizations. If the providers dealing with one organization were successful in convincing that organization to resist innovation, other organizations would still be free to adopt new methods.

One can easily imagine controls on psychotherapy sanctifying the currently predominant form of therapy—individual fifty-minute sessions. Extent of treatment might be defined in these terms. If in the context of such controls a group of psychiatrists discovered, for example, that an intensive pair of marathon sessions was particularly effective in treating bipolar affective disorder, adequate payment for this form of therapy might not be possible under an existing set of rules for coverage. The more innovative the treatment, the less likely it would be eligible for coverage. Technology for treatment of mental illness is highly imperfect. A policy that retards improvement in that technology, such as attempts to control moral hazard by specifying what is and is not eligible for payment, may be in the long term severely counterproductive.

It is not clear, however, that any set of third-party rules, whether instituted by government or private insurers, would be successful in preventing therapists and patients from obtaining payment for the services they wanted performed. There is scope for deception to avoid the restriction in any set of rules. Providers may use their discretion in reporting the diagnosis and seriousness to select, in effect, the form and length of treatment they and their patients desire. Discretion in diagnosis of mental disorder clearly exists and some diagnostic fudging to circumvent insurers' rules has already been discovered. Aetna found that some psychiatrists "will put an insurance acceptable diagnosis on a condition that is not a covered diagnosis" (1976: 9). Green (1969: 684) reports that in the California Kaiser–Permanente Group, when alcoholism became a covered diagnosis for federal employees, it came to light that psychiatrists had mis-labelled a full 5 percent of total patients who were alcoholics in order to provide treatment under other mental diagnoses. Health service providers are accustomed to acting in their own and in their patient's best interests. When controls work against these interests, and when deception is easy, many providers may be expected to use their discretion in diagnosis to the benefit of themselves and their patients and at the expense of the purpose of the controls. From experience in Canada, Evans is pessimistic that a system of outside controls can work to limit utilization in private practice: "The root of the problem is that although fee-for-service creates incentives for unnecessary care, private practice blocks any information channel that would enable a regulatory agency to determine necessity (or even accuracy of the billings" (1974: 480).

Peer Review

Reliance on the good judgment of professionals is unavoidable in any system for the delivery of mental health services. Peer review would rely on the collective good judgment of professionals to restrain moral hazard. Unless peer review works in the interest of individual providers it will encounter some of the same difficulties in application as controls by insurers. Providers will be able to manipulate the peer review formula to obtain the treatment they and their patients want.

Peer review can be prospective, concurrent, or retrospective, occurring before, during, or after the patient's treatment. Prospective review requires screening and has generally been applied only within organized care settings such as prepaid group practices or CMHCs. It seems to have been particularly effective in controlling costs, but it is not clear whether this is due to the screening or to the different incentives providers face in organizations that do screening.

For private practice providers, review must be concurrent or retrospective. Retrospective review, as has been implemented in the Professional Standards Review Organization program, has had only modest effect on utilization. Once treatment is completed, review committees deal harshly with only the most flagrant cases of overuse. In mental health where the acceptable dispersion around the mean for treatment for any particular disorder is probably exceptionally large, retrospective review might be expected to have little effect.

Concurrent review seems to offer more promise. Intervention can be creative, preventing "mistakes" in treatment rather than imposing a censure of unacceptable behavior. The American Psychiatric Association (APA) developed a specific model of concurrent peer review based on such principles (APA 1976). A psychiatrist would be automatically approved to treat a patient for the median number of visits used to treat patients with the given diagnosis in the region. An extension of the same number of visits would then be possible if the psychiatrist submits a form to the peer review committee explaining why the extra visits are necessary. On the APA's suggested form, the explanation for the extra treatment takes up two inches on the page. The committee never sees the patient. Under this system a length of treatment twice the median length would be virtually automatic. Further extensions would be possible upon request. As the APA admits this system of concurrent review is designed to "maintain professional autonomy" (1976: 4) and to promote a "high quality of psychiatric care" (pg. 5). It is not likely to do much to control moral hazard, however.

The median length of treatment in a geographic region is itself sensitive to insurance coverage and is nothing more than the typical behavior of the psychotherapists and patients in the region. If all psychotherapists and their patients exhibit moral hazard to the same degree, no psychotherapists would have their behavior restrained by a peer review system based on these standards. This was the experience in Canada with a similar system (Evans 1974).

A stricter version of peer review can be readily imagined, with lower limits on what is automatically authorized and more stringent requirements for demonstration of need for extensions of treatment. No peer review plan can avoid the fact, however, that peer review works like insurers' controls, against the interests of the individual provider and patient. Private practitioners can be expected to adapt to peer review, to learn how to manipulate reporting requirements to effect their and their patients' desires for treatment.

The California Psychological Health Plan (CHCP) (see Armer 1980) is a demonstration that peer review, despite its shortcomings, can help to restrain utilization. But the CHCP is a special arrangement in several important ways. It is a closed panel plan whereby psychiatrists and psychologists who volunteer to accept patients from the plan commit themselves to peer review after the first five visits. They are thus willing to accept the implicit behavioral norms of the organization, one of which is clearly "no excessive treatment." CHCP works no doubt in part because it is staffed by practitioners who feel comfortable in such a system. Peer review can help to restrain utilization, depending on the interest of the individual providers. In private practice, providers serving patients with traditional third-party coverage have no interest in being restrained and effective peer review would face an uphill battle. It would be reckless to rely on peer review as the exclusive or even general instrument for control of moral hazard.

Making Providers or Providers' Organizations Responsible for Cost

There are reasons to think that when providers or providers' organizations are made responsible for the cost of treatment, including the cost of overutilization associated with moral hazard, moral hazard may be effectively controlled. In private practice, providers are paid more the more they treat. In organizations where providers are employees, providers receive a salary and have no financial incentive to encourage patients to extend treatment. In many such organizations, patients do not pay on a fee-for-service basis but prepay for services, as in premiums to a prepaid group practice. Patients with coverage of this form have no more incentive to restrain utilization than in the fee-for-service private practice system, but providers do face a very different set of incentives. Providers' influence on treatment may offer a significant check on patients utilization.

Working in an organization, managers make individual therapists aware that the CMHC, the HMO, or the firm has limited resources to deal with its commitments to patients. The provider has a responsibility to the organization and to its patients to do a good job at rationing the organization's services. The Group for the Advancement of Psychiatry describes how this works at the Health Insurance Plan of New York, an HMO:

> Therapists are encouraged to be sparing of the time they give to a patient, who has become well enough to function independently. In the HMO there is no economic motivation for the provider to prolong treatment. Moreover, the presence of newly assigned patients waiting for service from the salaried staff exerts pressure to discharge patients as soon as possible. (1975: 538)

And further,

> because the amount of therapy which can be offered is limited by the budget, a feeling is engendered that one subscriber should not utilize therapeutic time indefinitely since this will be at the expense of another, who may need the service just as much.

Another advantage of an organized care setting is that organization is capable of a flexible response to a patient's problem. Organizations are capable of prospective screening, which may involve referring a patient for less elaborate treatment with less highly trained personnel. A provider in private practice has a narrower range of responses to a patient's problems and would lose business by referral.

Mamor (1973: 120) has gone so far as to say that psychiatrists have an obligation to patients to first try direct, less extensive forms of treatment for their mental problems. Mechanic has been a strong advocate of this form of organized care settings and HMOs, stressing the advantages of economical treatment and coordination of service providers: "Capitation plans [such as a prepaid group practice which receives a fixed premium in exchange for treatment] facilitating the provision of a broader range of services at reasonable cost, are potentially able to make use of the entire spectrum of suitable personnel, and forge a close alliance between general medical care and more specialized mental health services" (1978: 485–86). Organizations with

open-ended commitments to provide services as needed to their subscribers, such as prepaid group practices, also have the incentive to
provide preventive care, and to take advantage of offset effects of
mental health services on costs of other forms of care.

A considerable body of evidence has accumulated to support these
arguments in favor of provision of mental health services through
organized care settings where triage or screening is possible and
where providers do not benefit directly from extended treatment.
Prepaid group practices have demonstrated that they control moral
hazard and provide mental health service to their subscriber populations at reasonable cost. Reports of utilization experience at
Kaiser–Permanente (Green 1969), HIP (GAP 1975), the Group
Health Cooperative of Puget Sound (Spoeri 1974), and other organizations show that large populations can be offered services with a
relatively modest commitment of personnel, apparently much less
than would be required to cover the same population if services were
to be provided in private practice (Reed, Myers, and Scheidemandel
1972, GAP 1975, NIMH 1976).

Organized care settings have their drawbacks. The incentive not to
treat patients may work too well. It has been pointed out by Sloan
(1971) and others that in CMHCs providers spend a high fraction of
their work time in conference talking about providing for patients
rather than actually providing. No doubt some such discussion is useful and even essential if screening or rationing is to be conducted, but
conferences, referrals, and meetings consume resources just as treatment does. The system of incentives not to treat patients probably
influences cost comparisons of private practice versus organized care
settings. Organized care settings cost more to serve a patient per visit,
but because fewer services are provided per patient, cost is less per
episode of illness (Sharfstein, Taube, and Goldberg 1975). Sloan
(1971) believes that the incentive not to treat in CMHCs has so distorted provider behavior that it would be appropriate to restore some
of the incentive in the fee-for-service system by paying providers
partially on the basis of the quantity of services delivered.

Needed: A Mixed System

One clear conclusion from this review of ways to deal with moral
hazard is that no one way is *the* way. Each has its contribution to

make; each will be the preferred system for a subset of providers and citizens. One will offer more flexibility for exercise of professional autonomy but on balance will be more expensive. One will offer the patient a wider choice of providers but only at a cost greater than that of another system with less choice. *It is not necessary to pick one system.*

The main conclusion from this discussion is that a plan for financing psychotherapy should not discriminate against forms of control of moral hazard but should allow each its fair opportunity to work on behalf of the citizen and patient. It seems reasonable to suspect that each system would perform better in *competition* with other systems. Private psychiatrists are much more likely to submit to peer review if a significant proportion of their colleagues have signed with a closed panel plan or if there are viable HMO options for patients in the region. Providers within CMHCs will feel pressure to provide more services for subscriber's dollars if there are competing organizations that have been successful at dealing with moral hazard.

PROMOTING OFFSET EFFECTS

Over the past few years there has emerged a body of evidence that spending money for psychotherapy can save money elsewhere, in reduced productivity losses due to illness and absenteeism, medical costs, and other social costs. Most of the literature on offset effects suffers from a series of defects in research design, including small sample size, inadequate controls or insufficient identification of therapeutic intervention. The most convincing piece of evidence is the wide and growing acceptance in private industry that it is worthwhile to invest in providing mental health services to employees. Private firms are in a position to recoup some of the savings from psychotherapy in increased productivity or reduced medical benefits. That many firms believe this to be happening, whether researchers have "proved" it yet or not, is extremely significant. By 1977, there were over 1,200 programs in industry dealing with drug and alcohol abuse alone. (The role of private industry in providing mental health services to its employees is reviewed in a series of papers in Egdahl and Walsh (ed) 1980.)

When deriving the implications of offset effects for NHI policy, it is important to keep in mind the settings in which offset effects have been demonstrated. Jones and Vischi (1979) have recently reviewed twenty-five offset studies for the Alcohol, Drug Abuse and Mental Health Administration (ADAMHA). The settings of all studies in the United States were HMOs, health centers, CMHCs, or private firms. (The one foreign study was Duehrssen's of long-term psychotherapy in West Germany following World War II.) None of these studies was concerned with providers in private practice.

It is not clear that services provided by psychotherapists in private practice have the same offset effects of psychotherapy provided in the so-called controlled settings. If psychotherapy were a relatively homogenous service, it would be reasonable to generalize from what goes on in a controlled setting to what goes on in private practice. But as stated earlier, providers of psychotherapy in most controlled settings face a very different incentive structure than do therapists in private practice. The offset effects of services in private practice may be of a different type and magnitude from those discovered in settings in which the orientation of the therapist and the incentives facing the therapists are far removed from those characterizing therapists in private practice.

The point is, to promote offset effects private practice should not be treated more favorably than other settings under financing policies. In what is probably regarded to be the standard form of national health insurance, for example, coverage would automatically include services of psychiatrists (and possibly others) provided in private practice. This would be financed by compulsory taxation, perhaps a combination of payroll and income taxes. A narrow definition of qualified provider in national health insurance would undermine the incentive of private groups to continue the programs for which offset effects have been demonstrated.

Consider a firm that has an employee assistance program (EAP) for those troubled with mental problems or substance abuse. Suppose the firm has been contracting with a group of psychiatrists and psychologists to counsel employees through self-referral and referral of managers at the firm. Employees are entitled to twenty visits per year. From the employees' point of view this is a mental health benefit; from the firm's point of view this might be a worthwhile investment. Suppose the EAP pays off in that coverage costs the firm $5 per employee per year, but productivity is increased on average by $10 per employee per year. Now suppose national health insurance mandates benefits of the same twenty visits per year provided by psychiatrists and psychologists in private practice. Businesses run for profit, such as the firm in question, are ineligible to receive payment under national health insurance. The employees and employer are forced to pay for this coverage through taxes. The firm now faces the question of whether to continue its EAP given that it and its employees must in any case pay for coverage provided by independent practitioners. The firm may decide not to continue its EAP even if it were a more efficient way to deliver mental health services to its employees.

To further illustrate, suppose all the offset effects of psychotherapy appear early in treatment, so that services provided in private practice yield the same offset to the firm of an average of $10 per employee. But because of the different incentives facing private practitioners, the average treatment for employees treated in private practice is longer and costs the firm and its employees, through taxes, an average of $8 per employee. The firm, the employees, and society lose by the imposition of compulsory national health insurance for private psychiatry. Since the firm would get no additional benefits from spending anything on an employee assistance program, the incentives to set up the efficient means of service are eliminated.

An analogy can be made between educational and mental health services to illustrate this point again. Suppose studies of the effects of education in the home found that the time parents spend educating their children is a significant help to children's learning. Suppose on the basis of these studies it was decided that everyone should have education and a system of compulsory public education was set up to provide services by professional teachers in public schools. Even if the net benefit to children and families is higher when education is provided in the home, parents lose the incentive to bear the cost of their children's education because once the compulsory taxes are collected to pay for the public schools, parents regard it as free.

Since the tax cost of one alternative is unavoidable, firms contemplating EAPs or parents contemplating educating their own children must compare the *gross* benefits of the public alternative with the *net* benefits of the private alternative. This skews the terms of comparison and leads to inefficient choices of setting and treatment. The firm might choose the public alternative even if the net benefits of the public alternative are less than the net benefits of the private alternative. In short, the firm might choose the less efficient of two alternatives.

Thus compulsory insurance for psychotherapy covering only qualified, independent practitioners, can undermine the very programs that demonstrated offset effects. EAPs would be less worthwhile for firms than before. Programs like the California Psychological Health Plan, which exist because they can return to employers and employees reduced costs in the form of lower premiums, would lose their attractiveness. With employers' and workers' payments fixed by the tax code, there would be no incentive to restrain one's own utilization.

It would be terribly ironic if the existence of offset effects were the major argument in favor of compulsory insurance for psychotherapy and the resulting insurance program created incentives to destroy those for which offset effects have been demonstrated. Insurance for psychotherapy should be designed so as not to undermine the incentives private groups have to establish efficient mental health service programs. Ideally, the financing plan should not discriminate against service provided in such settings but should give private individuals and organizations the opportunity to compare the net benefits of services provided in different settings.

WHAT TO PAY FOR, WHOM TO PAY

Policy on national health insurance and psychotherapy will be on uncertain ground until issues of efficacy of treatment are satisfactorily resolved. Choices must be made in the absence of complete knowledge, and policy on what to pay for and whom to pay must take the form of balancing risks. Generous definitions of coverage for various procedures, professionals, and organizations carries the risk of paying for treatment not worth the cost. On the other hand a narrow definition of eligible services and providers may exclude some effective and less expensive therapy and may stifle improvements in mental health services.

One approach to this problem of balancing risks and related issues in the financing of psychotherapy is associated with the staff of the Senate Finance Committee. The approach is to pay only for psychotherapies that have been demonstrated to be safe and effective under "generally accepted principles of scientific research." Although it may sound reasonable to pay only for psychotherapies "proven" to be effective, it reflects a misunderstanding of the nature of scientific evidence to use "demonstrated effectiveness to generally accepted principles of scientific research" as the criteria for funding. These criteria are by nature conservative and they do not leave room for the possibility that unproven psychotherapy may be effective. To require proof beyond a reasonable scientific doubt is not a reasonable rule for individual or public decisions with regard to funding psychotherapy. Paying for something that is ineffective is only one of the mistakes government can make. Missing an opportunity is another. Exclusive emphasis on avoiding payment for ineffective psychotherapy, given the current state of clinical knowledge and research, would be a grave and harmful mistake itself.

A similar perspective should be applied to the question of whom to pay for services. Again, risks should be intelligently balanced. The risk of a permissive regulatory strategy is that patients will be improperly treated by incompetent practitioners or deprived of practitioners and settings that can truly help them. On the other hand, the risk of a restrictive regulatory strategy is the loss of the benefits of competition: more available services, lower costs, and probably most importantly, encouragement of diverse approaches to care for mental disorders and progress in treatment.

It is probably true that in general medicine innovation is stifled to some degree by channeling all research and treatment through physicians. Most people think this is sensible on the judgment that what innovation might be gained would probably not be worth the inappropriate treatment for people that would inevitably result from making standards for practice of medicine more permissive.

The weighting of risks comes out differently in mental health. It appears that there is less to lose in terms of inappropriate treatment with present technology by expanding the license of alternative providers. It also appears from performance in the past few years of psychologists, social workers, and others that there is more to gain by creating a research and service climate that permits development of numerous models for treatment of mental problems.

Progress in treatment for mental disorders is coming from a number of areas. Out of the research laboratories come advances in drug therapy and in behavioral psychotherapy. Increasing application of evaluation techniques in treatment settings generates a large body of common experience the professions and social scientists are using to help assess the contribution of alternative approaches. Many of the success stories of the mental health system, such as halfway houses or the integration of mental health services with work settings in EAPs, were conceived and are directed by nonmedical professionals. It is not necessary to be critical of any profession's model of care to recognize that a sufficiently advanced understanding of mental health has not been attained to rule out many models and to select a dominant one to which all our resources for care should be committed.

In this chapter some general principles for policy have been developed. The goal has been to describe a structure of financing to encourage effective, efficient and innovative supply of psychotherapy. The next chapter translates these general principles into concrete proposals for policy.

8 FINANCING PSYCHOTHERAPY

For some time, discussion of financing health services has centered around debate about national health insurance. This final chapter begins with a specific proposal for including coverage for psychotherapy within a NHI plan. The essential features of the proposal are a minimum benefit package, financing through tax credits, and coverage for a broad range of providers. It will be argued that this proposal is in close accord with the foundations for policy discussed in the last chapter.

It seems likely in the short term that compulsory insurance for psychotherapy will more often be the result of state rather than federal policy. State mandates for mental health coverage in health insurance policies are the counterpart at the state level to national health insurance. Both are forms of compulsory insurance. Discussion of the proposal for national health insurance indicates how it would need to be changed for implementation as a state mandate.

A PROPOSAL FOR PSYCHOTHERAPY WITHIN NATIONAL HEALTH INSURANCE

Benefits

A minimum benefit package should be compulsory to compensate for adverse selection and to encourage offset effects of psychotherapy. Compulsory benefits should be strictly limited to contain cost. An example would be coverage for $1,000 of psychotherapeutic services. Copayment on the first five visits should be low, no more than $10, for example. Everyone would be forced to enroll in a plan that offered at least this much coverage; people may choose to buy more. However, it is compulsory to have and pay for some coverage under national health insurance. As will be clear as the rest of the proposal is described, it is not necessary or desirable to put the government in the role of the insurance carrier or provider of care. Coverage for psychotherapy would need to be coordinated with coverage for other mental health services, particularly inpatient care, and general health services.

Financing

The method of financing should ensure fair distribution of the burden of paying for compulsory coverage, and in choice of plans, give consumers the incentive to take account of the cost of care. These two goals are accomplished by a tax credit scheme in which the bulk of the cost is paid out of general tax revenues (distributing the burden roughly in proportion to income), but the "marginal" dollar spent in weighing quality versus cost is almost entirely paid directly by the consumer.[1]

Each citizen would face a choice of many plans offering the minimum benefit package for a premium price. Some plans, for an increased premium, would offer more coverage than the minimum benefit package. Consumers would pay the premium to the plan they select for themselves and their families from their personal income. Employers could include partial payment for premiums to qualified plans as a fringe benefit, but under this proposal employer contributions to premiums would be counted as income and taxable. Thus there would be no incentive for the employer not to increase salary rather than provide this fringe benefit. Tax credits would largely offset consumers' premium costs. Consumers would receive a tax credit of 25 percent of the cost of the average minimum benefit package in their state for joining any mental health plan at all. For each dollar spent on premiums, consumers would receive a full $1 tax credit up to 50 percent of the cost of the average minimum benefit package in the state. Premiums paid after this level would be a credit against income tax at 25 percent of each dollar in premium.

Consider how this tax credit scheme would work for a typical consumer. Suppose for the previous year the average cost of the minimum benefit package in the state was $50 for a family of four. (For the first year of the program the cost would have to be estimated.) Suppose the family chooses an average plan that charges a premium of $50 for the minimum benefit package. The family gets an immediate tax credit of $12.50 (25 percent of $50) for joining the plan. A tax credit of $25 (100 percent of one-half of $50) is available for premiums up to one-half the cost of the average minimum benefit package in the state. The remainder of the premiums, $25, generate a $6.25 tax credit at the rate of 25 percent per dollar. Total tax credits are $43.75. Even though the family is paying 75 percent of the *marginal* dollar in premiums and thus has a strong incentive to choose an efficient plan, the family has seven-eighths of the cost of the premiums paid for by tax credits. An inexpensive plan is better than free to the family. A plan costing $35 per year, for example, would generate $40 in tax credits. It would be irrational for consumers not to choose some plan. Since tax credits bear the large bulk of the total premium cost, the financing for this program would be borne largely through the federal tax system distributing the burden roughly in proportion to income. It is virtually certain that compulsory insurance for psychotherapy in this form would be especially beneficial to lower income groups.

For individuals not paying taxes, the tax credit would be refundable, thereby retaining all of the incentives for choice of a plan, ideally an efficient one. Alternately the government could supply nontaxpayers with vouchers for purchase of a plan for delivery of mental health services.

Qualified Providers

A broad range of qualified providers and providing organizations creates competition for serving clients. This competition would pressure suppliers to provide services effectively and economically and to improve the quality of care. Psychiatrists and psychologists in private practice; medical organizations such as prepaid group practices and IPAs, CMHCs, and other mental health clinics; and nonmedical organizations such as departments of firms would all be eligible to receive payment for psychotherapy under the proposal. Some qualified organizations would supply insurance coverage to patients directly along with services, as do prepaid groups, IPAs, or EAPs. Mental health clinics and CMHCs would be expected to offer this prepayment service to some of their clients. Individual providers in private practice could conceivably, through prepayment plans, insure patients and bear the financial risk of patients, but it is more likely that most private providers would wish to work on a fee-for-service bases and rely on third parties such as insurance companies to bear risk.

A state board would be charged with licensing all providers. Physicians could provide psychotherapy in all states. Psychologists are certified as licensed to provide psychotherapy in all states. Twenty-nine states and the District of Columbia, including 80 percent of the U.S. population have put psychologists on equal footing with physicians in providing psychotherapy, allowing qualified psychologists to bill third-party payers independently of a physician. This predominant regulatory stance should be made part of national health insurance for psychotherapy. Physicians and qualified psychologists should be eligible for independent payment for psychotherapy. Other professionals would work under the supervision of a physician or a psychologist.

Including only physicians and psychologists as independent providers qualified under national health insurance may be too narrow a definition. Psychiatric social workers and nurses, in particular, have claim to acceptance, although these professions are not generally licensed or certified to provide psychotherapy independently of physicians. As the definition of independent provider becomes looser, the issue of professional quality control becomes more worrisome. At this time it is prudent to take the first step of including psychologists as independent providers.

It is clear that a good deal would be lost by excluding or severely restricting the practice of psychologists under national health insurance. For the development of innovative forms of mental health delivery, it is essential that there be adequate supply of qualified mental health professionals capable of taking a leadership role in a variety of organizations, professionals without rigid preconceptions of the institutions within which mental health services are properly delivered. Psychiatrists alone would be too few and too inflexible. After the increase in demand, under a NHI plan, any psychiatrist would be able to make a very good living based on independent private practice; there would be little pressure to innovate. To give further encouragement to forms of mental health delivery that have recently shown great promise—prepaid groups, EAPs, CMHCs, and others—it is necessary to include psychologists as independent providers.

Licensed organizations could be nonprofit or profit-making enterprises. Licensing psychiatrists, psychologists, IPAs, prepaid groups, and CMHCs would pose no new problems for such a board. The new problem would be licensing nonmedical organizations, particularly EAPs. This is an important detail that needs to be worked out. It is obviously necessary to require these and other organizations to offer services at a minimum level of availability and quality; it is also important not to require them to meet standards or provide services not required of other forms of delivery. For example, it would be a mistake to require that all EAPs offer weekend service (as some now do) if such a requirement is not a part of all qualified mental health plans. Doing so would put EAPs at a competitive disadvantage in relation to unburdened alternatives. To meet additional licensing criteria, the EAP should be under professional supervision of a psychiatrist or a psychologist and should meet the minimum benefit package with facilities judged adequate for the population served.

A concern about EAPs is that they would be a management tool rather than a service organization oriented to the interests of the workers. Many of these plans exist because EAPs *are* in part a management tool. The fear is that management might use an EAP to punish or control workers. Problems in the social organization of the workplace, from excessive stress to unrelieved repetitive job tasks, might be redefined as personal problems of workers through the use of such a program. Workers having difficulty in the organization might be labeled "maladjusted."

The most effective check against this possible abuse of mental health services would be workers' option to reject the EAP offered by management. Currently, many EAPs are the only mental health benefit available to employees. In this monopoly where providers are hired by management and not chosen by workers, programs are most open to possible misuse by management. Under the proposal here the EAP would simply be one of the options available to workers. EAPs would be subject to the same competitive pressure for good performance as would other providers under this proposal. If they were truly potentially effective organizations, firms would have the incentive to set them up in a manner acceptable to employees. Any system with a locked-in clientele is subject to mismanagement in many forms. This is true when the monopoly is held by a firm, a government, or a provider-dominated group. Consumers' alternatives are the most effective check against abuse of this kind.

Eligibility of EAPs in a NHI plan would be a marked departure from existing health policy. EAPs would be, of course, a small part of a larger, for-profit business. Eligibility for third-party payment under health insurance has up to now been granted only to organizations exclusively devoted to health care, ensuring professional control of treatment. Most of these organizations are non-profit, further deleting the power of any organizational goal unrelated to health. While I believe EAPs should be eligible for direct payment, there are other ways to structure the financing plan to encourage firms to set up EAPs when these are an efficient way to provide psychotherapeutic services to workers, without making EAPs eligible for direct payment.

The key is that the firm must be in a position to reap the benefits of an EAP. One way for this to happen is for the EAP to be eligible for direct payment under the NHI plan. Any savings produced by the EAP would be shared by the firm in increased productivity, and by the workers in better services and lower premiums. Benefiting the workers ultimately benefits the firm by making employment more attractive. If the EAP is not eligible for direct payment, experience-rating by the insurance carrier will tend to return benefits of the EAP to the workers and firm. The firm would still reap productivity gains and the workers enjoy lower premiums, since many problems would have been taken care of effectively by the EAP, and workers at the firm could be covered by insurance at low cost. The disadvantage to this is that by disqualifying EAPs, employees may not choose the EAP as their exclusive provider. Elimination of this choice makes reliance on experience-rating the less preferred alternative.

One advantage of the proposal here is that it would allow all existing institutions currently involved in the supply of insurance or delivery of mental health services to continue to operate. There would be minimal disruption in the supply of services. After a time, a citizen would, it is hoped, be faced with a rich variety of choices or organizations qualified to provide mental health services. Choice would accommodate the various tastes of consumers and producers of care and serve to police the behavior of all organizations. Blue Cross and Blue Shield and private insurance companies would offer insurance coverage similar to that offered today, third-party coverage for services provided by psychiatrists and psychologists. Insurers would offer a minimum benefit package and might differ in the range of optional services covered. Insurance companies would also differ in the means and strenuousness with which they review claims, with the more cost-conscious companies able to offer their policies at a lower premium. The local prepaid group practice(s) would offer a comprehensive plan covering mental and regular health benefits, and possibly a separate contract for just mental health services. If the prepaid group found it worthwhile to encourage those enrolled for regular medical services to enroll also for mental health services, the prepaid group could offer mental health coverage at a favorable price relative to alternatives. The local CMHC and IPA would offer contracts to provide covered services. More than one of these organizations might offer differentiated products to consumers, a pair of IPAs with more or less strict peer review for instance. The firm or union of an employee might set up its own EAP offering services in the workplace. Combinations of organizations are easy to imagine: an IPA that reinsures with a private insurance company, a firm that contracts with a CMHC to supply services to its employees, private practitioners affiliated with CMHCs, and so on.[2]

In an annual marketing season each plan would send out information on its services and premiums; in an open season citizens would be free to join the plan of their choice. To ensure accurate comparable information, descriptions of the plans might be prepared and distributed by the state licensing body.

DISCUSSION

Dealing with Adverse Selection

Everyone would buy the minimum benefit package. This requirement attempts to control adverse selection, but it might not be enough to ensure that everyone receives effective coverage for a minimum level of services: organizations would have an incentive to compete for the best risks in the population by offering services in name only for the smallest premium possible. The screening device before care is provided might be so fine that there is no effective coverage. Joining such a plan would be equivalent to dropping out of the insurance pool altogether, reintroducing the problem of adverse selection. Plans that offer meaningful coverage would draw an adverse selection of the risk pool and be at a competitive disadvantage.

The proposal's solution is to limit the domain of price competition to prices exceeding one-half of the average cost of the minimum benefit package in the state. Under the tax credit scheme that meets one's contribution dollar for dollar up to one-half the cost of the average minimum benefit package, there would be no incentive to offer a plan costing less. Plans offering policies for this minimum price would compete on the basis of service rather than price. The danger from adverse selection can thereby be controlled. A continued subsidy of 25 percent of premiums beyond one-half the average cost of the minimum benefit package would also work against the problem of adverse selection.

A New Role for CMHCs

Under the proposal Community Mental Health Centers would be brought into more direct competition with other parts of the mental health service delivery system. CMHCs could offer contracts for purchase by individuals or serve as the mental health component of another plan's health insurance package. As governmentally sponsored institutions, CMHCs could become the Tennessee Valley Authority of the mental health industry. It would be important that CMHCs not be given a perpetual unfair advantage through access to governmental subsidy. CHMCs were originally intended to wean themselves eventually from the federal government, and the proposal set out here, generating a demand for outpatient services and opening up individuals' choice of how they are to receive services, might be an incentive for the change. The advantage of a CMHC is a relatively low-cost treatment. In a system of financing where the individual has everything paid for with little regard to cost, a system offering services at lower cost is unattractive. But when consumers pay the marginal dollar of premium cost, an efficient CMHC service will be recognized and appreciated by the public, as reflected in their choices for setting for care.

One purpose of the CMHC program is to ensure services in underserved, largely poor areas. By putting purchasing power in the hands of the poor, CMHCs may do well financially under this proposal. If this does nöt happen, a case may still be made in favor of continuing special subsidy to CMHCs or other organizations to locate and service especially needy areas.

Confidentiality of Patient's Record

An important concern for any system of mental health services is the confidentiality of the patients' records. The proposal here offers two important advantages. First, records are not centralized into one data bank, so outsiders would not have convenient access to records. The purpose of record keeping is control. Because there is no central control in this proposal and because cost control and organizational standards are set decentrally by individual plans, a centralized system of records is not necessary. Certain area and national data would be useful for analyzing the working of the system, but these could be provided in aggregate or anonymous form to avoid breaches of confidentiality.

The second major advantage is that there would be no pressure in many organizations to "label" the patient. When a third party is the insurer, as in the conventional relationship between providers in private practice and insurance companies, there would probably be a need for the insurer to receive a "diagnosis" of the patient.[3] In organizations like CMHCs, prepaid groups, EAPs, and others that use an informal system of cost control relying on the incentives of the individual providers, the very existence of a label would not be as necessary. A possibly embarrassing record might not even exist. Some service organizations may even decide to market themselves stressing this "nonjudgmental" aspect of their services. These organizations may suffer in cost control but extra safeguards on confidentiality may appeal to a significant segment of the population.

Flexibility and Innovation

The need for a flexible and potentially innovative system for mental health delivery is repeatedly stressed in policy discussions by authors from many different backgrounds. Mechanic wrote,

> The risk we face with the new opportunity for extending psychiatric benefits under NHI is that a poorly designed scheme may help to fix in place some of the weakest features of our existing mental health delivery system (1978: 483–84).

Berwick and Zeckhauser wrote,

> Flexibility is an important feature of a mental health treatment system. One should be willing to sacrifice some efficiency in today's system in return for the assurance that the system will more easily adapt to tomorrow's possible pattern of demand (1975: 12–13).

and the Group for the Advancement of Psychiatry stated,

> Providers with different approaches [should be] allowed to operate in suitable delivery contexts without being forced to conform by financial or other constraints, to one inflexible model (1975: 633).

The proposal should receive high marks for encouraging flexibility and innovation. In national health insurance and other insurance plans that simply pay for "whatever the doctor orders," there is no incentive for cost control and, possibly worse, there is no incentive to introduce cost-saving technology. Under the proposal presented in this book, saving would benefit providing organizations and, as passed on in lower premiums, patients as well. The proposal would retain the full incentive for organizations to introduce better, more efficient ways to provide mental health services.

The technology of treatment of mental disorders is primitive. Mental illness is too serious a problem to forego improvements in the methods of treatment. Avenues to improvement should be kept open by encouraging diverse approaches to treatment. Government should not be obsessed with waste and legislate an exclusive list of technologies that would be supported. The NHI plan should structure the service environment to encourage effective, low-cost treatment, and let the system run itself through the decisions of providers and users. Stultifying, heavy-handed government regulation of the method of treatment must be avoided.

Psychotherapy and the Rest of the Mental Health and Health Systems

Extensive coverage for inpatient mental health services is part of almost every NHI proposal. The major financial risk of mental illness, as with physical illness, is the need for extended hospitalization. This should receive coverage under any NHI plan. Since a convincing argument for coverage of psychotherapy is to promote use of these services—where appropriate, to substitute for more expensive inpatient care—it is sensible to have providers make the initial decision for hospitalization. These providers recognize and have the incentive to act on trade-offs in costs and services in the patient's and society's best interests. The provider's plan should bear part of the cost of hospitalization to make sure the costs as well as the benefits of alternatives would be taken into account.

Although it is important to have mental health service providers make choices between inpatient and outpatient services, with attention to both quality of care and cost, it does not make sense for these individual plans to bear the full financial risk of treatment for the severely mentally ill—those with serious and chronic illness needing regular and long-term care. Seriously ill patients should be cared for in public facilities and in private facilities under contract with the government. Therefore, the mental health benefit package should include limited coverage, for example, for thirty days per year, 120 days lifetime of inpatient coverage, with coverage after these limits assumed by the government. The cost of coverage for the very sick would not be reflected in premiums to enrollees, but would appear on government budgets.

Most mental health plans would probably be too small to offer their own inpatient services, even of a limited amount, and would have to reinsure through an insurance company or other organization. An independent professional association might contract with Blue Cross, for example, to pay for inpatient mental health benefits for its enrollees. Providers in the independent professional association would retain the decision to hospitalize, but would not want to overuse inpatient services since Blue Cross would be free to experience-rate its customers. Other small mental health plans, primarily oriented to outpatient services, would enter into similar relationships. Large plans, such as prepaid group practices or community mental health centers, with some of their own inpatient services, would be in a position to offer at least short-term hospitalization directly. Independent professional associations, EAPs, and other small mental health groups could associate with a community mental health center or a mental hospital directly and avoid third-party reinsurance. This would make economies of direct service provision available to many forms of mental health plans.

The present proposal for psychotherapy in national health insurance is intended to serve people with acute mental problems. The chronically mentally ill, who require long-term care and supervision and who have difficulty holding a job and performing other everyday tasks, have problems that need to be addressed outside of the proposal for including psychotherapy in national health insurance. There are good arguments to be made in favor of giving even this difficult population meaningful choices about settings for care and living and other arrangements. Creation of a diverse structure of supply of mental health services, as envisioned in this proposal, would work toward that end. The usual notions of insurance are not applicable to this group.

The general health sector and the specialized mental health sector are related to one another in important ways: Effective treatment for physical illness can save on mental health treatment costs; effective treatment for mental illness can save on physical treatment costs. General health personnel can often provide services—drugs and rudimentary psychotherapy—practiced by specialized mental health providers.

The central fact about this interrelationship is that the best division of labor between the general and specialized medical health sectors in screening and treating mental disorder is not known. On one hand is the argument that generalists are the best all-around initial contacts for the health system, and should be encouraged to deal directly with all the "easy" health problems, including mental health problems. Under this argument the capability of generalists should be upgraded by helping them to recognize and to treat mental disorder. The increasing effectiveness of drug therapy strengthens this argument for the role for the generalist.

On the other hand is the argument that it is important to place patients with mental problems immediately into contact with a mental health specialist by making these personnel part of the early screening process or by quick referral by generalists. The argument to support this is similar to that justifying any specialized intervention, that generalists cannot be expected to treat special problems with the effectiveness of a specialist.

It would be inappropriate for public policy to force or even to encourage one division of labor in preference to another, since so little is known about their relative merits. A flexible approach would appear best. In plans such as the prepaid group practices, providing both physical and mental health services, uncomplicated psychotherapy and drug therapy might be handled by general medical personnel, with referrals needed only for serious problems. Other comprehensive plans might structure their practices differently, with more routine referrals to mental health personnel. It should also be permissible for mental health providers to offer services directly without forcing patients through a medical screening. An EAP or a community mental health center would offer this.

It is not obvious whether mental health services should stand alone or are better integrated with medical services or with work, education, or other settings. The proposal outlined here would allow for diverse approaches to integration and organization, with efficiency and advantages, as they emerge, conferring a competitive advantage on their respective organizations. It would be a mistake to force through a rigid policy on the organization of the delivery of mental health services in relation to general health services and other social activities.

In the proposal here, mental health coverage is potentially separate from other health coverage under national health insurance. This is important to provide scope for nonmedical organizations and providers, such as EAPs, to be chosen in conjunction with more conventional general health providers.

Separate plans for health and mental health insurance coverage could be awkward and expensive to administer, and could be confusing to consumers. These difficulties could be diminished considerably if coverage for mental health were offered as a subcontract to the general health coverage chosen by an employee. For example, if an individual chooses health insurance through an Independent Professional Association (IPA) of physicians, the individual might then have choice in the contract of receiving psychotherapy by members of the IPA, at a CMHC, or with the IPA in conjunction with the EAP at the workplace. Subcontracting is attractive both for its administrative simplicity and for its ability to take into account interactions among consumers' choices. Coverage for psychotherapy with an EAP might impose different additional costs on a total health insurance package, depending on the terms of the other coverage. Subcontracts can be priced to reflect cost given choice of the general plan.

It is clear that this proposal fits in best with a health insurance system in which consumers have meaningful choice of many aspects of their health insurance coverage and an incentive to choose an economical plan. This approach to health insurance coverage is best exemplified by proposals by Entoven (1978) and McClure (1978). The proposal for psychotherapy does not, however, require a philosophically compatible plan for general health care financing. State mandates, discussed below, represent a partial approach to financing psychotherapy.

Cost Control and Cost

An overriding concern about including psychotherapy in national health insurance is cost. The fear is that subsidizing demand for psychotherapy would lead to large increases in utilization. The demand for psychotherapy is not unlimited. Research on insurance and utilization indicates that the demand for psychotherapy is, however, more responsive to insurance coverage than the demand for other outpatient medical services. Vigorous cost controls on the use of psychotherapy appear prudent.

Costs are controlled in two ways in this proposal. The first is by the yearly limit of $1,000. Although the justification for this restriction is primarily one of cost control, another effect would be to reorient treatment away from intensive services for a few toward less intensive service for more. This would have favorable distributional impacts. Evidence on effectiveness is strongest in support of the effectiveness of the first few visits. Evidence for the effectiveness of long-term therapy is especially tenuous.

The other method to control costs is to enlist private incentives for cost control. An NHI plan should not discriminate against forms of cost control but should allow each its fair opportunity to work on behalf of the taxpayer and the patient. It seems reasonable to suspect that each system would perform better if it were in competition with other systems. Private psychotherapists are more likely to be willing to submit to peer review if a significant proportion of their colleagues have signed with a closed-panel plan or there are viable HMO options for patients in the region. Providers within community mental health centers will feel pressure to provide more services for the subscriber's dollar if there are competing organizations that have been successful in dealing with cost control.

The cost of providing psychotherapy in a minimum benefit package of $1,000 of services per year would be quite modest, probably between $5 and $10 per person per year. (See pp. 56–59 in Chapter 3.) Precise estimates of costs are impossible because it is not known to what extent consumers would prefer more cost-conscious mental health plans, such as EAPs or prepaid group practices, to plans involving private practitioners that would be appealing on grounds other than cost.

Third-party coverage for psychiatrists and psychologists in private practice would likely be the most expensive choice for the minimum benefit package. But even this option would appear to cost less than $10 per enrollee in 1979, based on the behavior of federal employees in the Blue Cross/Blue Shield high-option plan.[4] Other mental health benefit plans would offer the minimum benefit package at a much lower cost, possibly as much as 50 percent less. Use of these cost estimates presumes the existence of significant consumer choice and adequate supply of services. Restricting qualified providers and settings could severely disturb these modest cost estimates. If demand were channeled by restriction into a limited supply, only psychiatrists, for example, cost per unit of coverage and cost per person covered could go up dramatically. Addition of required coverage for inpatient mental health services would add to the yearly cost of mental health services. Experience with federal employees and others suggests it might double the yearly cost for the working population. But this portion of mental health care costs would be paid automatically under virtually all national health insurance plans.

The cost of providing the minimum benefit package to all Americans should therefore be less than $2 billion per year. The estimates presented here for the cost of psychotherapy do not represent added costs since much of the $2 billion would be offset by savings in other governmental programs (such as CMHCs and Medicaid), elimination of the tax deductibility of employer contribution to mental health insurance premiums, and reductions in personal expenditures for insurance and services for mental health. Many people now buying extensive coverage for mental health services might, with the new options available, buy less in joining one of the new plans. This reduction in insurance coverage for some plus the added competition in supply of services might actually reduce the total cost of psychotherapy.

State Mandates for Psychotherapy

Ten states have mandated coverage for psychotherapy for residents of the state covered by health insurance GLS (1979). In some ways these mandates are in close accord with the policies recommended here. They require a minimum benefit package (usually $500) and expand eligibility to direct payment to include psychologists in private practice, and in some cases, qualified mental health clinics (one state, Minnesota, reserves eligibility for psychiatrists). In this way they deal effectively with adverse selection and may promote offset effects of psychotherapy.

In some other ways state mandates are not ideal. There is little incentive for a consumer to choose the most efficient locus for care. A mandate requires all insurers in a state to add or amend benefits. Some insurers, such as a prepaid group practice, may have been able to add the required benefit at less cost than a conventional insurance plan. Consumers will then have some chance to choose coverage on the basis of cost, but the choice between plans may be dominated by other factors. Moreover, employees who pay a small portion of their health insurance costs have little incentive to economize in any case.

CONCLUDING REMARKS

The application of the market failure framework reveals opportunities for governmental intervention to improve psychotherapy markets' allocation. Economic theory, including analysis of adverse selection and other market failures, has been used to suggest reasons why collective, compulsory action to insure psychotherapy might be appropriate. Opportunities for improvement may include risks of mistakes or costs that could be imposed by governmental activity. Drawing on empirical research into the private practice of psychiatry and on the work of others, this book has assessed the importance of each of the opportunities and risks. A policy has been proposed that attempts to exploit the opportunities while avoiding the major risks. Efficiency and equity considerations led to a recommendation of a pluralistic, flexible system with a specified minimum benefit package but with considerable choice offered to consumers in the form of supply. In addition, the proposal purposely allowed for nonmedical organizations, such as EAPs, to offer mental health services. This would be an innovative step in health policy.

This proposal would give consumers choice of coverage for psychotherapy from among a wide variety of organizational options, thereby enlisting competition in the creation of a high quality and efficient system of care. Proposals to increase competition in the general health sector, such as Entoven's (1978), have stressed the cost-containing advantages of competition. Arguments in favor of competition on these grounds have largely been of a theoretical nature, with no solid evidence to support the contention that costs would be reduced following introduction of competition. It should be stressed that the proposal for psychotherapy set forth here does not rely primarily on competition to hold down costs; the modest minimum benefit package does that. Competition is put to another purpose—promoting choice and a flexible, innovative delivery system. Two facts can be taken for granted: Mental illness is a very serious problem, and much improvement is needed in current methods for dealing with mental illness. A system for financing psychotherapy must permit and encourage experimentation and progress in pursuit of the important but distant goal of mental health. The system must encourage progress in clinical techniques and in the social organization of mental and health services. This proposal fulfills these aims.

Empirical research is essential to assess the magnitude of problems or opportunities suggested by theory. The evidence on the demand and supply of psychotherapy, and the interrelation between psychotherapy and use of other services, is not always solid. Continued empirical research by economists and other social scientists is warranted in a number of areas. Regarding demand, a good deal is currently known about how treatment progresses within mental health service settings. The National Institute of Mental Health has collected useful data on services within organized settings for some time. The study reported in this book provides some good information about demand for services of psychiatrists in private practice. Much less is known about how patients first get into these settings. What influences patients to seek care? How are choices made among alternative settings, including the general medical sector? A comprehensive model of choice of setting would bear on the full set of behavioral issues of patient behavior dealt with here: adverse selection, moral hazard, consumer ignorance, offset effects, and distributional questions. In the context of a pluralistic mental health delivery system, demand behavior becomes particularly important to understand. Regarding supply, a related and similar set of questions remains to be answered. What are the influences on mental health professionals' choice of line of work, location, and setting? What are the determinants of the quantity and quality of supply of various personnel to localities? Economists should contribute to the study of interprofessional relations in mental health services and the need for and effect of various regulationships and reimbursement practices. In addition, much more research needs to be done on the workings of alternative controls on moral hazard, the various forms of rules, and incentives to patients and providers.

The major empirical weakness of the case for national health insurance for psychotherapy lies in the clinical sphere. Consumer ignorance of the effectiveness of psychotherapy may be either an opportunity for beneficial governmental action (if consumers undervalue services) or a risk of inappropriate action (if consumers overvalue services). Although this might ultimately be the most significant question regarding the advisability of national health insurance (if consumers are "way off" in one direction or another), it is currently uncertain in what direction consumers are most likely to err.

Public policy cannot be paralyzed in the presence of uncertainty. Risks must be assessed and balanced and decisions made. It is particularly important that public policy not have the effect of forcing uniformity and stifling innovation in mental health service. This is the major danger in much of public policy toward financing mental health care. Legislating payment for only certain treatments or narrowly defining eligible providers and organizations would be a grave mistake in an area of service where progress in treatment methods can be so beneficial.

The proposal put forward in this book ensures that everyone receives basic mental health services without the government specifying how those services must be provided. Without knowing the best course of action, any one choice of treatment philosophy, setting for care, or method of cost control is likely to be wrong. The government should confine itself to setting up a flexible system that encourages providers and patients to respond to effectiveness, quality, and cost. This proposal would encourage effective treatment in the least costly manner, provide for an equitable distribution of services, and encourage innovation and progress in treatment.

NOTES TO CHAPTER 8

1. This method of financing is similar to that proposed by Entoven (1978).
2. Entoven (1980) discusses the response of interest groups to his proposal for a "consumer-choice health plan."
3. GAP (Group for the Advancement of Psychiatry) notes that under a third-party payment plan, confidentiality of patients' records can be compromised in a number of ways: insurees may be forced to sign waivers granting the insurer access to their health records; employers may have access to mental health records; or confidential information may "find its way into centralized computer banks and become available to outsiders" (1975: 526). Under the present proposal, consumers would have choice of plans for which danger of such breaches would be minimized.
4. This is based on the information presented on the distribution of changes for this program in Reed (1975: 19). A twenty-visit limit cuts off over one-half of covered visits. The figures for 1973 reported in Reed (1975) are probably better suited for prediction than more recent figures since in 1975 Aetna, the major alternative for third-party coverage for federal employees, restricted its patients' psychiatric benefits to twenty visits per year. This has added to the adverse selection problem faced by Blue Cross/Blue Shield and made more recent statistics of utilization from their plans even less representative of federal employees.

APPENDIXES

SURVEY OF PRIVATE PSYCHIATRIC OFFICE PRACTICE

Part A. Data on the Practitioner

1. Your age: _____

2. Location of office: City _____ State _____

3. Average number of hours per week spent in private office practice: _____ hrs.

4. Your primary subspecialty, if any:
   _____ Psychoanalysis
   _____ Child psychiatry
   _____ Other subspecialty (Specify: _____)
   Percent of private office practice time devoted to subspecialty: _____ %

5. Number of *individual persons* seen during your most recent full week of typical private office practice:
   Individually   _____
   In group therapy   _____
   In conjoint therapy   _____
   In family therapy   _____   (Number of families: _____)

Source: Taken from Judd Marmor et al., *Psychiatrists and Their Patients: A National Study of Private Office Practice*, The Joint Information Service, Washington, D.C., 1975.

6. In your current office practice estimate the proportion of your patients who will be seen for the following total number of visits:

Under 5 visits   _____ %
5-9 visits   _____ %
10-19 visits   _____ %
20-49 visits   _____ %
50-99 visits   _____ %
100 visits and over   _____ %
          TOTAL   100 %

7. Indicate your typical fee ($ _____) for a typical outpatient visit (_____ minutes).

Part B. Data on last 10 consecutive patients seen in office during week ending _____ .

Instructions: Fill out a form for each patient.

1. Patient's age: _____

2. Patient's sex: Male _____ Female _____

3a. Race/Ethnicity: White _____ Black _____ Latin American _____
    Other _____ (Please specify: _____)
3b. _____ Patient born in the U.S.
    _____ Patient born outside the U.S.

4. Patient's marital status:
    _____ Never married   _____ Divorced
    _____ Married   _____ Separated
    _____ Widowed   _____ Unknown

5. When did you first see this patient in private office practice? (Month and year) _____

6. Where did you have your first professional contact with this patient?
    _____ In my private office practice
    _____ In an inpatient setting
    _____ In a clinic or other public outpatient facility
    _____ In other (Specify: _____)

7. Have you at any time admitted this patient to an inpatient service?
    yes _____ no _____
    If "yes," for what length of stay?
    10 days or less _____ 11-20 days _____ 21-30 days _____
    More than 30 days _____

8. Approximate number of office visits of this patient during last 12 months:
    _____ visits

9. Your primary diagnosis of this patient's disorder:

_____ Psychosis associated with organic brain syndrome

_____ Nonpsychotic organic brain syndrome

_____ Schizophrenia

_____ Affective psychosis (including manic-depressive illness)

_____ Other psychosis

_____ Depressive neurosis

_____ Other neurosis

_____ Alcoholism not otherwise diagnosed

_____ Drug abuse not otherwise diagnosed

_____ Personality disorder

_____ Psychophysiologic disorder

_____ Mental retardation

_____ Behavior disorder of childhood or adolescence

_____ Transient situational disturbance

_____ Other (Specify: _____)

_____ No mental disorder

Degree of functional impairment at time treatment began:

Very mild _____ Mild _____ Moderate _____ Severe _____

10. Services received this week:

_____ Consultation or diagnostic evaluation

_____ Chemotherapy

_____ Psychoanalysis

_____ Individual therapy other than psychoanalysis

_____ Group therapy (other than family/conjoint)

_____ Family therapy

_____ Conjoint therapy

_____ Therapy through collateral

_____ Electroshock therapy

_____ Other (Specify: _____)

11. Duration of this patient's final visit this week: _____ minutes

12. Current frequency of visits: _____ per month

13. Has this patient ever had a drinking problem? yes _____ no _____
don't know _____ inapplicable _____
Does this patient currently have a drinking problem? yes _____
no _____ don't know _____ inapplicable _____

14. Has this patient ever had a drug abuse problem? yes _____ no _____
don't know _____ inapplicable _____
Does this patient currently have a drug abuse problem? yes _____
no _____ don't know _____ inapplicable _____
If "yes," which drug(s)? _____

15. Expected future duration of treatment: _____ months

16. Expected number of visits in next 12 months: _____ visits

17. Patient's principal occupation: _____

18. Patient's annual family income (before taxes):
    _____ Under $10,000
    _____ $10,000–$20,000
    _____ $20,000–$30,000
    _____ Over $30,000

19. Does the patient currently have insurance that pays part of the cost of care in your office practice? yes _____ no _____
    Has insurance but has exhausted benefits _____
    Has insurance but declines to use it _____
    If "yes," what percent of the fee is covered? 75–80% _____
    50% _____ Less than 50% _____

FINDINGS OF THE JIS SURVEY

This appendix presents some of the findings of the JIS survey. The purpose is to give the reader easy access to some of the results of this excellent survey and to introduce the data that serve as the basis for the empirical investigation reported in Chapters 5 and 6. Marmor 1975 contains thoughtful interpretation of much of this material. Unless otherwise indicated, the tables that follow are the result of our own tabulations.

One caution before proceeding. These tables are presented simply to give the reader a sense of the data. They do not constitute valid tests of hypotheses, such as, "Do higher income persons make more use of private psychiatrists?" The sample of last ten patients oversamples heavy users. A patient making five visits per week is much likelier to show up in the sample than a patient making just one visit per week. This nonrandom method of sampling turns out to have important consequences for some statistics derived from this data. Table B-12, for instance, vastly overstates the frequency with which the rich see psychiatrists relative to the poor because of the oversampling of heavy users. (Compare with the analysis of this question in Chapter 6.)

PSYCHIATRISTS

Psychiatrists classified themselves into one of four subspecialties: psychoanalysis, child psychiatry, other subspecialty, or none, or general psychiatry. Responses are shown in Table B-1. Almost one-half of all psychiatrists had a subspecialty. The most common subspecialty was psychoanalysis; about one-third of all psychiatrists indicated that they were psychoanalysts. Child psychiatrists accounted for just less than 10 percent and other subspecialists about 4 percent of the total of all psychiatrists.

Psychiatrists in the survey varied considerably in the number of hours per week they devoted to private practice, reflecting the availability of part-time work for psychiatrists in mental health facilities (Table B-2). Only a few psychiatrists in the survey worked fourteen hours or less in private practice. The survey was directed to psychiatrists who had reported in an earlier survey by the American Psychiatric Association that they spent at least fifteen hours per week in private practice. Between surveys some psychiatrists may have cut back their time in private practice. The average number of hours per week in private practice in the sample is thirty-four; 43 percent of all psychiatrists worked at least forty hours a week. The distribution of hours worked per week is roughly the same over the various subspecialties.

The practice of psychoanalysts differed in some important ways from the practice of other psychiatrists. Although the average fee and minutes per visit were not much different, psychoanalysts saw many fewer patients per hour than other psychiatrists (Table B-3). Psychoanalysts saw an average of 0.69 patients per hour; other psychiatrists saw 1.11 patients per hour. Individual psychotherapy was

Table B-1. Self-Designated Subspecialty.

	Number	Percentage
Psychoanalysis	148	33.6
Child psychiatry	41	9.3
Other	19	4.3
None or general	232	52.7
Total	440	100.0

Table B-2. Hours per Week in Private Practice by Subspecialty (*Percentages in Parentheses*).

| Hours | | Subspecialty | | | | |
	Child	Other	None or General	All but Psycho-analysis	Psycho-analysis	Total
0-14	1	1	6	8	2	10
	(2.4)	(5.3)	(2.6)	(2.7)	(1.4)	(2.3)
15-19	4	0	16	20	6	26
	(9.8)	(0.0)	(6.9)	(6.8)	(4.1)	(5.9)
20-24	6	2	36	44	10	54
	(14.6)	(10.5)	(15.6)	(15.1)	(6.8)	(12.3)
25-29	1	2	24	27	16	43
	(2.4)	(10.5)	(10.4)	(9.2)	(10.8)	(9.8)
30-34	7	3	34	44	16	60
	(17.1)	(15.8)	(14.7)	(15.1)	(10.8)	(13.6)
35-39	2	4	23	29	19	46
	(4.9)	(21.1)	(10.0)	(9.9)	(11.5)	(10.5)
40-44	12	5	39	56	35	91
	(29.3)	(26.3)	(16.9)	(19.2)	(23.5)	(20.7)
45-49	3	0	21	24	19	43
	(7.3)	(0.0)	(9.9)	(8.2)	(12.8)	(9.8)
50-54	4	1	14	19	21	40
	(9.8)	(5.3)	(6.1)	(6.5)	(14.2)	(9.1)
55-59	1	1	2	4	2	6
	(2.4)	(5.3)	(0.9)	(1.4)	(1.4)	(1.4)
60-64	0	0	6	6	2	8
	(0.0)	(0.0)	(2.6)	(2.1)	(1.4)	(1.8)
65-69	0	0	2	2	0	2
	(0.0)	(0.0)	(0.9)	(0.7)	(0.0)	(0.5)
70+	0	0	1	1	0	1
	(0.0)	(0.0)	(0.4)	(0.3)	(0.0)	(0.2)
Not indicated	0	0	8	8	2	10
	(0.0)	(0.0)	(3.0)	(2.7)	(1.4)	(2.3)
Total	41	19	232	292	148	440
	(100.0)	(100.0)	(100.0)	(100.0)	(100.0)	(100.0)
Mean	34	35	32	33	37	34

Table B-3. Average Fee, Minutes per Visit, and Patients per Hour
of Practice by Subspecialty.

	Child	Other	None or General	All but Psycho-analysis	Psycho-analysis	Total
Fee	37.30	32.50	34.03	34.40	37.30	35.36
Minutes	45.8	49.3	47.0	47.2	48.9	47.8
Patients/hour	1.05	1.15	1.11	1.11	0.69	0.96

Table B-4. Distribution of Patient's Length of Treatment
by Subspecialty (*in percentages*).[a]

	Subspecialty					
Number of Visits	Child	Other	None or General	All but Psycho-analysis	Psycho-analysis	Total
Less than 5	11.5	20.5	11.9	12.4	5.5	10.1
5-9	12.5	18.2	13.1	13.4	4.4	10.4
10-19	15.6	14.6	18.0	17.5	4.1	13.0
20-49	23.3	21.1	25.6	25.0	7.4	19.1
50-99	14.9	14.0	15.5	15.3	15.3	15.3
100+	22.1	11.6	15.9	16.5	63.3	32.1
	100.0	100.0	100.0	100.0	100.0	100.0
Median	20-49	10-19	20-49	20-49	100+	20-49

a. Fourteen psychiatrists did not provide enough information to be included in this
table. The sample size here is thus 426 psychiatrists.

the predominant form of treatment by all types of psychiatrists:
over 80 percent of patients seen by psychiatrists in the survey were
treated individually. Psychoanalysts used individual psychotherapy
almost exclusively. Only 2 of 148 (1.4 percent) psychoanalysts saw
20 or more patients in group therapy in the week of the survey,
whereas 48 of 292 (16.4 percent) other psychiatrists saw 20 or more
patients in group therapy.

Psychoanalysts' patients made many more visits than did other
psychiatrists' patients, as Table B-4 shows. Figure B-1 displays the

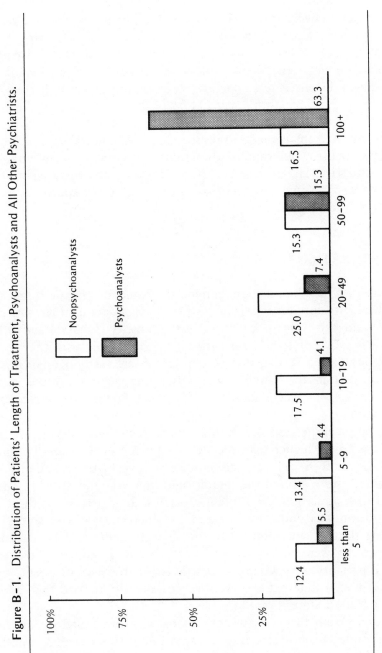

Figure B-1. Distribution of Patients' Length of Treatment, Psychoanalysts and All Other Psychiatrists.

difference between psychoanalysts and other psychiatrists. Psychoanalysts were almost four times more likely to treat a patient for
more than 100 visits. This is an example of how an uncontrolled
association between two variables—subspecialty and number of visits—might be interpreted incorrectly as indicating causality in one
direction. Psychoanalysts may not cause their patients to make more
visits; patients who want more visits may choose to see psychoanalysts. An attempt is made to resolve this in Chapter 5 where a model
is developed for determining the number of visits a patient makes to
a psychiatrist. The average age of psychiatrists was forty-eight years
(Table B-5). None were less than thirty, and a few continued practice into their eighties.

PATIENTS

The tables in this section summarize some of the personal and
medical information reported by psychiatrists about their patients.
Comparing the age, occupation, sex, ethnicity, income, and other
characteristics of the 4,300 patients in the sample with the overall
U.S. population reveals that certain groups are vastly over- or underrepresented in the sample. This raises important questions about
the relation between social and personal factors and psychiatric
utilization.

Fifty-seven percent of psychiatrists' patients were female, six percentage points higher than females' frequency in the overall population (Table B-6). The age distribution of psychiatrists' patients was
weighted more around the middle ages than was the distribution of
the U.S. population. As Table B-7 shows, 36.2 percent of the U.S.
population was under twenty and 14.4 percent was over sixty; yet
among the patients, only 11.6 percent were under twenty and only
4.3 percent were over sixty years old. Over one-half of all psychiatrists' patients were young adults, between the ages of twenty and
thirty-nine. Adult patients were less frequently married than adults
in the United States overall (Table B-8).

Twenty-four of every twenty-five patients of private psychiatrists
were white. From Table B-9 it appears that the overrepresentation
of whites came entirely at the expense of blacks. Blacks were 11.8
percent of the U.S. population in 1973 but less than 2 percent of
the private psychiatric patients. Latin and other ethnic groups (pri-

Table B-5. Age by Subspecialty (*Percentages in parentheses*).

| Age | | Subspecialty | | | | |
	Child	Other	None or General	All but Psycho- analysis	Psycho- analysis	Total
30-34	0 (0.0)	0 (0.0)	8 (3.5)	8 (2.7)	3 (2.0)	11 (2.5)
35-39	8 (19.5)	4 (21.1)	42 (18.2)	54 (18.5)	23 (15.5)	77 (17.5)
40-44	11 (26.8)	4 (21.1)	40 (17.3)	55 (18.8)	37 (25.0)	92 (20.9)
45-49	10 (24.4)	4 (21.1)	45 (19.5)	59 (20.2)	29 (19.6)	88 (20.0)
50-54	6 (14.6)	0 (0.0)	45 (19.5)	51 (17.5)	19 (12.8)	70 (15.9)
55-59	2 (4.9)	1 (5.3)	22 (9.5)	25 (8.6)	15 (10.1)	40 (9.1)
60-64	2 (4.9)	2 (10.5)	18 (7.8)	22 (7.5)	12 (8.1)	34 (7.7)
65-69	2 (4.9)	1 (5.3)	7 (3.0)	10 (3.4)	4 (2.7)	14 (3.2)
70-74	0 (0.0)	2 (10.5)	3 (1.3)	5 (1.7)	2 (1.4)	7 (1.6)
75-79	0 (0.0)	0 (0.0)	0 (0.0)	0 (0.0)	2 (1.4)	2 (0.5)
80+	0 (0.0)	1 (5.3)	1 (0.4)	2 (0.7)	1 (0.7)	3 (0.7)
Not indicated	0 (0.0)	0 (0.0)	1 (0.4)	1 (0.3)	1 (0.7)	2 (0.5)
Total	41 (100.0)	19 (100.0)	232 (100.0)	292 (100.0)	148 (100.0)	440 (100.0)
Mean	47	51	48	48	48	48

Table B-6. Sex of Patients.

Sex	Number	Relative Frequency	Adjusted Frequency	Frequency, U.S., 1973[a]
Male	1,829	42.3	43.0	48.8
Female	2,425	56.0	57.0	51.2
Not indicated	0.73	1.7	...	...
	4,327	100.0	100.0	100.0

a. Source: *Current Population Reports* Series P-25, No. 519 (April 1974, p. 12).

Table B-7. Age of Patients.

Age	Number	Relative Frequency	Adjusted Frequency	U.S., 1973[a]
0-9	86	2.0	2.0	16.5
10-19	413	9.5	9.6	19.7
20-29	1,065	24.6	24.8	16.1
30-39	1,225	28.3	28.5	11.6
40-49	899	20.8	20.9	11.2
50-59	429	9.9	10.0	10.5
60-69	140	3.2	3.3	7.9
70-79	33	0.8	0.8	4.5
80-89	7	0.2	0.2	2.0
Not indicated	30	0.7	...	
	4,327	100.0	100.0	100.0

a. Source: *Current Populations Reports*, Series P-25, No. 519 (April 1974, p. 12).

marily Oriental) were not underrepresented among psychiatrists' patients. About 95 percent of psychiatrists' patients were born inside the United States. This is close to the frequency in the United States overall (Table B-10). Table B-11 reports the rate per 1,000 of selected occupations in the U.S. work force and compares this with the rate per 1,000 workers in the sample of psychiatrists' patients. Professional and managerial occupations were overrepresented in the sample. The most overrepresented occupation was physicians. The underrepresentation of blue-collar employees compensated for the frequent appearance of professionals and managers. Among nonoccupational categories (not shown), the frequency of housewives in the sample, 227.2 per 1,000 patients, was about the same as their fre-

Table B-8. Marital Status of Patients Eighteen Years or Older
(N = 3,908).

Marital Status	Number	Relative Frequency	Adjusted Frequency	Frequency, U.S., 1973[a]
Never married˙	1,072	27.4	27.5	16.3 ("Single")
Married	2,178	55.7	55.9	71.2
Widowed	98	2.5	2.5	8.6
Divorced	383	9.8	9.8	3.9
Separated	154	3.9	4.0	(Not reported)
Unknown	8	0.2	0.2	
Not indicated	15	0.4	. . .	_____
	3,908	100.0	100.0	

a. Source: *Statistical Abstract of the United States, 1974* (p. 38).

Table B-9. Race/Ethnicity of Patients.

Race/Ethnicity	Number	Relative Frequency	Adjusted Frequency	Frequency, U.S., 1973[a]
White	4,095	94.6	96.1	87.2
Black	78	1.8	1.8	11.3
Latin American	56	1.3	1.3 ⎫	
Other	34	0.8	0.8 ⎭	1.4
Not indicated	64	1.5	. . .	. . .
	4,327	100.0	100.0	100.0

a. Source: *Statistical Abstract of the United States, 1974* (p. 26).

quency in the population, 202.3 per 1,000 people. In accordance with the age distribution of patients, primary and secondary school students were underrepresented in the sample by a factor of about 3. There were 91.1 primary and secondary students per 1,000 patients in the sample, but 292.7 students per 1,000 population in the United States.

As would be expected from the predominance of high-status occupations among patients, the distribution of patients' family income, reported in Table B-12, is skewed upward in comparison to the United States overall. Only 22.4 percent of U.S. families earned more than $20,000 in 1973, while 41.0 percent of patients' families earned more than $20,000.

Table B-10. Birthplace of Patients.

Birthplace	Number	Relative Frequency	Adjusted Frequency	Frequency, U.S., 1970[a]
United States	3,764	87.0	95.7	95.3
Outside United States	171	4.0	4.3	4.7
Not indicated	392	9.1	...	...
	4,327	100.0	100.0	100.0

a. Source: *Statistical Abstract of the United States, 1974* (p. 34).

Table B-11. Frequency of Selected Occupational Groups.

Occupation	Rate per 1,000 of Work Force in Sample	Rate per 1,000 of Work Force U.S. Population
Professional, technical, and kindred workers— selected professions	510.1	148.1
Physicians	71.6	3.7
Lawyers	44.8	3.4
Social workers	33.0	2.8
Writers, artists etc.	64.1	9.8
Teachers	114.2	42.1
Nurses	23.7	10.8
Managerial, administrative	154.7	83.1
Sales	75.6	71.0
Clerical and kindred workers	131.4	179.4

Source: Marmor (1975, p. 38).

Let us turn now to a summary of some of the medical information reported by psychiatrists about their patients. Almost 90 percent of patients were first seen by the psychiatrist in the psychiatrist's private office (Table B-13). Most of the rest were first seen in an inpatient treatment setting.

Diagnoses psychiatrists gave patients are indicated in Table B-14. Only about 1 percent of patients had no diagnosed mental disorder or were analytic candidates in training. The degree of patients' func-

Table B-12. Family Income of Patients.

Income	Number	Relative Frequency	Adjusted Frequency	Frequency, U.S., 1973[a]
$9,999 or less	993	22.9	23.7	38.9
$10,000-19,999	1,474	34.1	35.2	38.6
$20,000-29,999	783	18.1	18.7 }	22.4
$30,000 and up	933	21.6	22.3 }	
Unknown or not indicated	144	3.4	...	
	4,327	100.0	100.0	100.0

a. Source: *Statistical Abstract of the United States, 1975*, (p. 39).

Table B-13. Location of First Professional Contact.

Location	Number	Relative Frequency (percent)	Adjusted Frequency (percent)
Psychiatrist's private office	3,833	88.6	89.9
Inpatient setting	311	7.2	7.3
Clinic	65	1.5	1.5
Other	54	1.2	1.3
Not indicated	64	1.5	...
Total	4,327	100.0	100.0

tional impairment at the time treatment began is indicated in Table B-15. Over three-quarters of patients were judged by their respective psychiatrists to be moderately or severely functionally impaired. Slightly less than 18 percent of patients were ever admitted to an inpatient service by the psychiatrist treating them at the time of the survey (Table B-16). Patients diagnosed with depressive neurosis, schizophrenia, and affective psychosis account for over two-thirds of the patients admitted.

According to the psychiatrists, of the 3,908 patients eighteen years of age and older, 522 (13.4 percent) had a drinking problem in the past, 221 (5.7 percent) had a drinking problem at the time of the survey, 359 (9.2 percent) had a drug abuse problem in the past, and 127 (3.2 percent) had a drug abuse problem at the time of the sur-

Table B-14. Patients' Primary Diagnosis.

Diagnosis	Number	Relative Frequency	Adjusted Frequency
Psychoses	853	19.7	19.8
Depressive neuroses	1,114	25.7	25.9
Other neuroses	968	22.4	22.5
Personality disorders	797	18.4	18.5
All other diagnoses	529	12.2	12.3
No mental disorder	37	0.9	0.9
Psychotherapist in training	8	0.2	0.9
Not indicated	21	0.5	...
Total	4,327	100.0	100.0

Table B-15. Degree of Functional Impairment at Time Patients Began Treatment.

Degree of Impairment	Number	Relative Frequency	Adjusted Frequency
Very mild	192	4.4	4.6
Mild	766	17.7	18.2
Moderate	2,127	49.2	50.4
Severe	1,134	26.2	26.9
Not indicated	108	2.5	...
Total	4,327	100.0	100.0

vey. Drug and alcohol problems often accompanied each other. Of the adult patients who had drinking problems, 34 percent also had drug abuse problems, while of the adults who had no drinking problem, only 11 percent had drug abuse problems.

Table B-17 shows the services psychiatrists provided to patients in the week of the survey. Almost 5 percent of patients were simply evaluated. About one-quarter of all patients received some form of chemotherapy, almost always in conjunction with other services. The large bulk of patients received individual psychotherapy of some kind. About 13 percent of all patients received individual psychoanalysis. Less than 1 percent of all patients received electroshock therapy during the week of the survey.

Table B-16. Admission to Inpatient Service and Length of Study.

Admitted by Psychiatrist		Number	Relative Frequency	Adjusted Frequency
Yes		759	17.5	17.7
	10 days or less	177		
	11-20 days	210		
	21-30 days	182		
	31 or more days	174		
	Not indicated	16		
		759		
No		3,534	81.7	82.3
Not indicated		34	0.8	. . .
		4,327	100.0	100.0

Table B-17. Services Received.

Service	Number	Percentage of Total Patients
Not indicated (or no therapy)	28	0.6
Consultation or diagnostic evaluation		
Only	196	4.5
With other services	75	1.7
Total	271	6.3
Chemotherapy		
Only	70	1.6
With other services	948	21.9
Total	1,018	23.5
Psychoanalysis		
Only	541	12.5
With other services	19	0.4
Total	560	12.9
Individual therapy other than psychoanalysis		
Only	2,083	48.1
With other services	1,089	25.2
Total	3,172	73.3
Group therapy (other than family or conjoint)		
Only	61	1.4
With other services	138	3.2
Total	199	4.6
Family therapy		
Only	39	0.9
With other services	92	2.1
Total	131	3.0
Conjoint therapy		
Only	105	2.4
With other services	92	2.1
Total	197	4.6
Therapy through collateral		
Only	2	< 0.05
With other services	24	0.6
Total	26	0.6
Electroshock therapy		
Only	7	0.2
With other services	16	0.4
Total	23	0.6

CONSTRUCTING HECKMAN'S
λ IN A TRUNCATED SAMPLE

To construct λ we need to estimate $-\phi$, the probit index determining the probability an observation appears in the sample. Let $V > 0$ stand for "among the last ten." Recall that the probability desired, $P(V > 0|X)$ cannot be estimated directly from a truncated sample, but that using the formula for conditional probability, $P(V > 0|X)$ can be expressed in terms of known or estimable probabilities.

$$P(V > 0|X) = \frac{P(X|V > 0)}{P(X)} \quad P(V > 0) \qquad \text{(C-1)}$$

Putting information on these three right-hand-side probabilities together, it can be observed how the probability of entering treatment depends on X.

$P(X|V > 0)$

This is the probability a patient exhibits certain X characteristics, given the patient is in the sample of last tens. This is estimated by the relative frequency of appearance of the set of X characteristics in the sample. For this reason, and since $P(X)$ is estimated from Census Bureau publications, a limited number of X variables is used, and the values of these variables were categorized. The X variables and categories for the variables were as follows:

Sex (male, female)
Age (18–40, 41–60, 61+)
Race (black, Spanish, white, other)
Marital status (single, married, widowed, divorced)
Occupation (physician, professional technical or managerial non-physician, employed nonprofessional technical or managerial, not working)
Income (less than $10,000, $10,000–19,999, $20,000–29,999, $30,000+)

Unfortunately, insurance could not be included as one of the X variables.

$P(X)$

This is the unconditional probability that a set of X characteristics appears in the U.S. population aged eighteen years and older. The problem is to transform Census Bureau definitions and categories into those corresponding to the sample's. *Earnings by Occupation and Education* (Subject Report PC(2) 1970 Census of Population) provided the basis for the computation of $P(X)$ with a five-way breakdown of the number of people in the United States along the following lines:

Sex (male, female)
Age (18–24, 25–34, 35–54, 55–64, 65+)
Race (black, Spanish, white)
Occupation (extremely detailed)
Income (less than $6,000, $6,000–9,999, $10,000–14,999, $15,000+)

Based on a series of tedious calculations, the census categories were transformed to our own (accounting for inflation in income). The interpolative assumption used throughout was that the distribution of observations within a range was uniform.

Income in *Earnings by Occupation and Education* is earned income of individuals, while the data are all income of families. Unearned income is most important for upper income groups. For the $15,000+ category information reported elsewhere in the census on the distribution of family income was used to proportion these people among our income categories. If someone was married, spouse's income was added to get family income. To find a wife's income for example, the percentage was found of women by age and race who were in the labor force. For those men with working wives it was assumed half had wives making income in the same range as their husbands and half making incomes of the average woman. Thus of a group of high-income married men earning a certain income, some would have family income of a little more (those with wives with "average jobs") and some would have much higher family income (those married to women with a career on par with their own). A similar procedure was followed for married women, whose spouses were more likely to be working. Unmarried individuals not working were assumed to have family income less than $10,000.

To incorporate marital status, left out of *Earnings by Occupation and Education*, tables reporting marital status by age, sex, and race were used (*Statistical Abstract of the United States*, 1974, tables 48 to 49). Thus it was necessary to assume that the distribution of marital status was independent of occupation and income within age, sex, and race categories.

$P(V > 0)$

There are three published estimates of the number of patients seeing private psychiatrists in 1973: 2,400,000; 896,000; and 495,000. The subjectively weighted average of these—the number used here—is 800,000. Ninety-one percent of the patients in the sample were eighteen years or older. Taking the same figure as applicable to the whole United States, 728,000 adults saw private psychiatrists in 1973. $P(V > 0)$ scales the probability for all sets of Xs, so differences in the $X\beta$ index for different sets of the Xs are not sensitive to changes in $P(V > 0)$. There were 133,546,000 people in the United States in 1970 eighteen years of age or older. The unconditional probability that someone saw a private psychiatrist is thus:

$$P(V > 0) = \frac{728,000}{133,546,000} = 0.00545 \qquad (C-2)$$

This categorization of six X variables results in a six-way contingency table with each cell containing an estimate of the probability a person with this set of characteristics will become a patient of a private psychiatrist. The categories of the X variables imply a contingency table with $2 \times 3 \times 3 \times 4 \times 4 \times 4 = 1,152$ cells. In fact there are only 1,037 cells because the census does not report the number of Spanish women separately for some occupations, and a few cells have no people in the United States fitting all the characteristics specified.

With these 1,037 observations one can summarize the dependence of the probability a person sees a private psychiatrist by specifying a functional form for $P(V > 0|X)$ and estimating that function. Heckman's method calls for a probit index, based on the cumulative normal distribution. For computational convenience, a logit index has been estimated, based on the logistical distribution, which is very close to the cumulative normal distribution. Thus, it is supposed:

$$P(V > 0|X) = \frac{1}{1 + e^{-XB}} \qquad \text{(C-3)}$$

so that

$$\log(P/(1 - P)) = XB \qquad \text{(C-4)}$$

This equation can be estimated with standard regression techniques. XB is a logit index, but simply dividing by 2 gives a very close approximation to a probit index. To make sure $\log(P/(1 - P))$ was never minus infinity, where there were no patients appearing in the sample with a certain set of characteristics—for example, young black, widowed women physicians making more than $30,000—it is supposed that 0.001 patients appeared.

The estimated logit indices are reported in Table C-1. All variables are dummy variables. Each original X variable, of course, has an omitted category. One set of interaction terms, sex with all other variables, was included in the regression. Column 1 lists the indices for an unweighted regression. Column 2 is based on an equation that takes note of the fact that the variance of the estimate of P is proportional to $P(1 - P)$ and weights the observations by the inverse of the square root of this estimate of the variance.

Table C-1. Logit Index for the Probability of Seeing a Private
Psychiatrist in 1973 (t-statistics in Parentheses).[a]

Dummy Variable	Unweighted Regression	Weighted Regression
Male	-1.254 (1.97)	-.113
Single	1.142 (3.31)	1.300
Widowed	.5770 (1.67)	1.154
Divorced	1.447 (4.15)	2.146
Black	-2.106 (7.39)	.3705
Spanish	-1.062 (3.24)	1.050
Middle aged	-1.108 (3.73)	-.3777
Old	-1.693 (5.54)	-.5063
Income ($10,000-19,000)	.08093 (0.23)	.7404
Income ($20,000-29,000)	.2720 (0.79)	.4478
Income $30,000+)	1.455 (4.13)	2.269
MD	2.125 (6.34)	3.805
Blue collar	-1.795 (5.40)	-1.830
Not working	-2.523 (6.65)	-2.844
Single male	-.4286 (0.88)	-.6699

(Table C-1. continued overleaf)

Table C-1. continued

Dummy Variable	Unweighted Regression	Weighted Regression
Widowed male	-.4413 (0.91)	-.3412
Divorced male	-.5168 (1.06)	-.6786
Black male	1.036 (2.58)	-.02611
Spanish male	.6044 (1.33)	.06548
Middle aged male	-.2642 (0.63)	.5203
Old male	.2455 (0.58)	.3398
Male income ($10,000-19,000)	.09459 (0.19)	-.02598
Male income ($20,000-29,000)	.2787 (0.57)	.7201
Male income($30,000+)	.3095 (0.63)	-.07569
Male MD	-.6778 (1.45)	-1.661
Male blue collar	-.6114 (1.31)	-.5028
Male not working	.5027 (0.94)	.5502
Constant	-4.856	-11.351
Adj R^2	.3707	.451

a. Not reported for the weighted regression.

INSTRUMENTAL ESTIMATES
FOR INSURANCE COVERAGE

COINHAT is the estimate of COINRATE. Defining a new variable Y, which equals 1 if an individual has insurance coverage and 0 if not, the expected value of COINRATE is

$$E(\text{COINRATE}) = \text{Prob } (Y = 1) \; E (\text{COINRATE} | Y = 1) \qquad (D-1)$$

To estimate the E(COINRATE), or COINHAT, as a function of pre-determined X variables, estimate equations for each of the two terms on the right-hand side of this expression. Each equation was esti-mated by ordinary least squares using the same set of X variables. Explanatory variables are various characteristics of the individual, income, sex, and so on, plus state demographic variables such as income, employment, mobility, education, and insurance coverage.

Table D-1 reports the results. All independent variables are dum-my variables, (1, 0) unless otherwise indicated.

Table D-1. Equations for Probability ($Y = 1$) and E (COINRATE $Y = 1$) (t-statistics in Parentheses).

Independent Variable	Dependent Variable: Sample:	Y All	COINRATE Y = 1
Sex not indicated		.04293 (0.56)	.03685 (0.64)
Male		-.02521 (1.12)	.008227 (0.47)
Race not indicated		-.1503 (1.72)	.02827 (0.38)
Black		.2194 (2.99)	.1402 (2.96)
Spanish		.005141 (0.05)	-.07042 (1.01)
Race "other"		-.1611 (1.52)	-.04525 (.44)
Birthplace not indicated		.04095 (0.98)	.02574 (0.83)
Born outside United States		-.03962 (0.87)	-.01980 (0.54)
Birthplace unknown		-.04290 (0.82)	.01531 (0.38)
Marital status not indicated		.06406 (0.47)	.02209 (0.23)
Married		.09264 (3.59)	.04891 (2.38)
Widowed		.03436 (0.52)	.02775 (0.55)
Divorced		.02000 (0.60)	.06820 (2.47)
Separated		.06550 (1.36)	.05337 (1.43)
Marital status unknown		.5318 (2.21)	.04905 (0.39)
Occupation not indicated		.02864 (0.17)	.2417 (1.83)

Table D-1. continued

Independent Variable	Dependent Variable: Sample:	Y All	COINRATE Y = 1
Professional		.1268 (2.93)	−.04888 (1.35)
Physician		−.09320 (1.59)	.01550 (0.25)
Psychologist		.1307 (1.19)	−.1144 (1.45)
Medical student		−.1005 (0.51)	.2310 (1.28)
Semiprofessional		.9514 (2.76)	−.02426 (0.79)
Skilled labor and lower white collar		.08153 (2.03)	.007908 (0.23)
Homemaker		.08878 (2.21)	.01798 (0.52)
Unemployed		.02270 (0.35)	.7150 (1.19)
Retired		.2202 (2.41)	.06531 (0.99)
No or unknown employment		.1967 (3.06)	.02883 (0.58)
Religious order		.2299 (2.39)	−.03525 (0.51)
Disabled		.5676 (4.54)	.02092 (0.29)
Patient's age in years		.0008542 (0.91)	.0004856 (0.68)
Income not indicated		−.2503 (2.37)	.07654 (0.65)
Income $10,000−19,999		.07338 (2.82)	−.02059 (1.01)
Income $20,000−29,999		.02708 (0.87)	−.03375 (1.38)

(Table D-1. continued overleaf)

Table D-1. continued

Independent Variable	Dependent Variable: Sample:	Y All	COINRATE Y = 1
Income $30,000+		-.1234 (4.04)	-.1223 (4.67)
Income unknown		-.07541 (1.11)	-.04171 (0.75)
Percentage of state population employed in 1970		-.1480 (3.27)	-1.142 (3.35)
Percentage of state population under sixty-five covered by hospital expense insurance in 1973		-.3895 (1.01)	.8333 (2.94)
Percentage of state population under sixty-five covered by regular medical insurance in 1973		.2442 (1.11)	.4957 (2.93)
Growth of regular medical insurance in state, 1970-73		.1473 (1.55)	.2505 (3.42)
College students per population in 1970		1.267 (1.41)	-.01803 (0.03)
State population density in 1970		.00001553 (1.12)	.00001557 (1.45)
State population growth, 1960-70		.02499 (2.81)	.0005327 (0.08)
Percentage of state population immigrants in 1970		-.02667 (2.88)	-.0007226 (0.11)
Percentage of state population female in 1970		.0008158 (0.05)	.01178 (0.90)
Percentage of state population in urban areas in 1970		-.002341 (1.96)	-.003027 (3.32)

Table D-1. continued

Independent Variable	Dependent Variable: Sample:	Y All	COINRATE Y = 1
Percentage of state population black in 1970		-.0001179 (0.37)	.0003630 (1.53)
Percentage of state population younger than sixty-five in 1970		.01993 (0.48)	-.01845 (0.61)
Percentage of state population eighteen or older, 1970		-.003397 (0.36)	.01637 (2.11)
Percentage of state population sixty-five or older, 1970		.001307 (0.10)	-.01764 (1.58)
Median age in state, 1970		.02704 (2.22)	-.00007425 (0.01)
Median years of schooling in state, 1970		.03670 (1.16)	-.02752 (1.08)
Percentage of state population with 4+ years of higher education		-.01370 (2.19)	-.009719 (1.92)
Percentage employed in manufacturing in state, 1970		.006195 (0.06)	-.001497 (0.97)
Percentage employed in government service in state, 1970		.008418 (3.52)	.003211 (1.76)
Percentage of families with income $10,000-15,000 in state, 1969		-.02185 (2.49)	-.003173 (0.44)
Percentage of families with income $15,000-25,000 in state, 1969		.008941 (0.95)	-.01598 (2.35)

(Table D-1. continued overleaf)

Table **D-1.** continued

Independent Variable	Dependent Variable Sample:	Y All	COINRATE Y = 1
Percentage of families with income $25,000+ in state, 1969		.006205 (0.52)	-.01032 (1.11)
State median family income ($000s), 1969		.001238 (0.28)	.01019 (3.24)
Percentage of state housing into 1965–70		.0008622 (0.26)	.003686 (1.45)
Constant		-.9114	-.4812
R^2		.108	.169

REFERENCES

Aetna Life and Casualty. 1974. "Study of 1973 Mental and Nervous Claims Under the Government-Wide Indemnity Benefit Plan." Mimeo.

Akerloff, G. 1973. "The Market for Lemons." *Quarterly Journal of Economics* 84, no. 3 (August): 488–520.

Albee, G. 1977. "Does Including Psychotherapy in Health Insurance Represent a Subsidy to the Rich from the Poor?" *American Psychologist* 32, no. 9 (September): 719–21.

Alcohol, Drug Abuse and Mental Health Administration. 1979. "Alcohol, Drug Abuse and Mental Health Services Under National Health Insurance: Alternative Levels of Benefits and Estimated Costs." Washington, D.C.: Office of Program Planning and Evaluation.

American Medical Association. 1978. *Physician Distribution and Medical Licensure in the U.S.* Chicago.

American Psychiatric Association. 1975. *Confidentiality and Third Parties.* Task Force Report No. 9, Washington, D.C.

Armer, J. 1980. "Is Mental Wellness an Answer to the Runaway Cost of Health Care?" In *Mental Wellness Programs for Employees*, edited by R. Egdahl, D. Walsh and W. Goldbeck, pp. 213–220, New York: Spring–Verlag.

Arrow, K. 1963. "Uncertainty and the Welfare Economics of Medical Care." *American Economic Review* 53, no. 5 (December): 941–73.

Arrow, K. 1971. *Theory of Risk-Bearing.* Chicago: Markham Publishing.

Auster, S. 1969. "Insurance Coverage for 'Mental and Nervous Conditions': Developments and Problems." *American Journal of Psychaitry* 126, no. 5 (November): 698–705.

Bass, R.A. and R.B. Craven. 1978. "Manpower Issues in Community Mental Health Programs." In *Report of the ADAMHA Manpower Task Force*, edited by D. Kole, pp. 142–58. Washington: Alcohol, Drug Abuse and Mental Health Administration.

Berwick, D. and R. Zeckhauser. 1975. "A Framework for Assessing the Efficiency of Mental Health Care Delivery." Final Report, Contract No. ADM–42–74–57(OP). Washington, D.C.: National Institute of Mental Health.

Blum, J.F., F.C. Redlich, and R.F. Mollica. 1979. "Mental Health Practitioners: Old Stereotypes and New Realities." In *Trends in Mental Health*, 1950, 1975, Final Report, Contract No. 278–77–0072(OP). Washington, D.C.: National Institute of Mental Health.

Brown, B. 1976. "The Life of Psychiatry." *The American Journal of Psychiatry* 133, no. 5 (May): 489–95.

Castelnuovo–Tedesco, P. 1975. "Brief Psychotherapy." In *Treatment*, edited by Freedman and Dyrud, Vol. V of *American Handbook of Psychiatry*, edited by A. Silvano. New York: Basic Books.

Davis, K. and R. Reynolds. 1976. "The Impact of Medicare and Medicaid on Access to Medical Care." In *The Role of Health Insurance in The Health Services Sector*, edited by Rosett, pp. 391–425. New York: National Bureau of Economic Research.

Davis, K. and L. Russel. 1972. "The Substitution of Hospital Outpatient Care for Inpatient Care." *Review of Economics and Statistics* 54, no. 2 (May): 109–20.

Dörken, H. 1977. "The Practicing Psychologist: A Growing Force in Private Sector Health Care Delivery." *Professional Psychology* 8, (August): 269–74.

Dörken, H. and J. Webb. 1978. "California Licensed Psychologists in Health Practice." University of California. Mimeo.

Dörken, H. and J. Webb. 1979. "Licensed Psychologists in Health Care: A Survey of Their Practices." In *Psychology and National Health Insurance*, edited by C. Kiesler, N. Cummings and G. Vandenbos, pp. 129–160. Washington, D.C.: American Psychological Association.

Dorris, W. and T. McGuire. 1980. "Community Mental Health Centers and Competition in Mental Health Services." In *Federal Health Programs: Improving the Health System?*, edited by S. Altman and H. Sopolski, pp. 83–102. Lexington: D.C. Heath.

Duehrssen, A. 1962. "Katamnestische Ergebnisse bei 1004 Patienten rach Analytischer Psychotherapie." *Zschr. Psycho-som Med.* VIII, 2/62. Goettingen: Verlag Fuer Medizinische Psychologie.

Edwards, D.; L. Greene; S. Abramowitz; and C. Davidson. 1979. "National Health Insurance, Psychotherapy, and the Poor." *American Psychologists* 34: 411–19.

Egdahl, R.; D. Walsh; and W. Goldbeck. 1980. *Mental Wellness, Programs for Employees.* New York: Springer–Verlag.

Entoven, A. 1978. "Consumer Choice Health Plan." *New England Journal of Medicine* 298, no. 12 (March 23): 650-58, (Part I) and 298, no. 13 (March 30): 709-20, (Part II).

Evans, R. 1976. "Beyond the Medical Marketplace: Expenditure Utilization and Pricing of Insured Health Care in Canada." In *The Role of Health Insurance in the Health Services Sector*, edited by Rosett, pp. 437-92. New York: National Bureau of Economic Research.

Feldstein, M. 1970. "The Rising Price of Physicians' Services." *The Review of Economics and Statistics* 52, no. 2 (May): 121-33.

Feldstein, M. 1973. "The Welfare Loss of Excess Health Insurance." *Journal of Political Economy* 81, no. 2 (March/April): 251-80.

Feldstein, M.; B. Friedman; and H. Luft. 1972. "Distributional Aspects of National Health Insurance Benefits and Finance." *National Tax Journal* 25, no. 4 (December): 497-510.

Foote, A. 1977. *Cost-Effectiveness of Occupational Employee Assistance Programs*. Detroit: Institute of Labor and Industrial Relations, The University of Michigan—Wayne State University.

Freedman, D. 1978. "Psychiatry." *Journal of the American Medical Association* 239, no. 6 (February): 510-12.

Freedman, D. and J. Dyrud. 1975. *Treatment*, Vol. V of *American Handbook of Psychiatry*, edited by A. Silvano. New York: Basic Books.

Freiberg, L. and F. Scutchfield. 1976. "Insurance and the Demand for Hospital Care: An Examination of Moral Hazard." *Inquiry* 13, no. 1 (March): 54-60.

Freund, J. 1971. *Mathematical Statistics* Second Edition. Englewood Cliffs, N.J.: Prentice-Hall.

Fuchs, V. 1978. "The Supply of Surgeons and the Demand for Operations," *Journal of Human Resources* 13, supplement: 35-56.

General Accounting Office. 1979. *Legislative and Administrative Changes Needed in Community Mental Health Centers Program*. HRD-79-38. Washington, D.C.

Glasser, M. and T. Duggan. 1969. "Prepaid Psychiatric Care: Experience With UAW Members." *American Journal of Psychiatry* 126, no. 5 (November): 675-81.

GLS Associates. 1979. "Analysis of State Programs Which Mandate Mental Health Benefits Under Private Health Insurance." Final Report, Contract No. 278-78-0040(MH). Washington, D.C.: National Institute of Mental Health.

Goldberg, I.; G. Krantz; and B. Locke. 1970. "Effect of Short-Term Outpatient Psychiatric Benefits on the Utilization of Medical Services in a Prepaid Group Practice Program." *Medical Care* 8, no. 5 (September-October): 419-28.

Graduate Medical Education National Advisory Committee. 1979. *Interim Report*. Publication No. (HRA), 79-633. Washington, D.C.: U.S. Department of Health, Education, and Welfare.

Green, J. 1978. "Physician-Induced Demand for Medical Care." *Journal of Human Resources* 13, supplement 21-34.

Greene, E. 1969. "Psychiatric Services in a California Group Health Plan." *American Journal of Psychiatry* 126, no. 5 (November): 681-88.

Greenberg, W. ed. 1978. *Competition in the Health Care Sector: Past, Present and Future.* Washington, D.C.: Federal Trade Commission.

Group for the Advancement of Psychiatry. 1975. *The Effect of the Method of Payment on Mental Health Practice.* Report No. 95, Vol. 9. New York.

Guillette, M. 1976. "Is Psychotherapy Insurable?" Aetna Life and Casualty. Mimeo.

Hausman, J. and D. Wise. 1977. "Social Experimentation, Truncated Distributions and Efficient Estimators." *Econometrica* 45, no. 4 (May): 919-38.

Health Insurance Institute. 1973. *Source Book of Health Insurance Data.* New York.

Health Insurance Institute. 1976. *Source Book of Health Insurance Data.* New York.

Heckman, J. 1976. "The Common Structure of Statistical Models of Truncation, Sample Selection, and Limited Dependent Variables and a Simple Estimator for Such Models." *Annals of Economic and Social Measurement* 5, no. 4 (Fall): 475-92.

Herrington, B.S. 1979. "Blue Cross, Blue Shield Tighten Psychiatric Coverage in East, West." *Psychiatric News* (September).

Hill, D.B. and J.B. Veney. 1970. "Kansas Blue Cross/Blue Shield Outpatient Benefit Experiment." *Medical Care* 8, no. 2 (May): 143-58.

Hogan, D. 1979. *The Regulation of Psychotherapists.* Cambridge, Mass.: Ballinger Publishing Company.

Hollingshead, A. and F. Redlich. 1958. *Social Class and Mental Illness.* New York: John Wiley and Sons.

Hustead, E. and S. Sharfstein. 1978. "Utilization and Cost of Mental Illness Coverage in the Federal Employees Health Benefits Program, 1973." *American Journal of Psychiatry* 135, no. 3 (March): 315-319.

Johnston, J. 1972. *Econometric Methods*, Second Edition. New York: McGraw-Hill.

Jones, K. and T. Vischi. 1979. "Impact of Alcohol, Drug Abuse and Mental Health Treatment on Medical Care Utilization." *Medical Care* 17, no. 12 (December): 1-82.

Kennecott Cooper Corporation. 1974. "Insight." Mimeo.

Kiesler, C.; N. Cummings; and G. VandenBos. 1979. *Psychology and National Health Insurance.* Washington, D.C.: American Psychological Association.

Kole, D. 1978. "Trends in Private Practice by Mental Health Professionals." *Report of the ADAMHA Task Force.* Edited by Kole, pp. 192-201. Washington, D.C.: Alcohol, Drug Abuse, and Mental Health Administration.

Kole, D. and L. Metnick. 1978. "Utilization and Substitutability of Alcohol, Drug Abuse and Mental Health Personnel." *Report of the ADAMHA Task*

Force. Edited by Kole, pp. 107–17. Washington, D.C.: Alcohol, Drug Abuse and Mental Health Administration.

Krizay, J. 1979. "Utilization of Psychiatric Services Under the Federal Employees Benefit Program Over Five Years (1973–1977)." Washington, D.C. Mimeo.

Leibenstein, H. 1950. "Bandwagon, Snob and Veblen Effects in the Theory of Consumers' Demand." *Quarterly Journal of Economics* 64, no. 2 (May): 183–207.

Levine, D. and S. Willner. 1976. "The Cost of Mental Illness, 1974." Statistical Note No. 125, Washington, D.C.: National Institute of Mental Health.

Lewis, C. and H. Keairnes. 1970. "Controlling Costs of Medical Care by Expanding Insurance Coverage." *New England Journal of Medicine* 282, (June 18): 1405–12.

Liptzin, B. 1978. "Supply, Demand and Projected Need for Psychiatrists and Other Mental Health Manpower: An Analytic Paper." In *Report of the ADAMHA Manpower Policy Task Force,* edited by D. Kole, pp. 18–39. Washington, D.C.: Alcohol, Drug Abuse and Mental Health Administration.

Malan, D. 1973. "The Outcome Problem in Psychotherapy Research." *Archives of General Psychiatry* 29: 719–29.

Marmor, J. 1975. *Psychiatrists and Their Patients.* Washington, D.C.: Joint Information Service of the American Psychiatric Association and The National Association for Mental Health.

Mattera, M. 1979. "Why Psychiatrists are Behind the Eight-Ball." *Medical Economics* (February 5).

McClure, W. 1978. "On Broadening The Definition of and Removing Barriers to a Competitive Health Care System." *Journal of Health Politics, Policy, and Law* 3, no. 3 (Fall): 303–27.

McGuire, T. 1980. "Markets for Psychotherapy." In *Psychotherapy, Practice, Research, Policy,* edited by VandenBos, pp. 187–246. Beverly Hills: Sage Publishing.

Mckinlay, J. 1973. "Social Networks, Lay Consultation and Help-Seeking Behavior." *Social Forces* 51, no. 3 (March): 275–91.

Mechanic, D. 1978. "Considerations in the Design of Market Health Benefits Under National Health Insurance." *American Journal of Public Health* 68, no. 5 (May): 482–88.

Mills, D., A. Wellner and G. VandenBos. 1979. "The *National Register Survey*: The First Comprehensive Study of All Licensed/Certified Psychologists." In *Psychology and National Health Insurance,* edited by Kiesler, Cummings and VandenBos, pp. 111–28. Washington, D.C.: American Psychological Association.

Monsma, G. 1970. "Marginal Revenue and the Demand for Physician Services." In *Empirical Studies in Health Economics,* edited by Klarman, Baltimore: Johns Hopkins University Press.

National Institute of Mental Health. 1976. *Draft Report: The Financing, Utilization and Quality of Mental Health Care in the U.S.* Washington, D.C.: National Institute of Mental Health.

National Institute of Mental Health. 1977. "Provisional Data on Patient Care Episodes in Mental Health Facilities, 1975." Statistical Note No. 139. Washington, D.C.: National Institute of Mental Health.

Nemiah, J. 1975. "Classical Psychoanalysis." In *Treatment*, edited by Freedman and Dyrud, Vol. V of *American Handbook of Psychiatry*, edited by Silvano. New York: Basic Books.

Newhouse, J. 1970. "A Model of Physician Pricing." *Southern Economic Journal* 37, no. 2 (October): 174–83.

Newhouse, J. 1974. "A Design for a Health Insurance Experiment." *Inquiry* 11, no. 1 (March): 5–27.

Newhouse, J. 1978. "Insurance Benefits, Out-of-Pocket Payments, and the Demand for Medical Care." *Health and Medical Care Services Review* 1, no. 4 (July/August): 1–15.

Newhouse, J. and C. Phelps. 1976. "New Estimates of Price and Income Elasticities of Medical Care Services." In *The Role of Health Insurance in The Health Services Sector*, edited by Rosett, pp. 261–319. New York: National Bureau of Economic Research.

Nordquist, G. and S. Wu. 1976. "The Joint Demand for Health Insurance and Preventive Medicine." In *The Role of Health Insurance in the Health Services Sector*, edited by Rosett, pp. 35–65. New York: National Bureau of Economics Research.

Offenkrantz, W. and A. Tobin. 1975. "Psychoanalytic Psychotherapy." In *Treatment*, edited by Freedman and Dyrud, Vol. V of *American Handbook of Psychiatry*, edited by Silvano. New York: Basic Books.

Office of Technology Assessment. 1980. "The Efficacy and Cost-Effectiveness of Psychotherapy." Background Paper No. 3 of *The Implications of Cost-Effectiveness Analysis of Medical Technology*. Washington, D.C.

Panzetta, A. 1973. "Cost-Benefit Studies in Psychiatry." *Comprehensive Psychiatry* 14, no. 5 (September/October): 451–55.

Parloff, M. 1978. "Can Psychotherapy Research Guide the Policy-maker? — A Little Knowledge May be a Dangerous Thing." Paper presented at the 9th Annual Meeting of the Society for Psychotherapy Research, Toronto, Canada.

Parloff, M.; B. Wolfe; S. Hadley; and I. Waskow. 1978. "Assessment of Psychosocial Treatment of Mental Disorders: Current Status and Prospects." NIMH Working Group, Advisory Committee on Mental Health, Washington, D.C.: National Academy of Sciences.

Pauly, M. 1968. "The Economics of Moral Hazard: Comment." *American Economic Review* 58, no. 3 (June): 531–37.

Pauly, M. 1974. "Overinsurance and Public Provision of Insurance: The Roles of Moral Hazard and Adverse Selection." *Quarterly Journal of Economics* 88, no. 1 (February): 44–62.

Pechman, J. and B. Okner. 1974. *Who Bears the Tax Burden?* Washington, D.C.: Brookings Institution.

Perlman, M. 1974. *The Economics of Health and Medical Care.* New York: John Wiley and Sons.

President's Commission on Mental Health. 1978. *Report*, Washington, D.C.: U.S. Government Printing Office.

Redlich, F. and D. Freedman. 1965. *The Theory and Practice of Psychiatry.* New York: Basic Books.

Reed, L. 1975. *Coverage and Utilization of Care for Mental Conditions Under Health Insurance—Various Studies 1973-74.* Washington, D.C.: American Psychiatric Association.

Reed, L.; E. Myers; and P. Scheidemandel. 1972. *Health Insurance and Psychiatric Care: Utilization and Cost.* Washington, D.C.: American Psychiatric Association.

Reinhardt, U. 1978. "Comment on the Paper." In *Competition in the Health Care Sector*, edited by W. Greenberg, pp. 156-90. Washington, D.C.: Federal Trade Commission.

Regier, D. and I. Goldberg. 1976. "National Health Insurance and the Mental Health Services Equilibrium." Paper presented at the Annual Meeting of the American Psychiatric Association, Miami, Florida. May 13.

Regier, D.; I. Goldberg; and C. Taube. 1978. "The De Facto U.S. Mental Health Services System: A Public Health Perspective." *Archives of General Psychiatry* 35, (June): 685-93.

Research Triangle Institute. 1980. "Costs to the Society of Alcohol, Drug Abuse and Mental Illness." Contract No. 382-79-001. Washington, D.C.: Alcohol, Drug Abuse and Mental Health Administration.

Rosenstein, M. and C. Taube. 1976. *Staffing of Mental Health Facilities, United States 1976.* Washington, D.C.: National Institute of Mental Health.

Rosett, R. 1976. *The Role of Health Insurance in the Health Services Sector.* New York: National Bureau of Economic Research.

Rosett, R. and L. Huang. 1973. "The Effect of Health Insurance on the Demand for Medical Care." *Journal of Political Economy* 81, no. 2 (March/April): 281-305.

Scientific Manpower Commission. 1978. *Professional Women and Minorities: A Manpower Data Resource Survey*, Second Edition. Washington, D.C.

Scitovsky, A. and N. Snyder. 1972. "Effect of Coinsurance on Use of Physician Services." *Social Security Bulletin.*

Sharfstein, S. 1978. "Third-Party Payors: To Pay or Not to Pay." *American Journal of Psychiatry* 135, no. 10 (October): 1185-88.

Sharfstein, S. and H. Clark. 1978. "Economics and the Chronic Mental Patient." *Schizophrenia Bulletin* 4, 3: 399-414.

Sharfstein, S. and H. Clark. 1980. "Why Psychiatry is a Low Paid Medical Specialty." *American Journal of Psychiatry* 137, no. 7 (July): 832-33.

Sharfstein, S. and B. Dean. 1977. "Washington Psychiatry—Boom or Bust?" Paper presented at a meeting of the Washington Psychiatric Society, Washington, D.C., September 29.

Sharfstein, S.; C. Taube; and I. Goldberg. 1975. "Private Psychiatry and Accountability: A Response to the APA Task Force on Private Practice." *American Journal of Psychiatry* 132, no. 1 (January): 43–47.

Sloan, F. 1971. *Planning Public Expenditures on Mental Health Service Delivery.* New York: Rand Corporation, RM–6339–NYC (February).

Sloan, F. 1976. "Physician Fee Inflation: Evidence from the Late 60's." In *The Role of Insurance in the Health Services Sector*, edited by Rosett, New York: National Bureau of Economic Research.

Smith, M.L. and G.V. Glass. 1977. "Meta-Analysis of Psychotherapy Outcomes." *American Psychologist* 32: pp. 752–6.

Spence, M. and R. Zeckhauser. 1971. "Insurance, Information and Individual Action." *American Economic Review* 61, no. 2 (May): 370–87.

Steinberg, S.S.; D.A. Freeman; C.A. Steel; I. Balodis; and A.L. Batista. 1976. *Information on Manpower Utilization, Functions and Credentialing in Community Mental Health Centers.* University Research Corporation.

Taylor, L. 1975. "The Demand for Electricity: A Survey." *Bell Journal of Economics* 6, no. 1 (Spring): 74–110.

VandenBos, G. and C. Pino. 1980. "Research on the Outcome of Psychotherapy." In *Psychotherapy: Practice, Research, Policy*, edited by VandenBos, pp. 23–70. Beverly Hills: Sage Publishing.

Weisbrod, B. 1979. "A Guide to Benefit-Cost Analysis, as Seen Through a Controlled Experiment in Treating the Mentally Ill." Discussion Paper No. 559–79, Institute for Research on Poverty, University of Wisconsin—Madison.

Yates, B. 1980. *Improving Effectiveness and Reducing Costs in Mental Health.* Springfield, Illinois: Charles C. Thomas.

Zeckhauser, R. 1970. "Medical Insurance: A Case Study of the Trade-Off Between Risk-Spreading and Appropriate Incentives." *Journal of Economic Theory* 2, no. 1 (February): 10–26.

INDEX

ABOUT THE AUTHOR

Thomas G. McGuire is an assistant professor of economics at Boston University. He received degrees in economics from Princeton and Yale University, and is author of numerous articles on economics and mental health policy. He was recently co-chair of a conference on Economics and Mental Health sponsored by the National Institute of Mental Health. His current research centers on the effects of regulation and reimbursement practices on mental health service delivery.